MADOCKS
AND THE WONDER OF WALES

by the same author

DESIGN AND DETAIL OF
THE SPACE BETWEEN BUILDINGS
(Architectural Press)

DESIGNED TO LIVE IN
(Allen and Unwin)

MADOCKS
AND THE WONDER
OF WALES

The Life of W. A. Madocks, M.P., 1773–1828
Improver, 'Chaotic',
Architectural and Regional Planner,
Reformer, Romantic;
with some account of his Agent, John Williams

by

ELISABETH BEAZLEY

FABER AND FABER
24 Russell Square
London

First published in mcmlxvii
by Faber and Faber Limited
24 Russell Square, London W.C.1
Printed in Great Britain
by Ebenezer Baylis and Son Limited
The Trinity Press, Worcester, and London

To Clough Williams-Ellis

ACKNOWLEDGEMENTS

I am tremendously indebted to a great many individuals who, whether or not in an official capacity, most generously gave of their time and knowledge in showing me papers or allowing me to look at buildings which were in some way connected with this book.

To Mrs. Wright (née Juliet Madocks) for her most kind permission to see family papers and portraits; Mr. Clough Williams-Ellis for taking me to see Tremadoc and thus first introducing me to its founder; and to Dr. M. J. T. Lewis whose research on the history of the Festiniog Railway and related matters has been of the greatest help to my work.

To all those now living in Tremadoc or in houses which are connected with this story who so kindly allowed me to wander round their property; particularly Captain Livingstone-Learmouth the present owner of Tan-yr-allt.

To the clergy and members of numerous parish churches for help in searching registers and finding wall tablets, including Cray, Edmonton, Gresford, Llandyrnog and Talgarth.

The following have given very helpful information and advice on matters ranging from family history, architecture, planning and land-drainage to those concerning William Madocks' interest in politics: Mr. Robert Adams; Mr. Robert L. Arrowsmith; Mr. John Beazley; Mr. Michael Dalby; Mrs. J. O. Davies, Trefecca College; Mr. J. J. Evans; Mrs. Fairbairn-Eyton; The Rev. D. Hamilton; Doctor Quentin Hughes; Professor R. T. Jenkins; Mr. Bedwyr Jones; Mr. Jonah Jones; The Rev. R. G. Jones; Miss Gwenneth Lewis; The Rev. Tom Morris; Mr. Bob Owen; Mr. W. Morgan Richards; Sir John Summerson; Mr. G. Thomas; Mr. Keith Williams-Jones; and Mr. Charles Wrangham. The archivists, keepers and librarians in the National Library of Wales; the University College of North Wales; the British

Museum; the County Record Offices of Caernarvon, Flint, Lincolnshire, Merioneth and Wiltshire; L'Administrateur de la Section des Cimitières, Direction de l'Architecture et des Affaires Domaniales, Préfecture de la Seine; the Ashmolean Museum; Bexley and Greenwich Public Libraries; the Central Record Office; Chief Engineer, Gwynedd River Board; Guildhall Library; History of Parliament Trust; House of Commons Library; the House of Lords Record Office; National Museum of Wales; the National Portrait Gallery; National Register of Archives; River Boards Association; St. Davids Cathedral Library; Search Room, Somerset House and Twickenham Parish.

The book is chiefly based on letters of W. A. Madocks and contemporary papers in the National Library of Wales, the County Record Office, Caernarvon, and the Library of the University College of North Wales, Bangor. These are listed in the bibliography and I am most grateful to the Librarians for permission to quote from them.

My thanks are due to Miss Anne Cundy-Cooper and the Peter Coxson Typing Service for their patient work on the typescripts, and finally I am most indebted to Mrs. J. R. Beazley and Miss Eileen Tulloch for their invaluable help in reading and checking, and to Mr. Alan Pringle of Faber and Faber Ltd. for all his work on this book.

NOTE

In transcribing quotations, no attempt has been made to 'correct' spellings.

Contents

Illustrations

PLATES

*Permission to reproduce these illustrations is gratefully acknowledged.
1, 2, and 3, Mrs. Wright (photographed by Olive Kitson); 4 and 5, Mr.
Kenneth Rowntree and the National Museum of Wales; 6–9, the
National Library of Wales.*

MAPS AND PLANS

LINE

Other line drawings in the text are taken from W. A. Madocks' letters, but are reduced in size.

INTRODUCTION

The Background
Eighteenth-Century Wales

'I AM AT the utmost extent of England west, and here I must mount the Alps, [and] traverse the mountains of Wales . . .'[1] wrote Daniel Defoe, creator of the intrepid Robinson Crusoe, during the tour he made of Great Britain in 1724. After he had crossed the border, Defoe found his expectations of the 'inmost provinces' to be correct: 'Even Hannibal himself would have found it impossible to have marched his army over Snowdon, or over the rocks of Merioneth and Montgomeryshire,' he wrote, and recorded that much of Wales was sparsely populated and exceedingly wild.

Defoe was one of the first of the eighteenth-century travellers to explore the Principality. During the succeeding hundred years others were to follow in ever increasing numbers; they made their sketches, wrote their journals and returned to the familiar comfort of Georgian England to sort out their notes and impressions often with the intention of publishing their own particular *Tour*. Discernible throughout these fascinating guide-books is that glow of achievement which can result from lonely travels among strange people. It was certainly justified. To take a chaise into the heart of Merioneth or to hire a pony in Llangollen and follow the bridle-tracks over the hills into Snowdonia was every bit as much an achievement as the journeys now made to the remoter parts of Persia or Afghanistan. To travel by stage-coach on what passed for main roads was not much less hazardous.

While we can, with some effort, imagine the discomforts

which the early traveller had to endure, it is less easy to remember his pioneering frame of mind. What he went to admire is still, to us, so admirable, that it is easy to forget that the idea of making a journey into the wild for any but strictly practical ends was quite new. The early eighteenth-century gentleman had been educated to admire order above all else whether it was entirely man-made as in his country houses, town planning or works of art, or in nature laid out by man in his gardens, parks and newly enclosed fields. The Grand Tour was first made to admire classical order; to admire nature unimproved was a new and odd notion which only began to get around towards the middle of the century. It had certainly not occurred to Defoe who travelled primarily to report on the works of man despite nature; he describes the relatively small hills of Monmouthshire as 'these horrid mountains' and regards with 'astonishment' but with little else, except perhaps distaste, 'the prodigious height of the un-passable mountains' of central Wales; it is with real relief that he reached Anglesey, 'a much pleasanter Country than any part of North Wales, that we have yet seen; and particularly is very fruitful in corn and cattle'. It would not enter his mind to praise anything so bleak, unproductive and fraught with danger as a mountain.

It was not until the second half of the century when the avant-garde of the Romantic movement was beginning to discover Wales that the *Tours* began to show a diametrically opposite attitude to the landscape through which their writers travelled. Now they were prepared to admire it for its own sake without even an object of archaeological interest in the view. The horrid mountains were fast becoming sublimely picturesque.

'The romantic beauties of nature are so singular and extravagant in the principality, particularly in the counties of Merioneth and Caernarvon, that they are scarcely to be conceived, by those, who have confined their curiosity to other parts of Great Britain,' wrote one such enthusiast,[2] and he went on to enumerate the practical advantages of the Welsh tour which he felt 'has been hitherto strangely neglected; for while the English roads are crouded [*sic*] with travelling parties of pleasure, the Welsh are so rarely visited, that the author did not meet with a single party during his six weeks journey in Wales'. In addition he found the Welsh themselves 'universally civil and obliging' and could not recommend the Tour highly enough. This was in 1774.

Among the first to discover the wonders of these mountains were the painters. Richard Wilson's years in Italy and England seem to have given Cader Idris and Snowdon a classic serenity. But to him, Montgomeryshire born, this was a homecoming. To Gainsborough, Turner, the Varley brothers and many others, it was a revelation to see what lay beyond the homely English counties. Our vision is so strongly influenced by theirs that the mountains today, particularly in light sun through rain or dispersing mist, still suggest a late eighteenth-century sketch or journal. Perhaps this is because both they, and the strange illusive lights and mists which so often hang over them, are so exactly in tune with the romantic ideal of the picturesque as it has come down to us.

Very important to the general appreciation of Welsh scenery was the spread of the engraving. Paul Sandby, who made his Tour in the early 'seventies, also introduced the technique of aquatint to England. Many of his own drawings were published, as were those of his contemporaries, and through them the popularity of the summer Tour in the Principality spread further. Later the French wars, by making continental travel and the Grand Tour less easy, combined with the thirst for the romantic and picturesque to put Wales firmly on the map.

Although the eighteenth-century traveller always had an eye to appreciate the awful peak or chasm, his interests were as diverse as his curiosity. Some went to botanise; many to search for archaeological remains, or for ruins of any kind provided they were sufficiently melancholy; others, in the early nineteenth century, recorded the splendid iron aqueducts and bridges which, thanks to Thomas Telford, were then in the vanguard of anything yet designed, not only in Britain but throughout the world. Everyone recorded the habits of the people, what they wore, what they ate, their religion, education, their weddings and funerals, the attractions of their daughters, their farming and

17

fishing. . . . The only thing not recorded was the conversation because, being in Welsh, it was incomprehensible to all but a very few. From the journals of these undaunted travellers the liveliest but most unexpected picture is gradually filled in; lively despite much desperate poverty and unexpected because it is so utterly foreign to the contemporary English scene.

At this period Wales still had a social structure which was completely different from that in England, where the middle classes had been steadily growing in both importance and numbers since Elizabethan times. The contrast was less marked in the richer border counties where the majority of the few great landowners had their seats but in the mountainous interior there was only a thin scattering of small squires and richer farmers; the peasants were both numerous and poor and lived precariously from one harvest to the next. Middle-class professional men were rare; lawyers, doctors and shop-keepers were to be found in the principal towns, but these were few and far between; the miserably paid clergy usually held several livings in order to make ends meet.

Food, and particularly any difference from that to which he is accustomed, was then, as now, one of the first things to be noticed by any tourist. The material poverty of the interior was reflected in the monotony of the basic diet. Wheat bread, then considered essential by most Englishmen, was a rare luxury to ordinary people. Instead the usual food was a kind of porridge (*llymru*), and oatmeal cakes were eaten throughout most districts of Merioneth and Caernarvon (where the prejudice against growing wheat was described as 'rivetted') 'except in genteel families, towns, and inns upon the post-roads'.[3] There, too, the Englishman had some hope of the cup of tea[4] to which he had become addicted, but as late as 1802 it was still unknown in parts of Wales, and was uncommon in the remoter districts until the end of the Napoleonic Wars.[5] Buttermilk took its place, or ale when something stronger was wanted.

In spite of this poverty the life of a Caernarvonshire peasant may have compared favourably with that of his children and grandchildren who migrated to find work in the industrial towns, but the nostalgia of our vision of pre-industrial Britain often blurs the true picture. The hard facts must have been very hard indeed; the average standard of living was so near subsistence level that one poor harvest meant real hunger; two could be disastrous. The tourists, who delightedly described the civil and picturesque peasantry who so obligingly acted as their guides, travelled during the summer.

The mud-walled and thatched cottages looked attractive enough in the sun. But to those who knew them better they were 'truly habitations of wretchedness. One smoky hearth, for it should not be styled a kitchen, and one damp litter-cell, for it cannot be called a bedroom, are frequently all the space allotted to a labourer, his wife and four or five children. . . .'[6] Conditions were slightly better in the villages near the lead and coal mines (e.g. Flintshire and Denbighshire) since the need for labour pushed up wages.

In good years the farm labourer's life had many compensations; it had great variety not only in the type of work done but in the atmosphere in which it was done. The loneliness of shepherding contrasted with the excitement and bustle of the shearings on the big farms; the all-out effort of the harvest and the all-out festivities which followed it were very different from the long toil of each cottager on his own stony potato plot and patch of oats. The hired servants had the compensations of the singing and story-telling that accompanied their weaving in the farm kitchens in the long winter evenings, while the smallholding (*tyddyn*) gave a sort of spiritual independence to its owner which the landless man could never possess. But it could not give security, or the actual independence that went with it. Methods of farming were far too primitive and the holdings too small for this to be possible.

The wool trade made the greatest difference to prosperity at every level in the weaving and knitting counties. It was then still a home industry, very few manufactories having yet been built. Thomas Pennant, whose famous *Tours*[7] (first published 1778) were as much a social survey as a search for the picturesque, gives an unexpected picture of Bala, with 'its vast trade in woollen stockings, and its great markets every *Saturday* morning, when from two to five hundred pounds worth are sold each day, according to the demand. Round the place, women and children are in full employ, knitting along the roads; and mixed with them *Herculean* figures appear, assisting their *Omphales* in this effeminate employ.' Travellers on the Holyhead coach found knitters at every halt selling stockings, gloves and Welsh Wigs (a woollen cap which provided snug comfort in draughty coaches).

Although the industry was still almost entirely unmechanised at the turn of the century, production seems to have been high. Merioneth and Montgomeryshire were particularly famous for the export of flannels and webs (a measure of cloth). Pennant records that before the American war £10,000 worth of stockings and £40,000 of web or flannel were exported in one year from Barmouth to the continent. At the other side of the country the weekly wool market transformed Shrewsbury into a Welsh town, English scarcely being heard in the streets. As the Yorkshire wool industry grew, some felt bitter that so much good Welsh wool was exported to England when it might have provided both labour and wealth at home had modern wool mills been constructed in the interior of Wales.

Social customs were reported with great interest but, probably because of the language difficulty, many travellers fell back on earlier *Tours* to provide details. This meant that the same event, not necessarily typical, might be reported a number of times and become regarded as a custom.

Some travellers had the luck to meet a bidder who, carrying a ribboned crook, rode from house to house bidding people to a wedding. It was the custom for the guests to bring presents in kind or money for the newly wed couple. This was for the wedding proper. There was also the 'Little Wedding' or the custom known as bundling, considered by some tourists to be an American habit, scarcely known in England. It was said 'to have originated in the scarcity of fuel, and in the consequent unpleasantness of sitting together, in the colder parts of the year without a fire. Much has been said of the innocence with which these meetings are conducted. This may be the case in some instances. . . .'[8] However it was pointed out that 'both parties are so poor, that they are necessarily constrained to render their issue legitimate, in order to secure their reputation, and with it a mode of obtaining a livelihood'. One reviewer[9] at least was riled by such an account and firmly stated that it did not 'form one of the general usages of the lower classes in Wales' which were much as in 'the purlieus of London'. He described other customs such as that of strewing flowers on the new graves in church-yards and found that it 'produces a sentiment of pleasing melancholy in the living'.

The churches themselves with few exceptions were then sadly neglected. The root cause was the low pay of the clergy, resulting in pluralities which in turn led to the practice of livings going to men who actually lived in England and visited their parishes once a year at the most; many of the clergy could not speak Welsh nor could their parishioners understand English. Bad pay also meant that livings went to uneducated and even illiterate men. Conversely there were others who, besides being conscientious parish priests, had advanced views on such practical subjects as agriculture and architecture, and some were first-class scholars. Despite the efforts made in the seventeenth century, the prevalent ignorance among the poor was one of the greatest barriers to the teaching of the Church and this had led a few of the clergy to a practical interest in education.

Among other outstanding achievements in this field had been the famous Circulating Schools—intended primarily to give religious instruction, to which end reading and writing were first taught. Men and women as well as children attended and these classes were an important source of the Welsh Sunday School movement which was to have such a profound effect on the country. As the shortage of teachers was acute dissenters were employed as well as churchmen.

Among the clergy themselves the distinction between anglicans and dissenters was far less clear cut than might be imagined. Thomas Charles (Charles of Bala) for instance, who was one of the leading figures of the Calvinistic Methodists, had been ordained an anglican curate. He made no final break with the established Church until just before his death when, in 1811, after long pressure, he ordained eight of his foremost lay preachers, thus breaking the tradition of the Church by which only priests who had been episcopally ordained might administer the sacrament.

Throughout the eighteenth century, among those who preached to the vast concourses of people who gathered to hear the gospel some wished to remain within the Church; but with buildings in ruins and few able to accommodate a congregation of more than two or three hundred, to preach outside was often the only practical answer. The eighteenth-century Welshman, basically religious and ever appreciative of a fine performance whether of eloquent argument from the pulpit or singing to the harp, would walk miles to hear a good sermon. Open-air preaching reached its numerical zenith in North Wales in the Bala Revival meetings (1790). It is extraordinary to think of these vast throngs of people, starting off from their remote villages and lonely farms in ones and twos, joining forces with others on the hill paths until the lonely groups became a steady stream on the turnpikes leading to Bala where a crowd of up to forty thousand might congregate in the great open field outside the town. In addition to their religious significance, these meetings were important occasions in the life of the countryside, providing a chance for the scattered population to forgather.

Generally speaking neither the gentry nor the tourists had much sympathy with these Revivalist meetings: a conventional anglican background gave little notion of the vacuum caused in Wales by the lethargy of the established Church. The rift was accentuated by the fact that only men who professed the anglican faith were able to go up to Oxford and Cambridge, so the establishment and nonconformists were insulated from each other's point of view just when they might be best able to appreciate it. Thus the richer landowners had little contact with the educated members of the movement; and, if not indifferent, they actually opposed it.

On the other side of the coin there is little doubt that some of the dissenting preachers played on the emotions of the people to an appalling degree. At this range it is again difficult to know how typical are the descriptions of dissenting meetings given in the *Tours*. What may well be a description of the same event is repeated in various publications: 'The phrensy spreads among the multitude. . . . Men, women and children, indiscriminately cry, laugh, jump and sing, with the wildest extravagance. That their dress becomes deranged, or the hair dishevelled, is no longer an object of attention—And their raptures continue, till, spent with fatigue of mind and body, the women are often carried out in apparent insensibility.'[10]

By the end of the eighteenth century the hostelries were beginning to cater directly for tourist trade. Although the roads were still very poor, once arrived at the inn most travellers enjoyed themselves and felt the more comfortable for the spice of danger in the journey ahead for which 'guides were to be hired, pillions for the ladies provided, and a long list of anxious questions about fords, tides, etc., etc., to be stored up for use as the necessities of their application occurred.'[11]

There were other problems; the most irritating was undoubtedly that dealt with in an advertisement in the *North Wales Gazette* under the head HOW TO PUZZLE BUGS. These creatures can have been by no means universal since tourists sometimes noted when they had spent a particularly restless night. They commented with refreshing lack of restraint on the inns where they put up. Tan-y-bwlch Inn, a famous stop on the road down from Snowdonia to central Wales, apparently gave a warm reception to those travelling in style but others were less fortunate.

For instance, the painter, Rowlandson, and his companion had begun as they neared the inn 'to calculate on the comforts of good beds and a good supper, and had scarcely decided whether to order chicken or chops, and confidently drawn up to the door, when *mine host*, with petrifying phiz, approached to say he had no room'.[12] Another party 'extremely wet and much inclined to seat ourselves by a comfortable fire-side' got a similar reception. 'It was six in the evening, we had 8 miles to walk, over the wildest and most desolate road in Wales.'[13]

On the other hand, a traveller by post-chaise found it 'small

but good' and its owner 'civil and attentive'. The best compromise, apparently, was to take a pack-horse to carry baggage;
the tourist was then received with more cordiality at inns and
could cover about thirty miles a day while, as a 'pedestrian', it
was easy to 'step aside to botanise and examine the beauties of
nature and art'.[14]

But much as they delighted in the wilds of Wales for a short
spell, by the end of August the tourists had mostly returned to
the more civilised border country or had crossed into England.
Charles Apperley, better known as Nimrod, the famous sporting
writer of the early nineteenth century, who knew north and
mid-Wales very well, wrote of it: 'Although myself three parts a
Welshman, I am no admirer of the interior of Wales as the residence of a well-educated gentleman, still less of one of a highly
cultivated mind.'[15] Admittedly Nimrod's main interest was fox-
hunting and in this respect Wales could hardly compete with the
English shires. But like many of his contemporaries he had wide
interests based on a classical eighteenth-century education (he
always carried a copy of a Latin poet on a fox-hunting tour) and
he liked to have similar minds and kindred spirits around him.
In this respect the country was sparsely provided.

There were however two parts of North Wales which contrasted strongly with the mountainous regions of Caernarvon and
Merioneth: the Vale of Clwyd, and the border country centred
on the great market town of Wrexham.

Even those bent on admiring the awful and melancholy relaxed
into lyricism when they discovered the gentle, fertile vale sheltered by the Moel Famma range to the north and buffered from
Snowdonia by the rolling Denbigh moors; today it might still
be described as the 'Cambrian Paradise'. Walter Davies in his
famous agricultural report[16] told how he found a cottager who
'was literally *sitting under his vine*; for the wall was covered with
grapes. A smile of complacency sat on his countenance' and
Davies wrote of the enormous quantities of corn exported and the
thirteen acres of lavender which were grown near Ruthin to be
distilled in an elaboratory adjoining for sale in London. In Cam-
den's *Wales* (1806) an old tale showing the fertility of the Vale

claimed that 'a stick thrown into it would be covered with grass overnight'. The cattle chewed contentedly in the deep meadows watered by the Clwyd and the Elwy and the tourists journeyed leisurely between hedgerows covered with honeysuckle and dog-rose. A botanising contributor to the *Cambrian Traveller's Guide* recorded with evident satisfaction both *vinca major* and *campanula trachelium*.

While the Vale of Clwyd remains wonderfully unchanged, Wrexham, by contrast, would be scarcely recognisable to the eighteenth-century traveller. The iron works and coal mines had then made little impression visually on the predominantly agricultural scene but it was soon to change irrevocably. The mines grew steadily busier and with them the foundries flourished.

In addition to Wrexham's industrial prosperity, its market and fairs were the most important in the whole of North Wales since they acted as a clearing-point for both Welsh and English goods. It is hardly surprising that this important, busy, but rural-seeming market town with its splendid parish church was included in the itinerary of most tourists. Another attraction for these travellers was the number of big houses in the surrounding country whose hospitality they could enjoy. Being on the very edge of Wales, bordered by the rich counties of Cheshire and Shropshire and easily accessible to London, the country was populated by big landowners, prosperous squires and rich gentlemen farmers. The fertile land, and the possibility of a secondary means of livelihood in the expanding industries, meant that the peasants too were better off than those in the interior. From Sir Watkin Williams Wynn whose seat at Wynnstay was run on a scale fabulous even to eighteenth-century England, to the itinerant tinker or hired labourer, life was more prosperous than any known in Snowdonia or the wilds of Merioneth.

It was in these two rich and pastoral regions, near Wrexham and in the heart of the Vale of Clwyd, that the Welsh property of the Madocks family lay. By eighteenth-century standards the estates were small, not more than five or six thousand acres in all; but it was prosperous land well cared for by generations of farming squires.

1

The First Twenty-five Years
1773 – 1798

WILLIAM ALEXANDER MADOCKS, third surviving son of John and Frances Madocks, was born in London on 17 June 1773. His father, then a bencher of Lincoln's Inn, was soon to become one of the most eminent King's Counsel in England. His mother comes down to us through her portrait; a lively, intelligent young woman with widely spaced brown eyes in a heart-shaped face, painted, as was fashionable at the time, in fancy dress. But this portrait[1] see Plate 2 was made twenty-six years before William's birth. His arrival and, more important, his survival after a gap of ten years during which two other children had died in infancy, meant the greatest joy to his middle-aged parents. Their elder sons, John Edward and Joseph, were due to leave home for school at Harrow when the baby was christened at St. Andrew's Church, Holborn. He was called William after his grandfather; Alexander was not a family name but that of the Macedonian who conquered half the world. The family lived in a plain brick house in Bedford Row: a surprisingly modest dwelling for a flourishing barrister with an established family, but convenient enough for Lincoln's Inn and the Middle Temple where John Madocks spent so much of his time.

Such origins sound entirely English, but this was far from being the case. Frances, who was the daughter of Joseph Whitchurch, a London merchant, had English blood through her mother but the Whitchurch family, though now living in the fashionable village of Twickenham, was of Loughborough, County Down.

The Madockses were quite Welsh if six hundred years in the Vale of Clwyd qualifies for this description; certainly they had plenty of Celtic blood by the eighteenth century. Their descent is traced directly from Sir Robert Pounderlinge of Aberchwiler, Bodfari, who lived at Pontryfydd in that parish. He was a governor of Diserth Castle in the reign of Henry II. Surnames were little used in Wales until much later but the name Madoc appears quite frequently in the family tree. The first to use Madocks was John Madocks of Bodfari, Esquire (1601–62). His eldest son, Edward, sold his property for the Royalist cause and was killed fighting at Edgehill. His younger son, John, Sheriff and Capital Burgess of Denbigh, married as his second wife Jane Williams, heiress to Vron Iw[2] in the neighbouring parish of Llangwyfan, and it became the chief family property. The old stone house stood on the rising ground to the north side of the Vale. Below lay the water meadows of the Clwyd[3] and beyond the moorland rolled away to the distant peaks of the Snowdon range.

The family tree gives the impression of the country squires serving the county as sheriff or occasionally in the militia, marrying into similar families and remaining peacefully in the Vale. William Madocks (grandson of Jane and John and grandfather of William Alexander) was the eldest son of a youngest son so had no hope of ever coming into Vron Iw. He turned to trade and so successful was his tobacco business in Ruthin that he was able to buy the old moated farm-house of Llay Hall near Gresford, a village close to Wrexham on the other side of the county. He married his first cousin Ann, one of the Pulestons of Pickhill, and it was their eldest son John (born 1723) who was the barrister who went south to practise with such outstanding success in London.

John Madocks inherited Llay Hall when still a young man and ten years later the Vron Iw property passed to him through the death of his father's cousin, Edward Madocks. Perhaps the possession of these two estates made him feel it was time to settle and to provide an heir to this very pleasant inheritance. At all events, it was in the same year (1758) that he married Frances and shortly after they went to live in Bedford Row where the first years of their married life were spent and all their children were born.

When William was five, he was painted by James Scouler, an eminent miniaturist of the day. In this case the portrait (see Plate 1) is near life size. A sturdy small boy looks squarely from the frame; he stands there in a manly manner, the back of one hand on his hip, as though prepared to address an audience. The other hand rests affectionately on the head of a large black retriever. He seems to be a thoughtful, friendly child, small for his age but confident and determined. His fair hair, not yet cut short, is slightly red and his cheeks have a warm glow. This colouring is set off well by his white ruffled shirt, open at the neck, and a mushroom-coloured suit, the coat also worn negligently open; the waistcoat buttons seem rather strained.

Despite the large gap in age between the boys, the Madockses were a remarkably close and affectionate family. One great bond between the brothers which lasted all their lives was their tremendous enjoyment in acting and singing. Private theatricals played a prominent part in late eighteenth-century social life and it was one in which a talented small brother could join as an asset rather than a barely tolerated liability, but the tall narrow house in Bedford Row allowed little space either for play acting or ordinary family life.

John Madocks by now had an extremely lucrative practice, his opinion as King's Counsel being much sought and respected, so there was no reason why these cramped conditions should continue. They wanted a country house but Wales was too distant; it was therefore decided to compromise, as scores of thousands have tried to since, and to find an ideal piece of unspoilt country within reach of London.

It was not then difficult: John Madocks was in the vanguard of a movement which was to become very popular by the turn of the century; when he bought the estate of Mount Mascall at North Cray in Kent the district was quite undiscovered. But it was not many years before guide-books were to describe the Crays with enthusiasm. They were 'judged by many persons to be the most beautiful spot in the county'[4] and Bexley, the next village on the London side, was to be extolled as a very superior suburb: 'Many persons of fortune are inhabitants of it. Several small but elegant houses have been erected here within a very few years; and it is highly probable that the salubrity of the air, with the convenience of it being only thirteen miles from the metropolis, will be a strong inducement to other opulent people to fix their country retreat upon this delightful spot.'[5] An excellent state of affairs for the sociable young Madockses and one which William remembered.

Mount Mascall itself was no such upstart; the house dated from Jacobean times and was of substantial size[6] but probably its greatest asset in the eyes of the family was its private theatre. Vale Mascall, just below, became John Edward's on marriage[7] and some years later when his first wife died their children came up to live with the grandparents. William was himself little more than half-way between the two generations so belonged in a sense to each and was thus at the hub of family life instead of being at a possibly lonely tail-end. Even so he was separated by over a decade from each.

The first real break in his life came a few days before his eleventh birthday when he was sent to boarding school. He went to Charterhouse, then on the original site of the monastic foundation which made a green oasis in the heart of London,[8] temptingly close to the excitements of the metropolis.

There were forty foundation scholars or gown-boys but William was an oppidan lodging in Mrs. Bathurst's house. Here his life would not have been so spartan, but it probably followed much the same pattern as that of the scholars. They rose at five, had breakfast of beer, bread and cheese at eight, a midday dinner and then more beer, bread and cheese for supper. Between dinner and supper hungry boys could apply for a hunk of bread. Accommodation was no more lavish than the food. It was not until 1805, when a new Master introduced one or two revolutionary improvements, that the gown-boys were provided with a bed apiece.[9] This was an existence very different from the comforts of home but William's naturally sociable nature and quick wit would stand him in good stead. Work was no worry and games, at which he does not seem to have excelled, were not then considered of much importance. At eleven his clear treble would be needed in the Charterhouse choir. This, coupled with an unusually gentle nature for so lively a boy and the fact that he was still small for his age, should have been enough to melt Mrs. Bathurst's heart and see to it that she did not allow school to be too harsh a shock.

William spent five and a half years at Charterhouse where he evidently absorbed a sound classical education. He left, suddenly, after Founder's Day in December 1789 and, since it was not uncommon for the celebrations to get out of hand on this annual occasion, his precipitate departure was probably connected with these festivities. Several boys were involved but their crime is not recorded. His cousin, who described the sequel but, tantalisingly, not the event, wrote: 'He might have gone back had he submitted with the rest of his form to be flogged. To this he vehemently replied "No Sir".' His father backed him and 'immediately entered into a paper war with the Master of the Charter House'.[10]

From what is known of John Madocks it is likely that he won. At sixty-seven he had nearly half a century of successful argument behind him and he had recently resigned his seat in Parliament since politics took up precious time that might have been devoted to the law. He was now Master of the Bench of Lincoln's Inn and Treasurer of the Middle Temple. In his portrait he appears as a splendidly conventional eighteenth-century gentleman with a shrewd but slightly amused face under his beautifully curled wig; he wears his pale grey coat and yellow waistcoat with sure aplomb. Although his politics were Tory he was not in all respects conservative. Welsh tradition,[11] which is probably not entirely without foundation, has it that he might have been knighted 'but, just as the sword was about to be held over him, he rose up, and said he had rather not. . . .' The writer adds, rather unnecessarily it would seem, 'he was one of the most independent minded men that ever was born, and the most liberal.' The same perhaps not entirely reliable source states that 'for a great many years together he made £10,000 a year by the efforts of his brain.' The rather less imaginative *Salisbury Journal*[12] had estimated some years before that he was the fifth most prosperous barrister in England, earning £3,800 per annum. It can anyway be assumed he was rich, highly intelligent, and not unoriginal.

From his few surviving legal letters John Madocks shows a nice directness and is always brief but conversational: 'Sir, I received your letter at a time when I was pretty much hurried and unluckily mislaid it. Otherwise I would have answered it sooner. The neglect requires an apology.'[13] He cared for his family in the widest Welsh sense of including relatives of a distant degree of kinship, and advanced money which there was little likelihood of seeing again to pay off the debts of his Flintshire cousins. His family, his profession and his responsibilities to those on his estates were more than enough to fill his busy life.

One preoccupation at this moment was William's immediate future. At sixteen he was revelling in the fine freedom of having finished with school and could doubtless have filled the time in acquainting himself with the life of a young gentleman of leisure, paying particular attention to the delights of Drury Lane and Covent Garden; but old John Madocks was taking no risks. Instead William was bundled off to work in a country solicitor's office during the short gap which had unexpectedly occurred between his leaving Charterhouse and going up to Oxford.

He was also entered at Lincoln's Inn for, with his good brain and quick wit, there seemed to be no reason why he should not follow in his father's footsteps at the Bar, and get equal satisfaction as well as a good income from that career. It was essential that William, as a third son, should have a profession, but John Madocks could see that his natural gifts and sociable nature might easily undermine this course. He spent much of his time with his brothers, and although it was natural enough for John, as the eldest son, to have no profession, their father had always wished that Joseph had stuck to the army and had not happily idled away his time in painting and theatricals, however gifted he might be. It would be sheer waste of William's brains if he did no more than that, and it was economically necessary that he should earn money. The work in the solicitor's office may have seemed excessively dry, but it gave him a fair picture of the workings of the practice; the few months he spent there were later to stand him in better stead than his father ever could have hoped (or feared). The drudgery was shortlived: three months before his seventeenth birthday William was up at Oxford surrounded once more by congenial companions with his own enthusiasms and interests.

Christ Church, of which he was now a member, was not only one of the most fashionable and overcrowded[14] colleges of the day but it also had a high scholastic reputation. It was still perhaps possible for a gentleman to go up for a term or two with the declared intention of reading only the Stud Book and the *Racing Calendar*,[15] but Cyril Jackson, the Dean, was taking a lead in educational reform. He also chose good tutors, implored his undergraduates to read Homer, and enjoyed parties, travel and archaeology. He sounds exactly the man to create an atmosphere in which William's embryonic talents might flourish. It may have been under him that William developed his unusual tact; for Jackson, who had once been tutor to the Prince of Wales, was reputed to have 'a wonderful tact in managing that most un-manageable class of undergraduates, Noblemen'.[16] Presumably he also used it in dealing with commoners for there is no record of undue flouting of authority during William's time at Christ Church.

Politics were in ferment. Although the university officially backed the Pitt administration, discussion among its under-graduates[17] naturally ranged to the opposite extreme. (Paine's *Rights of Man* was published during William's second year.) At home, parliamentary reform was very much alive, but, far more dramatically, events in France reverberated throughout Oxford. The Bastille had fallen during William's last summer at school: an event to shake the whole of Europe and not least to stir the imagination of a sixteen-year-old boy, already restless to get away from school and the physical oppression of London in high summer. Perhaps the first germs of radicalism had been planted then; they would be nurtured by a natural reaction to his

33

father's conservatism and the university's official face. Then suddenly, even before he came down from Oxford, the situation and political climate were to change completely: the storming of the Tuileries by the mob, the massacres in the prisons, the guillotine and the Reign of Terror, horrified Englishmen and caused much heart-searching; certainly a young man with William's romantic temperament and classical education would be utterly shocked. His political life was still a long way ahead and his opinions at nineteen are not on record but the bottom must have been all but knocked out of his most cherished ideals and it would be bewildering to know what line to hold. All Radicals were now regarded with deep suspicion and parliamentary reform, so recently supported by quite moderate Whigs, was to be conveniently forgotten.

A trickle of gentry had continued to wander about Europe even when England and France were officially at war but the Napoleonic Wars coupled with the growing enthusiasm for the romantic in both art and nature put a stop to the Grand Tour proper. It had gradually been replaced by travels to the more picturesque parts of Britain: notably the Lake District and Wales.

Whether or not William managed to slip over to the continent at this time he certainly went often to Wales; regardless of the conditions set by war or fashion, this was where he really belonged. These visits had all the satisfaction of a homecoming coupled with the exuberance of the house-parties, race meetings, private theatricals, balls and country festivities into which his friends and relations entered with such gusto. The Madockses were related to most of the close-knit society of North Wales gentry and a very hospitable society it was. There were plenty of houses where they were considered as an extension of the immediate family. The Wrexham district was particularly lively; its hub, where they often stayed, was Wynnstay, seat of Sir Watkin Williams Wynn who, with every territorial justification, was known as King of Wales. The Sir Watkin of William's boyhood was not only a great landowner but a distinguished patron of the arts: Joshua Reynolds and Garrick were among his friends and Wynnstay itself had recently been rebuilt by that most fashionable architect, James Wyatt.

The tradition of the Wynnstay theatricals was continued by the next Sir Watkin, who had succeeded to the title at the age of seventeen and had been a contemporary of William's at Christ Church. The plays lasted for six weeks each winter and two or three performances were given each week. R. B. Sheridan and his family were among the guests who took part (he held a high opinion of Joe Madocks' Sir Anthony Absolute) and Charles Apperley (Nimrod), who lived near by, was often there. He later referred to these parties in his autobiography:[18] 'There were at Wynnstay, often in the times to which I have been alluding, three very choice spirits, in the persons of John, Joseph, and William Madocks. . . . I have good reason to think that, in what may be called social accomplishments, few men approached nearer to the Sheridans than these three brothers did, the two juniors more especially. They had not only as much ready wit at their command as the human mind has capacity for . . . but there was no end to their singing; neither were they at all behind their friends in their devotion to Bacchus, as well as to Apollo in the social hour. I have no ear for music, still less taste; but I would ride a bad hack fifty miles tomorrow, could I hear half-a-dozen duets sung as Joe and Billy Madocks—for so they were called, *par excellence*—had wont to sing them. Then as rational companions of graver hours, they were all delightful; and, to complete the portrait, their tempers were "youthful and mellow" as the song runs, to the latest period of their lives.'

The house-parties offered every variety of entertainment. Since the majority of the guests were themselves landowners they had the typical eighteenth-century interest in agriculture and the improvement of property. After a night of play-acting and drinking or dancing, the gentlemen would ride out to inspect new crops or systems of tillage or drainage, or chaises would be brought to the door so that the ladies might view the latest improvements in landscaping. The liveliest interest was taken in new land reclamation schemes, fine woodland, new building projects . . . in anything that enriched the estate practically or visually; preferably both. All property was discussed with intense interest and enthusiasm.

While William was still up at Oxford his widowed brother John (who was soon to re-marry[19]) decided to build himself a house. He chose a site at Erith, a few miles north of Mount Mascall on the Thames estuary. This fashionable district, also easily reached from London, was utterly foreign to that other estuary in North Wales which was to claim much of William's life but there can be little doubt that it deeply influenced his later plans.

A contemporary writer described the neighbourhood:

'On the Thames opposite this town, the Indiamen, in their passage up the river, frequently come to anchor, and lay some time to be lightened of part of their burthen, that they may proceed with greater safety up the river.

'This makes a great resort of Erith, not only of the friends and acquaintances of those who are on board these ships, but for some continuance afterwards, in the carrying on a traffic with the inhabitants of the neighbouring country, for the several kinds of East India goods, which have been procured on board.'[20]

Erith may have first shown William the attraction of a neighbourhood which had something out of the ordinary as its *raison d'être* to make it hum socially as well as thrive economically. Fine landscape alone was not enough in unspoilt eighteenth-century England to encourage congenial spirits to take up residence; something more was vital. Erith was unique in having the Indiamen; other places might claim tamer diversions, medical springs or sea-bathing or perhaps simply the convenience of proximity to an important coaching-route. Some such advantage was essential if a place was to compete with the delights of Bath or the new resorts which, like Brighton, were fast developing.

Here he also saw, probably for the first time, the enormous possibilities of land reclaimed from the sea: the Thames marshland below his brother's house had been drained in Elizabethan times and now bore the 'most exuberant crops of corn'. The house itself, Holly Hill, was of most modest size and design. The same writer described it as 'a cottage, not improperly so stiled, being upon a very small scale indeed. . . . It is a neat and elegant box.' John, who had most of the extravagant tastes of the society to which he belonged and who as heir to the Madocks' fortune could well afford to indulge them, might have been expected to build on a much grander scale. Instead he was in the vanguard of that short-lived 'simple cottage' school of villa building which so soon developed the ornamental extravagance of a multitude of fashionable styles and in this he seems to have strongly influenced his younger brother.

Louis XVI's execution (during William's last winter at Oxford) and the horror with which this news was received in England had put an end to Pitt's precarious peace. On 1 February 1793 war was declared and, despite its awfulness, it came almost as a relief after the long uncertainty of the peace which had preceded it. Inevitably this meant untold misery for some but the everyday life of the majority of English people was remarkably unaffected. It at least put a brake on any wild schemes William may have cherished of continental travel. His father, now considering retirement, urged him to settle down seriously to read for the Bar. He had taken his degree and there now seemed every likelihood that he would get through the necessary work and dinners without letting them interfere with his growing social activities. He had no special wish to enter any other profession. His disgust at any form of violence ruled out the army or navy; he had no particular inclination to enter the Church which, incidentally, might have curtailed his theatrical activities. His father would naturally have discouraged his radical political leanings and he was still too young to stand for Parliament and had not sufficient income; should he wish to do so later a legal training would stand him in good stead.

The one thing for which William was particularly suited was the life of an eldest son. His real interests were too varied to be channelled solely in one profession, and they needed money. He was beginning to find that anything connected with the land, in its broadest sense, was of fascinating interest: scientific management of property, new methods of farming and forestry and, above all else, landscape design and town-planning. Had he been a less reluctant draughtsman he might have tried his hand at architecture but, unlike Joe, he sketched with difficulty and never except for strictly practical ends. So William settled into John Madocks' old chambers in Lincoln's Inn: a young man of twenty with good family connections, not much money and an irresistible enthusiasm for enjoying life. With this went his unusual charm, the contradictory mixture of seemingly boundless vitality and exceptional tact based on gentleness with other people's feelings.

Everything now seemed set fair for his father's retirement and William's call to the Bar but, by the following September, John Madocks was dead. True, he was seventy-one and had probably over-worked for most of those years; but this was small comfort to his widow who inherited not only Mount Mascall and a generous settlement but the sole anxiety of William's future. No one else was likely to take his career very seriously and now that he was to have some money of his own there would be less incentive to work. Neither of his elder brothers was much concerned; possibly they saw little point in working almost to the grave as their father had done.

Contrary to popular tradition which holds that William inherited a fortune at his father's death, by the standards of his background he had little. Naturally the bulk of the Welsh estates was entailed[21] and most of the remainder was left in trust also for John Edward's benefit. William personally inherited a few hundred acres of the Denbighshire property (scattered in several different parishes) which brought in a rental of only £190 per annum and, in a codicil made shortly before his father's death, a holding in an iron working near Wrexham (at Brymbo; this was to become one of the chief foundries in the country). He also inherited £5,000 in stock, £2,000 in ready cash, and his father's chambers in Lincoln's Inn and the Middle Temple, with their books. But perhaps one of the most important instructions in the will only indirectly concerned him at this stage. John Madocks willed that £50,000, 3 per cent Consolidated Bank annuities, were to be transferred to the names of trustees (of which William was one) 'to lay out the same or the money to arrive at the sale thereof in the purchase of Lands. . . .' These were to be freehold lands of inheritance, not copyhold nor leasehold.

In spite of long years in Kent, Wales claimed John Madocks in the end. The poor of the parish of Gresford were to be given £100, and he was buried in the family vault in that most splendid parish church. The sculptor, Rogerson,[22] was commissioned to carve his likeness in low relief below which the acute intellect, elegant manners and pure faith of the King's Counsel are gratefully remembered in Latin.

After his father's funeral it was hard to go straight back to London and William fell again under the spell which Wales so inevitably cast over him. Much as he always enjoyed Denbighshire and particularly the social life of that corner of the Principality, it was the remote interior that fascinated. Each year he escaped from civilisation for as long as possible to explore more of it.

One of the highlights of any Welsh tour was the Cader Idris region in Merioneth (now made famous by Richard Wilson). Based rather uncomfortably at Dolgelley which was generally not well thought of ('the streets are irregular and the houses principally small and most are ill-built') the tourists happily exhausted themselves and the 'poneys' which they hired, on this outstandingly grand and melancholy mountain. It was then something of a relief to leave both the wild precipices and the cramped, unarchitectural assize town to wend their way north up the beautiful valley of the Ganllwyd to the splendours of Snowdonia.

Some miles upstream came a highlight of the tour: a tributary joining the main river came cascading through the oak woods in a series of splendid falls. The water poured over the dark wet rocks which contrasted blackly with the whiteness of the foam and the pale lichen on the dry parts of the boulders. The Rhaeadrddu (black falls) were not to be missed.[23] Indeed no self-respecting tourist could pass them by. The guide claimed to have escorted Wilson, Gainsborough, 'and many other artists',[24] to see the cataract, and the Madockses would have naturally included it in their travels. To William this remote and idyllic valley, with its sheltered meadows protected by wild hills, held special charm and he was fascinated by the falls themselves with their constantly changing moods: their thunder after heavy rain when the water poured through like smoke; their brilliance when shafts of sun broke through the wet oak leaves and warmed the mossy banks where the wild orchids grew; or their quiet after a rare drought.

For him it was not enough to explore the river during a short break on a summer journey up to Snowdonia. He wanted to be free to be there whenever the spirit moved him: to see the young oak bursting in spring or the yellow glory of the woods after the first frost of October. He wanted somewhere to plant trees for himself and practise the picturesque landscape which he and his friends discussed with such verve. Last, but perhaps most important of all, he wanted somewhere deep in his beloved Wales which he could feel to be his own, where he could gather his friends under his own roof. At last this seemed possible.

The land in the valley at the junction of the rivers was divided between two small farms; together with their woodland and some open hill these amounted to only about a hundred acres. It was discovered that three Shrewsbury linen-drapers would be willing to part with it, the mill and fisheries, for £2,500; not so much perhaps, but enough to make a hole in William's capital which would have left little income if judged by the standards of his colleagues. But there was also that sum set aside in his father's will for the purchase of freehold property and William seems to have persuaded his fellow trustees of the soundness of the investment.

As soon as the transaction was completed he built a small house in the simple 'cottage' style of the early villa builders, perhaps a conversion of the existing farm-house.[25] Richard Fenton, the traveller and diarist, described it after one of his visits as having three rooms up and down and 'a wide verandah quite rustick about it'.[26] It was delightfully situated on a little knoll from which the landscape improvements could be enjoyed to the full, but space soon proved cramped and an extension was added: 'near one end of it, scarce seen amongst the shrubs and trees, is a

Gothick building to imitate a ruin overgrown with Ivy, which Mr. Maddox made a Ball room of.'[27]

William was now a Fellow of All Souls and was shortly to be admitted as a student to the Inner Temple but he managed to spend a good deal of time at his beloved Dolmelynllyn (the name was soon contracted by English tongues; letters from London arrived addressed 'Doly, Dolgethly'). Tourists noted with appreciation the new riverside walk which enabled them to admire the falls to much better advantage. On an angular rock facing the water they might have noticed a Latin inscription which had been newly carved. It came from Gray's lines *To the Deity of the Grand Chartreuse* in which the poet calls on the spirit of the woods and waters. 'And we are more conscious of the presence of a god among the pathless rocks, over the savage crests, the rugged steeps, amid the sounding waters, under the night of the groves, than we would be were his image placed under a roof of citruswood, shining with gold and graced with the art of Phidias – All hail to thee! Give thou peaceful rest to the youth who duly invokes thee!'[28]

The 'set' to which this youth belonged were known as *the Chaotics*; it was his greatest delight to lure them down to Doly. When they were not criticising his improvements, exploring the mountains, going on expeditions to see the curious copper-impregnated moss which turned their ponies' hooves a brilliant blue, admiring the medieval ruins at Cymmer Abbey, fishing, or sketching the waterfalls, the house-party was active in writing verse. When a contribution was completed, it was thrown into an old wooden salt-box, chosen with the intention that its contents should have the wit of Attic salt; after dinner when the party lacked sufficient energy for more active entertainment these literary efforts would be read aloud as they sat round the fire. Where actual happenings were described, they give a lively if esoteric picture of the daily events as they occurred to different members of the household. It was an age, too, when puns were exceptionally popular and William, ever a man of the times, was a regrettably apt punster. But the puns had to be new, as the advertisements in the mythical *Doly Gazette* hinted. There was

for instance, decorated with a vigorous pattern of triangles and written in a child's round hand, an ADVERTIZEMENT which ran: 'To be dispos'd of a large quantity of cast off jokes, Puns, Puzzles and conundrums but little worse for wear, some scraps of Greek and Latin in the hands of the owners, together with a large collection of anecdotes in high preservation. . . .'[29]
and another headed
'Advertisement for a *Good Pun*: it is expected when required he shall serve the whole family in turn. . . . Inquire at the Mad Dogs at Dolmelynllyn.'[30]

These house-parties took the keenest interest in the picturesque, and discussed it warmly, taking sides with the various fashions of the day. For William, nature herself was to be exemplified and made, if anything, more rugged, romantic and wild. Surprisingly, the salt-box verses show that the laid-out garden as well as the more recent vogue of Chinoiserie was still common in spite of the onslaught of picturesque propaganda:

> 'Oh! Dolly, may no impious wretch
> Thy native charms disorder
> No strait parterre around thee stretch
> Adorned with boxen border!
>
> No leaden shepherds with their crooks
> Be there, no Gods of Plaister,
> No Chinese bridges cross thy brooks
> No Yew hedge Square be past her!'[31]

This cult was not to be taken over-seriously. The property was advertised by another contributor as 'a most elegant and complete Ferme Ornée, most desirably situated for those, who are desirous of blending Taste with Rusticity, and Elegance with Retirement. This beautiful Bijou displays itself on the Verge of an extensive Goose Common. . . .'[32]

While the visitors also delighted in the rare and splendid trees which were planted, the results were seldom quick enough for their owner. Clearing and felling to improve the prospect was a satisfactory occupation but he found tree growing to be a slow business which sorely tried his patience. Transplanting was rather quicker in its results but in his enthusiasm he was constantly tempted both to move large trees and to transplant at the wrong time of year:

> 'Soon as the Vernal Tint appear'd
> The budding trees at Dolly heard
> Their Master's dread command
> That every individual twig
> Must run again another rig
> Which he hath lately plann'd . . .'[33]

and so for a dozen or more verses the silviculture of their impetuous host might be gently mocked by Doly's guests.

Expeditions were also a source of contributions and one from John Madocks gives a nice idea of the kind of mishap the Chaotics most enjoyed. It was entitled:

> 'Inscription
> Upon a rock supporting a bridge over the river
> Mawddach at Dolymelynllyn in Merionethshire'

> 'This Monument
> Was not erected in commemoration
> of the memorable escape
> Of The Rt. Honble. the Lady Baroness Stowell
> The Honble. Miss Legge
> W. A. Madocks, Esq.
> P. Francis Junr. Esq.
> J. W. Warren Esq.
> and
> The Chevalier Grog*
> Who after having eat a very good breakfast
> Seen two Waterfalls
> Been drenched in the rain and mud till their very nankeen
> Pantaloons and dimity petticoats cried out Shame!
> After being lost on untrod mountains

*William's dog

and pathless forests
and cut off by roaring cataracts from all hope
of Dinner
And confronted by Death and Rheumatism in various shapes
Here found rest at last!

'Upon a slippery pinnacle
Surrounded by raging torrents which roared destruction
on every side
Embracing and embraced they sat
Invoking the protection of Heaven and the assistance of
Thomas Paine *
Their vows were heard. . . .'34

'The Deluge – An Epic Poem' on the same subject bewailed this vogue for Welsh cascades and the miseries of cold, wet and hunger that had to be endured to admire them. There was no end to their verse making. Some were serious but few were political; unfortunately the Chaotics and the Radicals did not mix well, these last usually being too earnest in temperament and taste. Other poems were fashionably romantic; the female guests preferred to contribute this type. The Baroness Stowell, for instance, deposited a long and melancholy ballad in which a luckless youth searched 'for two long years absorbed in grief' for his unintentionally unfaithful Julia who, as it turned out, was already dead; but, finally, '. . . as a friend, to his relief, Death joined their souls in One.'35

In her farewell verse the Baroness hinted that her host should take note of this cautionary tale. Perhaps she felt he was nursing some hopeless passion; with an unmarried daughter on her hands such a state of affairs could not be allowed. However, if this was the case it would have been in character for him to mask it. Certainly his other guests had not noticed: he was described as 'Dolly's spouse, so young, so gay, so free' and at the break up of a billiard party during the same holiday he seems to be just that: 'William, who high upon the stairs, Reel'd with Madeira to and

* Agent to the property

fro . . .' was reported to have addressed a somewhat forward member of the fair sex in a gallant speech beginning 'Oh Suzette, fair as Cream of Tartar. . . .'[36]

It would be surprising if William's heart had not warmed to one, if not several, young women at this period. He enjoyed their company as they did his and had a spontaneous and affectionate nature. In an attractively contradictory personality, practical realism and romantic idealism were combined in interesting if uncomfortable proportions. But matrimony was to be out of the question for some time yet. He belonged to the eighteenth-century landowning gentry whose sons did not wed without some prospects, and whose daughters were still less encouraged to do so. It had been in order for John as heir to marry at twenty-one and a generous settlement was arranged for his needs. For William such a step could not be considered until he had been called to the Bar. Meanwhile he seemed to be in no hurry to settle; at twenty-five life was very enjoyable and it was obvious that marriage would mean harder work and less amusement; worse, it would mean much less freedom to run down to Wales. He might, by some happy chance, meet an heiress but since in William's mind it was first essential that she won his heart the chances of marriage were long.

However there seems to be evidence of one budding romance of the Dolmelynllyn days but, sadly, it does not seem to have prospered. In an exercise book, very neatly copied in a girl's hand, there is a series of letters from William to a 'Dear Coz'.[37] They were in fact only related in the friendly Welsh sense of claiming distant connections as kin but this form of address was probably used to avoid detection since all names in the correspondence were carefully changed to inverted initials. Her brother was Watkin Hayman who was one of William's closest friends. Although crippled from childhood he was one of the liveliest of the Chaotics and his sister seems to have been like him. The copying must have been a painstaking labour of love on her part and the contents suggest that William was very fond of her.

Whatever her identity,[38] we owe to this girl light on other facets of William's character. She shared his varied enthusiasms and, it is much to be hoped, his addiction to puns. The correspondence shows a scientific curiosity which is as surprising to find in William as in herself; they exchanged books on Chemistry and attended scientific lectures, and samples of manganese were sent from Doly to lure her to Wales where she was promised not only scenic grandeur but also microscopic wonder. His letters were mostly in a light vein but they were occasionally more serious. For instance, triggered off suddenly by the capture of Malta, William expressed remarkably twentieth-century sentiments: 'What do you think of Buonaparte's taking Malta? There's no end to him. I already begin to hate Heroes. . . . Providence . . . sends them as an affliction to the human race. They are only made to disturb and destroy. There is a plausibility about military glory which makes it doubly dangerous. A triumph is a fine shew & captivates the indiscriminate eye of the vulgar, but when the mind retraces in detail the horrible scenes which were contributary to that Triumph, Glory is death & Military fame, eternal disgrace.' The letter concentrated realistically on the appalling misery that war brings to the ordinary people whom it overwhelms. He foresaw a long war (this letter was written seventeen years before Waterloo). 'That one madman may play a principal part on the Theatre of Europe and go thro' 3 or 4 editions of the History of the World, the whole bulk of mankind are to be put in motion, their alarms & their fears raised to a pitch of torture. . . .

'A Hero or two in every country once in a Century, would soon drive us all back to Savages and my faith now goes to the belief that Heroes are sent to Earth to retard the too rapid progress of improvement towards civilization and Happiness. So much for Buonaparte but I fear you will be the real sufferer. With many apologies for so Riotous a Pen. Believe me no Hero but yours affectionately. . . .'[39]

William did not make a habit of disclosing his deeper feelings and in his next letter he expressed relief that she had 'looked indulgently on his nonsensical rhapsody about Buonaparte'. It seemed that he feared that she might find him pompous. Some of those

things about which he was beginning to care most were of little
interest to the confident generation of the landed families with
whom he had been brought up. But in other ways he felt completely at home in their company, talking the same language,
enjoying the same jokes, knowing the same people. The majority
of those zealous reformers whom he met in England were of a
different cast. The two could not mix and when the following
winter he wrote from the Temple or Oxford he was ever impatient to be in Wales. From All Souls he complained of 'being
locked up in the solemn gloom of a College, instead of revelling
in the Principality at its gayest and most fantastic season' and he
remembered that he was missing a dance in Wrexham that very
evening, hinting that had he been there he would have been on
the look-out for a 'Partner for Life' and not merely for a single
caper. But whatever may have been hoped this relationship seems
to have developed into a long friendship, with his cousin a
regular visitor to Doly and a confidante in many of his schemes.

Christmas, 1798, was a very anxious time for them. Both
Watkin Hayman and John's wife, Elizabeth, were seriously ill.
William himself was laid up in his rooms in the Temple with one
of the severe attacks of rheumatism which had already begun to
afflict him; to add to this misery he had a very sore throat. He
wrote to his cousin for news of Watkin: 'Pray let me here from
you *very often*' and commented on the profusion of advice offered
by all who wished one well: 'Those whose opinion one can't
respect one wished to the D – – –L. Those whose advice is respected generally distract by their contradiction' and he urged that
they should all meet in Bath early in the New Year.

But this reunion was not to be, for both Elizabeth and Watkin
died on January 3. William's first duty was to his own family
so he could not join his Coz. so he wrote at once: 'To your great
and good mind, with equal powers to bear as to feel your affliction
any attempt to offer consolation would be impertinent.' Instead
he reminded her of the idyllic days they had all spent at Doly in
the summer just passed. But he finished on a more philosophic
note and it is strange that the analogy he chose should so closely
describe the disaster which was to overwhelm him thirteen years

later. 'Life, like the sands on the shore, is often ruffled and dis-
turbed by storms, but time and circumstances repair the damage
as the tide gradually fills up the hollows, and smooths the
inequalities, but the loss of W. is irreparable. He has left a void
which nothing can fill up.'

The approaching spring and his cousin's letters buoyed his
spirits once more when they were soon to meet. Again the letters
slant light on a nice piece of introspection: 'I know not how to
feel so grateful as I ought when you have done little less than
set my greatest Enemy against me more than ever, and loaded
my vanity with fresh powers to maintain its dominion. I cannot
help acknowledging the kindness of your intention in endeavour-
ing to make me friends with myself & admiring the infallible
means you have selected to accomplish it.' But self-analysis soon
gave way to schemes for the summer during which he planned
'that we may exchange the festivities of Cader and Snowdon as
often as we please, & indulge in a full swing of Chaotic Caprice'.
Some new idea was evidently maturing.

2

Traeth Mawr and Boston
1798-1804

EVEN DURING that first idyllic summer at Doly a new and much broader scheme had begun to take shape in William's mind. While the valley provided all that could be asked for as a subject for picturesque improvement, and as a base for sociable house-parties nothing could be more agreeable, that was the full extent of the potentialities of the small estate. William had realised these limitations from the start. Many of his contemporaries would have been well content with things as they stood, and would have happily divided their time between Wales and London with numerous visits to English country-houses and perhaps inter-vening spells at Bath or some other resort. But for William's growing interests and enthusiasms this was not enough. Had the Law or even some more defined intellectual activity than his propensity for wide reading and book-collecting absorbed his energies, Doly would have provided an ideal retreat from the Temple and All Souls. With Mount Mascall, too, always available when he wanted a short break in the country, he would appear to have had an excellent assortment of bases from which to pursue his varied interests. But since at heart he was neither a lawyer nor a dilettante this was not enough.

The career into which he had been directed in his father's distinguished footsteps had become an absorbing sideline. Architecture and planning fascinated him. And yet, although he spent so much of his time in designing and shaping his new property, he still never sketched for pleasure as did so many far less creative

4

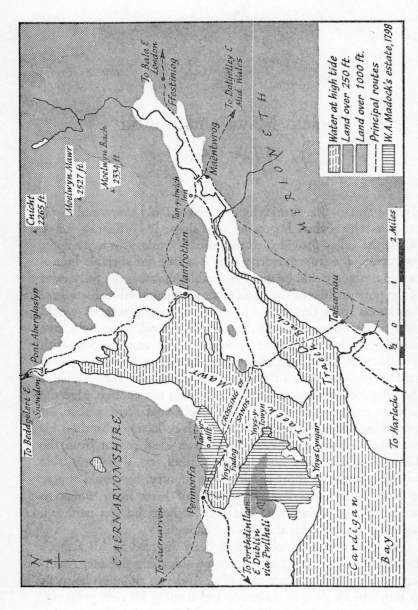

Traeth Mawr and region, 1798, when William Madocks bought the Penmorfa estate

Map labels:

N

To Beddgelert &
Snowdon

CAERNARVONSHIRE

To Caernarvon

Cnicht
2265 ft.

Moelwyn Mawr
2527 ft.

Moelwyn Bach
2334 ft.

Pont Aberglaslyn

To Bala &
London

Ffestiniog

Tan-y-bwlch

Tan-y-bwlch
Inn

Llanfrothen

Maentwrog

To Dolgelley &
Mid Wales

M E R I O N E T H

Penmorfa

Tan-yr-
allt

Ynys
Fadog

CROSSING OF
SANDS

Ynys-y-
Tywyn

Ynys Cyngar

T r a e t h   M a w r

T r a e t h   B a c h

Talsarnau

To Harlech

Cardigan Bay

To Portdinllaen
& Dublin
via Pwllheli

Legend:

Water at high tide
Land over 250 ft.
Land over 1000 ft.
Principal routes
W. A. Madock's estate, 1798

0   ½   1   2 Miles

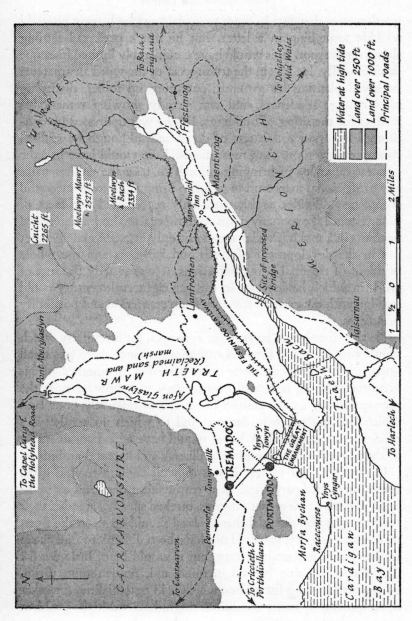

Traeth Mawr and region, 1836, after the completion of the Festiniog Railway

gentlemen in that day. In order to explain an idea by post he could scribble something in a letter, but he much preferred settling things on the spot. This would have considerably limited his scope professionally. He was in the truest sense of the word an amateur: he loved planting his grounds, conjuring up follies, discussing ideal cottage residences, and was already showing remarkable instinct for the siting of buildings. But he was oppressed by continuous attention to matters of detail and, although he realised its importance more than most men did, he would have had the greatest difficulty in bringing himself to take the endless pains any professional man must in order to bring a job to its successful completion. Besides, architecture only represented one facet of his interests. Like so many of his contemporaries, he was interested in affairs in a much broader sense: not only in estate management but in the development of roads and harbours and the whole problem of regional communications. It was exactly the sort of work in which landowners in the late eighteenth century could indulge with the greatest freedom from restriction and possibility of success.

He therefore began to keep his eyes open for a property which would provide scope for such enthusiasms. Since there was small hope of the Madocks estate trust investing in another of his ventures so soon, it would be necessary somehow to raise the money himself and to restrict his search to relatively poor land which was not much in demand and to which no gentleman's residence was attached. A house would have added considerably to the price, besides cramping William's architectural ambitions.

In the fifth year of war it was difficult enough to find good agricultural land anywhere at a reasonable price; and since he had lost none of his earlier interests, but had simply extended their range, it was also essential that his land should be set in the finest picturesque scenery. It would not have been difficult to find cheap property in a mountain setting, but it would be of little use for the kind of farming he had in mind and, remembering Erith, he was also looking for a place which held potentialities for other development. So many conditions might have made the problem seem insoluble: but William was not deterred.

A favourite expedition from Doly was an excursion to admire the splendours of Snowdonia. The party would travel due north to the junction at Maentwrog with the road which runs down the upper part of the Vale of Ffestiniog from Bala and England. They would probably stay the night at the famous Tan-y-bwlch Inn and next morning reach the great estuary of the Glaslyn which divided the counties of Caernarvon and Merioneth. Here they would turn inland and, with Snowdon looming ahead of them, make their way up the edge of the sands to Pont Aberglaslyn, where they could stop for a meal and watch for the fish at the famous salmon leap before entering the splendid pass which led up to Beddgelert and Snowdon itself.

For the sake of variety, on the return journey William might bring them back down the far side of the estuary. Although there was no track except a rather hazardous path at the foot of the cliffs, the discomforts of the journey were amply rewarded.

The scene set by Traeth Mawr (the Great Sands) was remarkably grand; it was far wilder than that of the better known Vale of Ffestiniog which ran down to Traeth Bach immediately to the south. Of that valley Lord Lyttelton had written on his tour 'With the woman one loves, with the friends of one's heart, and a good library of books, one might pass an age there and think it a day,'[1] but he had given a rather less tranquil picture of Traeth Mawr: 'The view of these sands is terrible, as they are hemmed in on each side with very high hills, but broken into a thousand irregular shapes. At one end is the ocean, at the other the formidable mountains of Snowdon, black and naked rocks, which seem to be piled one above the other; the summits of some of them are covered with clouds, and cannot be ascended. The grandeur of the ocean corresponding with that of the mountain, formed a majestic and solemn scene; ideas of immensity swelled and exalted our minds at the sight; all lesser objects appeared mean and trifling so that we would scarcely do justice to the ruins of an old castle. . . .'[2] This was indeed a warm recommendation.

William's detour not only gave an opportunity to admire this splendour from another viewpoint, but it enabled him to point out a small rocky island near the mouth of the estuary from which, legend had it, the famous Prince Madoc had sailed to discover America in the twelfth century. Although he did not claim descent from this illustrious explorer, their common name was a bond and the story would appeal to his romantically minded guests. (Robert Southey was soon to retell the legend in his epic and widely popular poem, *Madoc*.)

An awkward stage of William's expedition now had to be faced since the Traeth itself, a great inlet of the sea, barred their way south. It must either be crossed or they must retrace their steps back up the estuary to the lowest bridge, Pont Aberglaslyn.

If the tide was out travellers usually hired a guide to take them over the treacherous sands. Otherwise they waited for the small boat which acted as a ferry. This could be equally unnerving: a reverend gentleman from Bath,[3] for instance, recorded how his party crossed 'in a small leaky skiff with a heavy gale right against us', and the journey at low tide was sufficiently perilous for the intrepid Richard Fenton to write in his journal 'Crossed the sands without a Guide, safe thank God, the water in the Glas-lyn being rather low and not the least affected by the rain over-night'[4] and, on another occasion, 'Though in one sense the Ride is charming, yet it can't fail to excite a degree of horror, and after it is past, a degree of gratitude at our preservation. . . .' All in all the estuary was romantic, beautiful, dangerously unpredictable, and extremely inconvenient.

But Traeth Mawr also held possibilities of quite another kind: during the previous twenty-five years parcels of land had been reclaimed all along its shores (but chiefly from the Merioneth side) by means of simple earth embankments. The steady rise in the price of land everywhere in these war years had accelerated the enclosure movement throughout the country and, since the government had encouraged the enclosure policy, scores of bills had passed through Parliament chiefly for the fencing of common land or hill. But on the Traeth it was not even necessary to go to the expense of obtaining an Act of Parliament for such enclosure; ownership of the adjoining shore was in itself sufficient. Here then was an ideal place to search for relatively cheap property in unsurpassed scenery with seemingly boundless opportunities for agricultural improvement.

But first land for sale at a reasonable price had to be found, and this might mean a long wait. Again William's luck was in. In 1798, less than two years after the move to Dolmelynllyn, some small farms near Penmorfa on the Caernarvonshire side of Traeth Mawr were to come on the market.[5] Their acreage is not recorded but even allowing for the poorness of the land, which in general consisted of either rough hill grazing or boggy ill-drained ground on the edge of the estuary, a total annual rental of £221 10 0 cannot have represented anything very grand. They consisted of eight holdings in all. The smallest, Ynys Fadog, took its name from that rocky island from which Prince Madoc may have set sail for the New World; it was let for £1 0 0. The largest had a rental of £51 0 0; if wartime inflation had affected this property as it had most, these figures represent a humble estate. But to William they meant a kingdom of infinite possibility and a chance which might never occur again. It was essential that he should somehow raise the money to buy immediately. Fortunately there was the scattered Denbighshire property left to him by his father which could be used as security against which funds might be borrowed.

His mother listened to his latest schemes with anxiety. It was madness to embark on yet more property if he ever hoped to finish reading for the Bar but, at best, this now seemed a doubtful possibility. It might be better that he should have other irons in the fire if only she could believe that they would be properly forged. Despite the many anxieties that William had often caused her, it was impossible for Frances Madocks long to resist the combined onslaught of his own genuine conviction of the possibilities of a scheme coupled with that special affection she had for her youngest son. But she was determined that he should keep out of the hands of the money-lenders and, knowing that now his mind was made up he would go through with the deal somehow, she decided to lend the money herself. The dream thus became a reality with unhoped-for speed.

It was only possible to guess at William's ultimate objective when he first bought the Penmorfa farms in 1798, but whatever practical reasons he may have put forward there is little doubt that he completely fell for the place itself; for the ever surprising wonder of any country where water runs up into the mountains. Each full moon the spring tides transformed the Traeth into a great inland sea, five miles across at its widest point. On the Caernarvon shore, at the north end of the estate, the valley was walled by sheer crags, which, rising precipitously from sea level, seemed much higher than they in fact were. To the east the Merioneth hills climbed away less hurriedly to rise to the magnificent silhouette of the Moelwyns and the Cnicht. To the north, as a stupendous backcloth, lay the Snowdon range; the scale of the nearer crags gave it an almost Himalayan grandeur and added to the illusion of remote height. But what counted most was the ever shifting light. In sunlight after heavy rain, the mountains had that blueness seldom seen except on the west coast of Britain; everything was sharp and defined; the rain-washed rocks had the clarity of a wet sea shell, quite unlike the dry, hazy blue of landlocked mountains. Except after rare stretches of drought, here was none of that dusty, bloom of grape, distance. Often William would be there on quiet days of gentle mist when the Atlantic clouds hung about the mountain tops. It was never quite the same; for remote majesty there were days of September gales; or in spring when the wild daffodils were yellow in the meadows, the mountains might be astonishingly transformed, suddenly snow-covered against a pale blue east wind sky.

As the tide fell, the Traeth itself was equally unpredictable and the valley floor as well as the mountains took up the changing light. Sheets of water shrank exposing small sand banks left yellow and clean by the falling tide. Changing minute by minute, this inland sea became a diminishing lake which itself ebbed away leaving only the ribbon of river streaming quietly seaward across wide stretches of shining wet sand contrasting brightly with the stretches of dark marsh and the flats of salt grass. The only moving thing, except for the wind tearing across the rushes and changing their dark brown to khaki green as they bent, were the small black cattle, and the grey sheep, and the marsh birds. The curlews summed up the whole feeling of the Traeth; its untamed character of wildness, solitude, and near despair. They, and the peewits pairing in the spring, and the wild duck flocking in their thousands in winter, added to that undefinable melancholy that was so necessary to the romantic in the age of which William was so much a part.

His first scheme was the direct and practical undertaking of reclaiming about a thousand acres of the marsh and tidal sands which bordered the new property and turning it into good pasture. 1799, which had opened with so much personal anxiety for William and his family, ended with privation and hunger for thousands of others. A cold, wet summer had meant a poor harvest, and this, for the many who at best lived near subsistence level, could only mean one thing. While the better-to-do were shaken into some realisation of the general financial situation of the country through introduction of income tax by Pitt, others were wondering how their families were to survive.

During the hungry winter which followed William made his plans for the spring. Immediately the March gales were over he intended to make a start on his enclosure scheme. Since he owned land on both sides of an inlet which ran into the Traeth from Penmorfa an embankment could be built right across its mouth to protect it completely from the sea. No Act of Parliament was necessary but experienced advice was certainly needed. Since his neighbours showed little enthusiasm, and several actually opposed the scheme, William sought the professional help of an engineer, James Creassy, who had considerable experience of such schemes in England, particularly in Lincolnshire where he had surveyed and reported on the Bedford Level many years previously: sea banks therefore held few surprises for him. Creassy's confidence must have been particularly helpful at a time when so many others were antagonistic or indifferent. The engineer told later, in his report to the Board of Agriculture, how 'the works were carried out by him [Madocks] in a very spirited manner, not withstanding the rooted prejudices of the neighbouring inhabitants against all such improvements; and the whole of the works were in consequence finished between the two equinoxes.'[6] Creassy also stated that with forty-five years' experience behind him he 'entertained no doubt of the goodness and fertility of the land when reclaimed'. (See map, page 136.)

Not everyone opposed the scheme; for the workmen who were employed it meant far more than a hope of better things to come. The Rector of Penmorfa,[7] told the Board that 'this meritorious undertaking has been a great blessing to the country, particularly during the scarcity of 1800, when above 200 poor men were in constant employ, and kept off the neighbouring parishes, greatly to their relief and comfort, while all around were starving'. The bank thus had much the same effect as that of the destitution roads and other charitable building schemes which were instituted for relief of the potato famine in Scotland some forty years later. It was the greatest satisfaction to William, who was already feeling the need for more ready cash, to be able to relieve such suffering while prosecuting his own ends.

The embankment[8] which they built was over two miles long and varied in height from twenty to eleven feet. It was made simply of sea sand covered by sods so the slopes of its sides had to be very gradual and its base correspondingly wide (eleven acres of turf were needed just to cover it).

However simple this method of construction, the labour of moving those hundreds of thousands of yards of sand by shovel and wheelbarrow was colossal, and this was only a part of the work.[9] The report described how 'the sluices for venting the inland waters and freshes, were the greatest expense'. Their foundations, on shifting sands, necessitated sheet piling and 'expensive oak frame-work, before three large stone arches could be turned'. The cost of this embankment was £2,800 excluding fences, roads and land drainage, particularly the 'making of 2 great cuts or dykes under the high-lands to act as catch-water drains and to convey the waters off to the sea before reaching the flat'. Creassy was very particular about this provision; it was too often forgotten that the water from the surrounding hills could leave reclaimed land boggy and unproductive even when the sea had been effectually kept out. He described how in Lincolnshire the

Romans had cut 'that vast work called the Carr Dike'[10] for the same purpose and, true to form, William named the barely navigable ditch that drained the foot of his hills after the great Roman canal.

Work on the Traeth went with a swing. The first sod had been ceremoniously cut at the end of March and the men dug with gusto. Half-way through the summer William described the scene to his Dear Coz: 'I am now at Penmorva amidst 150 wheelbarrows and 200 Spades and hearts too all attempting Canute like to set boundaries to the Ocean and make old Neptune back his chariot. . . . I am just now sitting in a Fisherman's hut on the Seashore and am fancying I have learned that "Man wants little here below".' Such serenity was rare. The rhythm imposed by the tides which inevitably governed the timing of the work, and the sense of achievement both mental and physical which came from spending long hours in the open overseeing the scheme, gave William one of the happiest summers of his life. Luckily the weather was with him. Day after day the sun beat down. The squeaking of the barrow wheels, the thud of the spades as they thumped down load after load on the slowly growing bank and the intermittent shouts of the foremen's orders broke the drowsy midsummer. This local whirr of activity contrasted strangely with the quiet of the empty marsh. Then the steadily rising tide would put a halt to the work on the bank itself; a sudden silence would come over the Traeth as the men broke off for their oatmeal cakes and llymru. In the cold of the early morning, or towards sunset, they would build brushwood fires to keep off the damp chill and, as they squatted round them, their songs would rise from the misty estuary to the surrounding hills. It was then that William could come nearest to them. On the job, language difficulties confined communication to a technical minimum, but he could join easily in their singing, picking up new harmonies as quickly as any, and, in return, introduce them to the latest operatic successes which had reached London or improvise an 'interlude'[11] on some topical event, in the fashion of the day.

The land reclaimed (1,082 acres) varied from stiff to very light but it was said to be 'on the whole of a very productive nature'.

In 1801 a large tract was under oats, the year following wheat and rape, and the third year barley and grass seeds. The ultimate object was permanent pasture; 'the plough has been used with a view principally to bring the surface into good form, and prepare the land for being well laid down.' Another local rector wrote 'I can also assert that the finest clover I ever beheld, grew where there were only sands, prior to this great undertaking.'[12] Remarks like these together with Creassy's report had the gratifying result of causing the Board of Agriculture to award the project its Gold Medal.

William now wanted to set work going on the Traeth. Pig rearing was started; a rope-walk laid out; and the export of paving stones begun. He could never be enough in the Principality and whenever he was in England he was straining to be back. From All Souls he wrote to his cousin again. He was thinking a hundred times a day of Wales and, at all hours of the night, his thoughts flew there 'like a King's Messengar, at any time, Post Chaise'. Only a couple of years earlier when he had been enjoying himself at 'Lord R's, Midhurst, Sussex' he had implored his cousin's support at Mount Mascall. Then he had spent a very 'Anti-Chaotic evening' with his mother who had been urging that he should be more at Penmorfa. Matters were now quite different. With the bank completed, there would be time for things beyond the immediate concern of the estate: 'You must promise to spend a month with me in Snowdonia in the atumn,' he wrote, 'you have not half a notion of the chaos till you have explored these mountains. Cader Idris is a polished place to some of the lofty and rugged scenery I can show you. I am grown a great sailor and Cardigan Bay on a fine day is the rehearsal of Elysium. How should you like to play with a Solar Microscope? There is such an abundance of natural curiosities, particularly marine about these coasts. . . . I think we might venture to enlist one for next summer. The insects, fish and transparent vegetables are here beautiful and rare.'

The great drawback about such plans was that the property boasted no base for such hospitality. The dwelling-houses attached to the farms, besides being integral with the farm buildings to which they belonged, were mostly ill-constructed hovels as was to be expected in a poor district with an absentee landlord, which was typical of Wales at this time. The existing buildings also tended to be dank and low-lying on the edge of the marsh, or almost inaccessible in the rocky hinterland.

But, to William's sense of the site's potential, there was one cottage which held possibilities. It was narrow and dark and faced north straight into a steeply rising hillside, but was sheltered from the south-westerly gales. Tan-yr-allt means, very appropriately, 'under the wooded cliff'; the cottage was built on a shelf about a hundred feet above the level of the estuary. Probably the cowbyre and living quarters were under one roof, as it was a long building, one room thick; or it might have been a pair of cottages.

Shelter was of prime importance to a traditional Welsh house. Sun was not much considered, and the idea that there should be a view would be thought extraordinary, but this cottage only needed to be opened up at the back to command the most splendid prospect over the newly embanked land and the little wooded islands that studded the Traeth to the Merioneth hills or to the broad open waters of the estuary towards the open sea in the west. The spell of Tan-yr-allt still rests in this rare combination of sheltered seclusion and open aspect.

A new range of rooms was now added right across the south face of the cottage so that the back became the front (see painting facing page 96). Nothing at all grand; just two comfortable parlours with a stair hall in the middle and three bedrooms above. It could hardly have been more straightforward and sounds the kind of addition any of the neighbouring gentry might have made. Like their houses, it too was built of local stone with a slate roof, but there the similarity ends. The new style which Tan-yr-allt introduced to North Wales (as Doly may have to Merioneth) had a lightness and elegance which gave a sense of civilised ease quite foreign to the sturdy forthrightness of the vernacular building tradition. Travellers of the day were enthusiastic, but seem to have been slightly taken aback by its simplicity. A full-page engraving appeared in the *European Magazine* with the explanation 'Mr Madocks' cottage . . . was built more for a convenient residence than for splendour of show'[13] while the *North Wales*

Gazette described it as an 'elegant villa, the simplicity of which corresponds with the scenery around it'. (Surely only a native reporter could then have dismissed Snowdonia in such unexalted terms?) Perhaps some extravagantly romantic cottage ornée was expected of its fashionable owner who, it might be guessed, would have fancy London ideas. What they found was a long low house, with a shallow hipped roof and widely projecting eaves; on the ground floor was a generous verandah, roofed in slate like the house, onto which french windows led from the main rooms, so that there was, in effect, a colonnade on three sides, binding the old house to the new. The gently pitched roof with its deep eaves which was to become a hallmark of Regency houses in England gave the house a character utterly different from that of the clipped eaves and gables traditional to windswept coastal or mountain regions.

Such roofs were made possible by improved methods of slate quarrying which were beginning to be practised, notably at the Penrhyn quarries near Bangor. Much larger slates of standard size were now cut, and, where these were used, steep pitches were no longer necessary to make a roof waterproof. William knew Benjamin Wyatt,[14] one of the architect brothers of James Wyatt. He was agent and architect to the Penrhyn estate so it was possible through him to get the best material for Tan-yr-allt. Even so there was still the difficulty of finding slaters who knew how to fix it and, champing to be in residence but with the house still open to the sky, Madocks urged that a message be sent to Wyatt: '. . . state my predicament; that the house is uncovered and that I am *detained* in *London* for want of a couple of *Understanding Men* for a few days to put on Lord Penrhyn's slates.' So new was this fashion of a low pitched roof that when Horace Billington, the painter, who was a close friend of the Madockses, made a drawing of Tan-yr-allt it was automatically shown with a traditional pitch rather than what was actually there. It may have been the roof which surprised Fenton who commented: 'Mr Madocks has built himself a house of singular cast'[15] or perhaps it was the casement windows which were certainly an innovation after a century of sliding sashes in any self-respecting residence. Certainly there was nothing else remarkable about the design except its charm and extreme simplicity and in this it seems to reflect John Madocks' cottage, Holly Hill.

The new rooms in Tan-yr-allt were of pleasant but modest proportions. The walls of one of the parlours were lined with silk and it had the unusual but very attractive feature of a window over the chimney-piece. Most of these chimney-pieces were made of local slate and, probably, to copy-book designs supplied by William but one, in 'very handsome Marble', was shipped from London. A billiard room had been provided in the old cottage and a water-closet, perhaps the only one in this part of the Principality, had been installed in a converted pantry. William was particularly proud of this innovation but it caused considerable trouble. Anxious but technically unenlightening appeals concerning its well-being dot the correspondence: 'Drive on the house, the *Water Closet Remember*.' If the new bedrooms had shallow vaulted ceilings which added greatly to their charm, nowhere was there anything extravagant or luxurious. It was all on a modest scale; so modest that in a very short time it was necessary to build on. But William had every right to be proud of this conversion which bears all the marks of an exceptionally sensitive and knowledgeable amateur using his own wits to interpret a design seen in an architectural book, or possibly a sketch made by a friend back in England. The idea may have come via Doly which, judging from Fenton's description, seems to have been similar.

It was then still common for any educated man to take a keen interest in architectural matters. Large numbers of books were printed to satisfy this interest and these, with the excellent builders' copy-books which were published in profusion, meant that sound and even elegant design could percolate quite humble builders' yards. We can thank this system for the marvellous legacy of building of much of Georgian England. In Wales, the lack of demand for more stylish houses than the traditional farm, itself a most satisfying building, meant a lack of interest in innovation. Many of the charming Georgian and Regency buildings that are still to be found in some seaside resorts (Beaumaris or Aberayron for example) were actually built in Victorian times.

To William this was the beginning of the realisation of his dream. Long before Tan-yr-allt was completed house-parties at Doly had been interrupted to go to inspect works in progress, reluctant guests dragged from the comforts and beauties of that abode to enthuse, if they could, over the wonders of Tany.[16] Now, as his guests swept up the new carriage drive, amazed by the splendid panorama that lay at their feet, they were equally delighted to find the house with its broad sunlit verandah and the cool eating parlour behind where the sideboard was loaded with an ample collation for the refreshment of hungry travellers.

The garden too was quite modest in size but nothing was stinted: 'Mignionette & Sweet Peas, universally & in abundance' was a typical Madocks instruction. Roses were his favourite above all other flowers. 'I want 1,000's,' he wrote, the noughts ending in a descriptive squiggle trailing off into infinity. All old-fashioneds, their marvellous scents, sharpened by the tang of salt air, would drift through the house and, as the blooms fell, the petals would blow in shoals through the french windows. Vines were planted along the colonnade and the walled garden, sloping down the hillside towards the sun, was well stocked: peas, beans, broccoli, 'sallads', chervil and chicory. Raspberries and strawberries also flourished and Hugh, who like all gardeners took pride in early fruit and vegetables, had to be discouraged from having everything at its prime some weeks before a house-party was due to arrive.

It is easy to imagine William sitting under the colonnade in the late afternoon sun. The less politically minded of the Chaotics might have taken themselves off to explore the romantic pass to Beddgelert while their host talked with his knowing London guests about the Irish question or maybe the latest production at the Haymarket or the boundless possibilities of the estate.

A difficulty which was constantly to confront him, as it must have perplexed many other go-ahead landlords of that day, was the apparently insoluble contradiction of resolving his intense admiration for the picturesque with a typically rational eighteenth-century attitude towards the improvement of land. As soon as the new embankment was completed, the land was drained. The ditches and fences, like the bank itself, ran in straight lines. It was only logical that they should. The next objective was to establish a large nursery of trees; a particularly important project in such a barren area. The seedlings too were best planted in lines with long straight avenues between them. Admittedly those 'large drains and neat embankments' fencing the enclosed land on the neighbouring estate of Tan-y-bwlch were much admired by tourists, but William felt in his heart that it would have been much better without them. How could such things be tolerated after the romantic wilderness of Doly?

With Tany nearly complete the problem of letting Doly to a suitable tenant arose. But 'suitable' did not merely mean someone who would regularly pay the rent, although this was of importance in William's ever precarious financial position. His Coz had been active in the matter but he feared that a would-be tenant whom she had suggested might not be sufficiently *'chatoically* formed as to be completely worthy of Doly'. The tenant must be an 'incontestible disciple of Mirth, Taste and irregularity to take Doly in trust for such uses . . . that we may exchange the festivities of Cader and Snowdonia as often as we please, & indulge in a full swing of Chaotic Caprice. . . . I do not mean to exclude the Parties you allude to, but pray examine them if you have any further notion of them, as if they were candidates for the conclave, or lots of old china at an auction before the inquisitive spectacle of a connoiseur Dowager. . . .'

The 'full swing of Chaotic Caprice' seemed essential to William. In a more serious mood he had recently written a long doggerel on the importance of contrast to the real enjoyment of every aspect of living. This attitude was to be the greatest blessing in his own life which was to be coloured by extremes of light and shade, some of his own choosing but much unsought.

At this stage, he was still choosing, and although he was to be more and more occupied in schemes in Wales, he decided to stand for Parliament. The choice of constituency may not have been his, but Boston in Lincolnshire which he was to represent could hardly have been more remote geographically or spiritually from his beloved Caernarvonshire.

5

He got a chance to stand in the by-election of 1802. The freemen of Boston[17] were rightly proud of the fact that it was not a rotten or pocket borough, and to William, who was consistently to stand for parliamentary reform rather than for party, this was of great significance. In this matter he stood well to the left of the Whig party to which most of his political colleagues belonged. Boston's poll of some six hundred may now seem paltry, but in the context of the day, when the majority of seats were sold by those who held the interest to the highest bidder reflecting the political views of the landowner who traded it, this was indeed freedom. To his great delight William came top of the poll and was to hold his seat for the next eighteen years.

On visiting his constituency he exchanged the mountains and mists of Caernarvonshire for the great fenland of South Lincolnshire with its immense skies and towering cumulus clouds; the moist airs of the south-west winds for the clear dry easterlies, shrill as a whistle; the grey stone and slate for brick and tile; the independent poetic Celt, for the equally independent rational Bostonian. Although so much about the town was utterly foreign to his own property in Caernarvonshire, the ideas behind this bustling, expanding seaport were very similar to those which were quite soon to be the preoccupations of its M.P. He had had, from the start, a common interest with the neighbouring landlords in reclamation and drainage schemes. The first embankment on Traeth Mawr was built two years before he entered Parliament; he may have got to know the locality because of his schemes in Wales, or seen possibilities in Wales through the work done by colleagues in Lincolnshire. The Erith marshes were already familiar, so the connection may have been a chance matter, but it was obviously to be an important bond between William and his constituents.

Equally important was the fact that when William headed the poll in 1802 he started an association with a borough which, despite its long history, was to all intents and purposes rebuilding itself as a new town. Boston, having been a thriving port in medieval times, had become something of a backwater by the mid-eighteenth century. The River Witham, connecting it to the open sea, had been allowed to silt up; commerce had declined and buildings decayed. Towards the end of the eighteenth century new drainage schemes had been put in hand, land reclaimed and the channel deepened and widened. An 'exceedingly commodious and elegant' new bridge, in that still daringly experimental material cast iron, designed by Rennie, was put in hand in 1802, the year of Madocks' election.[18] During the first decade of the century 748 new houses were built, and places of worship for the nonconformist population erected (there was already a Baptist chapel and Jewish synagogue). The town hall held 'commodious rooms for convivial meetings' but new assembly rooms were felt to be necessary in 1811. There were three schools and a dispensary.[19] The gaol was a 'very damp and unwholesome place, a disgrace to civilised society'; the Corporation had for a long time intended to take it down but were delayed by the cost of building the iron bridge (£22,000) and other improvements. The Custom House was a 'respectable looking building' but no doubt William would have more interest in the theatre which he may have been instrumental in getting started: it did not open till 1806.[20] In view of the work which he himself was so soon to begin in Wales, it is tantalising that so few of these buildings have survived[21] since it is impossible to tell what influence, if any, they may have had on the embryo town on the reclaimed sands of Caernarvonshire that was beginning to take shape in his mind. Or, for that matter, what influence he may have had on the shape of Boston. But there can be little doubt that as the coach rattled over the long straight road on the last stage from Stamford, and the tower of the great church crept up the horizon like an immense three-decker, his thoughts were not solely political. Sitting up on the box with the coachman on a fine summer day and looking out over the unfamiliar geometric pattern of the drained land, with its great farms and parish churches anchored like ships in a vast flat sea, the extraordinary contrast of the country and close similarity of his own planning problems to those of his constituents, must often have occupied his mind.

Above all else he would never forget the bustle of the seaport. He was always stirred by the sight of ships both in their own right

and as indications of life and prosperity and, in this respect particularly, early nineteenth-century Boston must have delighted
him. A close-up of the town survives in a letter written by a
young currier, newly arrived from his Nottinghamshire village:
'Their is Ships lie within two minutes walk of the shop Can see
the tops of the Mast Poles of the ships over the houses as I walk
the streets their is Vast numbers of ships come to Boston they
appear sometimes like A Wood when the leaves are off when
they are close together have seen five sailing together. . . .'[22]

William's financial outlook was now more hopeful since the
Penmorfa property had already increased considerably in value;
but his recent expenses including those of the election had been
very heavy. His mother, realising how vital it was that he should
have money at this critical stage, again came to the rescue and
advanced another substantial sum against William's legacy in her
will (£8,487 8s. 8d.). That is to say, substantial in terms of a small
estate, but a pittance when reckoned against the schemes which
were taking shape in his mind.

But Frances Madocks had not long to live. Her death the next
year (1804) seems to have been sudden, for to his great sadness
William did not reach Margate, where she was then staying, in
time to see his mother before she died. She left various legacies.
Her silver plate and books were divided between her sons; her
sable muff and tippet, her jewels and trinkets, her laces and shawls,
and all her whole pieces of silks, muslins and dimity, as well as the
bound book of coloured prints and the camera obscura from the
dining-room, were divided between the two eldest grand-
daughters whom she had brought up. Numerous bequests were
made, but William certainly proved to be the favourite. As well
as the direct bequests, already advanced, all her real estate, including Mount Mascall, was left in trust for William and one John
Perryn[23] of Twickenham. It so happened that only a few months
passed before this unfortunate man 'lost his life by a fall from a
carriage in Lancashire'[24] so it was not long before the whole came
to William. He sold the property to his eldest brother to pay off
the debts already incurred and to finance his future schemes.

3

The Great Plan
1800 – 1811

REVELLING IN the excitement of the transformation that was to be made at Tan-yr-allt, William would turn from the tantalising smells of lime mortar and newly sawn timber to the marshy tang of the estuary immediately below. He saw it in two moods: sometimes as a great romantic landscape mirrored in the still waters of the flood tide; at others as a treacherous obstacle to the opening up of this very poor part of Wales.

The difficulties of crossing Traeth Mawr and, to a lesser degree, Traeth Bach were critical to serious travellers. The tourists might enjoy dramatising what was to them a rare event, but to those going about their business up the coast and between mid-Wales and the north and, in particular, to the sheltered anchorage of Porthdinllaen in the Lleyn peninsula of Caernarvonshire (then as important a harbour for the Dublin traffic as Holyhead) the crossings caused delays, inconvenience and often actual danger. True, Traeth Mawr presented a lesser hazard than some of those on the Anglesey route and many preferred to use Porthdinllaen. It was this Irish traffic which was to be the key factor in getting under way the great schemes of road building and improvement which were eventually to open up this remote corner of the Principality.

At that time the journey to Ireland was fraught with hazard. The great Holyhead Road[1] was unthought of (Thomas Telford, its engineer, was an unknown shepherd's son in Eskdale, just beginning to learn his trade as a stone mason). The Holyhead route from London to Dublin had several particular dangers

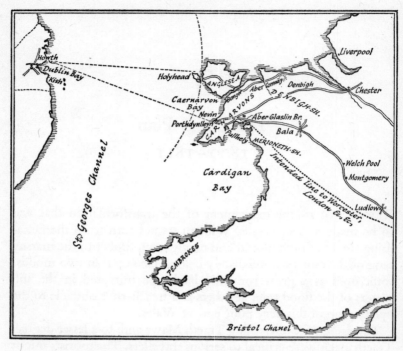

Map showing routes to Ireland via Porthdinllaen and Holyhead
after Thomas Rogers, 1807

whether the journey was made from Shrewsbury or from Chester.
That from Shrewsbury meant crossing the mountains; that from
Chester meant the Conway ferry had to be negotiated. This was
trying enough both to the passengers' nerves and to the driver's
timetable but the ferry at Bangor, which neither Holyhead route
could avoid, was far worse. The treacherous currents of the Menai
Straits were forbidding on a fine summer day; in winter, travellers
endured long delays while they waited for the tide, or for a storm
to ease, thankful at least that some consideration was being given
to reduce the likelihood of their death by drowning. But having
reached Anglesey in safety, there was still the crossing to Holy
Island to be made before they arrived at Holyhead. The Porthdinllaen route on the other hand, apart from the poorness of its
roads, had only one great drawback: the crossing of Traeth Mawr.

Various fantastic projects concerning this estuary had flared up and petered out spasmodically during the past two hundred years. Bold plans for embanking both it and Traeth Bach, by building a great dam across the mouth and thus solving problems of communication and enclosure in one grand scheme, had tantalised idealists for many years. But each scheme had been turned down by more practical men on account of its immense cost.

William would be well aware of these projects and it is likely that his ideas were quite as grand as those of any of his predecessors. Thomas Pennant, for instance, who was a Flintshire neighbour of the Madockses, had drawn attention to the most famous of these projects in his well known *Tours in Wales*:[2] 'In the year 1625, Sir *John Wynn*, of *Gwedir*, conceived the great design of gaining this tract, and a lesser called *Traeth Bychan*, from the sea, by embankment. He implored the assistance of his illustrious countryman, Sir *Hugh Myddleton* . . .' (the engineer famous for his design of the New River, 1608–13, which gave London its water supply). Sir John evidently had no notion of the likely cost: 'I am content to adventure a brace of hundred pounds to joyne with you in the worke' he wrote and Sir Hugh, after suitable cousinly and patriotic sentiments, replied 'Touching the drowned lands near your lyvinge, there are manye things considerable therein. . . . If to be gayned, which will hardlie be performed without great stones, which was plentifull at the Weight [the Isle of Wight where he had been working] as well as wood; and great sums of money to be spent, not hundreds but thousands–and first of all his Majesty's interest must be got. As for myself, I am grown into years, and full of business here at the mynes, the river at London, and other places–my weeklie charge being above £200; which maketh me verie unwillinge to undertake anie other worke; and the least of theis, whether the drowned lands or mynes, requireth a whole man, with a large purse. . . .'

No more was heard of such projects for nearly a hundred years. Then in the early eighteenth century a survey of the Traeths was made by some Dutchmen and in 1718 local landowners petitioned for a bill[3] to be introduced into Parliament, but it seems to have foundered in its early stages.

Later in the century, as land enclosure and reclamation which had become so popular among English landowners spread into the Principality, the Duke of Ancaster (who owned property in both Lincolnshire and Wales, and who was therefore familiar with large reclamation schemes) was encouraged[4] to take up the matter. The survey which was then made by an engineer named Golborne was part of a much wider plan[5] to link up north-west Wales with the English road network: in other words to provide at last a good route from London to Dublin.

It was pointed out that Golborne's route was thirty-seven miles shorter than that via Holyhead and Chester and that 'if this were made the General Post Road the conveying of the Mail would gain time in proportion; it would be the road for travellers and would bring much wealth to the country.'[6] But despite these advantages, and an optimistic report on the value of the land to be reclaimed, no more was heard of the scheme.

Back in 1770 when this last attempt had been made to improve communications with Dublin, few influential men in either capital had much interest in the matter so local apathy and natural conservatism had easily prevailed. Now, thirty years later, things were very different. In Ireland the bloody rebellion was over in fact, if not in its bitter memories, and the English had at last persuaded the Irish Parliament in Dublin to vote itself out of existence and to send members to Westminster instead.

William Madocks may have foreseen this event when buying the Penmorfa property. At all events he had immediately seen the regional implications in the proposed Act of Union. Communications between the two capitals would have to be improved for it was obvious that the Irish members, forced frequently to make the journey to attend sittings at Westminster, would be quick to appreciate the problem. Once the road was built the whole region would prosper and for Madocks there were special hopes. If the Porthdinllaen route was decided upon, travellers would actually pass through his property on the first leg of the journey to London. The estate would no longer be at the back of beyond, but could become a civilised stage on a journey between two capitals. What better way of attracting friends and colleagues to visit this distant corner of Wales? In the same sort of way as that in which the East Indiamen brought life to Erith, so the Irish traffic would automatically bring it to Caernarvonshire. By this, not only the Tan-yr-allt house-parties but the whole district would benefit. A coaching inn would be necessary where passengers could refresh themselves before crossing the Traeth. Stables would be needed for stage horses. A shop where travellers could buy small necessities for the journey would be useful for they were few and far between in the Welsh villages . . . and so the plan grew.

Such a scheme was a practical possibility whether or not the grand ambition of damming the Traeth materialised, provided the actual road to Porthdinllaen and the harbour itself were superior to those of the Holyhead route. A dam would clinch Porthdinllaen's claim and William almost certainly nursed the idea in secret as a more distant objective, but he was then in no position to tackle the enormous practical and financial difficulties of such a project (incidentally the 1800 embankment would automatically become redundant if ever the whole Traeth were embanked so, except in terms of useful experience, it would have been a pointless expenditure). But he could set going immediately both road and harbour improvements.

The roads, such as they were, were in a very primitive state throughout North Wales at the end of the eighteenth century. Accidents were frequent. In bad weather they were in no fit state to take wheeled vehicles. As much use as was practicable was made of the coastal shipping for heavy goods; it plied a busy trade but was far too slow and uncertain for most passengers. Travellers went on horseback and even those who were not in real poverty walked great distances. Only the main routes in summer were fit for chaises and coaches; in winter they were generally impassable.

Obviously then the road system[7] was the first matter to be tackled for, quite apart from its importance to the harbour, it was high time to improve communications between the western peninsula of Caernarvonshire and the rest of Wales. Unless use were made of bridle tracks to join the skeleton network there could be no connection between the south of the peninsula (Pwllheli,

Criccieth, Penmorfa etc.) and central North Wales (e.g. Capel Curig) without going round by Caernarvon and Bangor, a detour of close on fifty miles.[8] Roads within the peninsula stuck chiefly to the coast so that to Porthdinllaen from Traeth Mawr was indirect.

In June 1802, a meeting was held at the Crown and Anchor, Pwllheli, of Gentleman, Clergy and Free-Holders, to consider the road system in the Lleyn peninsula (William's neighbour, Colonel G. L. Wardle, soon to become a national figure in connection with the impeachment of the Duke of York, was in the chair). It was concluded 'that a good Road from Porth Dinnllaen Harbour across Traeth Mawr to communicate with other Roads leading to England will be of essential Service to the landed and commercial Interests of those Districts'. Inspired no doubt by the success of this meeting, another was held six weeks later at which it was resolved that this new road should be connected with a branch which was to link with that running through the Aberglaslyn Pass to join up with the Capel Curig turnpike. The junction of the two would be close to Tan-yr-allt for this second route ran along the foot of the crags on the north side of the Traeth: it crossed William's newly reclaimed land and passed within a hundred yards of his front door. In addition to its usefulness to the community at large, it turned out to be particularly convenient to the Tan-yr-allt house-parties, arriving as they so often did by the Capel Curig coach.

The Porthdinllaen Turnpike Trust Act[9] was passed the following year. Despite the many difficulties that constantly had to be overcome, both sections were set to work and progress, though inevitably slow, was gradually made. What had been described as 'a tedious foot-path over rocks which run close by an arm of the sea' was to become the Penmorfa–Pont Aberglaslyn road, soon to be capable of taking phaetons and carriages, and the 'spirited undertakings of Mr. Maddox and Mr. Parry [the High Sheriff]' were also praised for the 'good carriage roads [which] have been opened' including that 'excellent line of communication . . . to the little bay of Porth Dinnllaen'.[10]

The great object during the next few years was to make this

new route *the* main highway used by the mail coach and all the fast traffic between the two capitals. For this to become an undisputed reality much would have to be done to that 'little bay'.

Even William–whose mind's eye already saw the coaches thundering down the newly made turnpikes, carriages and postchaises halting at his new inn (as yet unbuilt) and the whole region opened up and prospering–realised that a start could not be made on the new packet station without Parliamentary sanction. He made himself responsible for the slow business of getting a harbour bill through the Commons; but it was not until 1806 that the Porthdinllaen Harbour Company[11] was formed, and a bill was before Parliament which would empower it to raise £12,000 in shares for the building of a harbour. This luckily coincided with the formation of the Ministry of Talents. Madocks wrote enthusiastically: 'We shall now have great interest in Dublin for all our plans, as I know almost all the Ministry going there and the Duke of Bedford, who is Lord Lieutenant. Huzza!'

It is difficult now, with Holyhead so long established and Porthdinllaen once more just a rocky bay, to realise how close was the contest between these two claimants to Dublin's traffic. In those days just before the coming of the steam packet, the position of a harbour in relation to the prevailing wind was all important and the protagonists of Porthdinllaen engaged Thomas Rogers, lighthouse builder and engineer, to report on its situation.[12] This he did most favourably and prospects seemed bright. 'We have got the Portdynlaen Harbour Bill and all our public works are going swimmingly. You will no doubt rejoice to hear that,' Madocks wrote. 'The Liverpool people, the Carnarvon and the Holly-head have been very troublesome and opposed us in various ways, but we have conquered them all, and we have got this great and important measure, I believe I may venture to say. . . .' This time Madocks was not being over optimistic: the Bill[13] actually received the Royal Assent two days later. That for the improvement of Holyhead had not even been petitioned, and the advantages of Porthdinllaen were plain.

Meanwhile William had developed the idea of a small coaching town a stage further. If the opening up of communications with the outside world was going to bring trade and prosperity to this remote and poor region, a market town would be needed. Lying at an important new road junction, and between the low-lying westerly Lleyn peninsula and the mountainous interior, his coaching stage would be well sited to serve in this capacity too.

But if the town and region were to prosper as he hoped, they would need their own outlet to the sea. Porthdinllaen was out on a limb near the tip of the peninsula; fine for Dublin but of little use to the interior. Something was needed nearer its heart. William therefore proposed to build a second new harbour at the mouth of Traeth Mawr in a small sheltered anchorage called Ynys Cyngar. From the new town a canal was to be dug to the nearest point on the Traeth so that goods could be taken by water direct to the harbour; fortunately this canal was already partly in existence as a drainage channel (the Great Sluice) to the embanked land.[14] Another bill was brought before the Commons and in no time the neighbourhood buzzed with petitions and counter-petitions. Madocks wrote an open letter[15] on the advantages of the harbour. Adam Smith and others were quoted on the 'natural and necessary consequences of an improved navigation' and foot-notes were added for the sake of those landowners and traders less familiar with political philosophy: 'Adam Smith: "every improvement in the circumstances of the society, tends, either directly or indirectly, to raise the real rent of the land, to increase the real wealth of the landlord, and his power of purchasing labour, or the produce of the labours of other people." ' After the usual set-backs typical of such enterprises this Bill[16] was eventually to receive the Royal Assent. And so, from a single coaching inn on the projected London – Dublin road, Madocks' scheme had developed into what would today be described as a regional plan, with the new town which was to act as its capital conveniently sited on his small estate.

Thus the formation of the turnpike trust (1802) coincided with the beginning of ten years' intense activity. The first embankment of 1800, although of considerable importance on the Traeth, was a local affair; the road system, the projected harbours and the

town were to ensure that Tan-yr-allt was on the map in a much
wider sense.

At this most critical moment William Madocks, himself a
complete amateur, had nobody to look after any of these diverse
projects or his new property. Thomas Payne,[17] the agent from
Dolmelynllyn, had already proved to be unsuitable. He was too
conservative either to put his employer's bolder schemes into
action or cheerfully to tolerate his sudden whims. He was, as
Madocks had said, 'too rivetted'. To be without an agent or
steward[18] was difficult enough at any time, but with so many
schemes on hand and with an owner who had to spend much of
his time in London the situation was serious. In addition to the
diverse problems with which an agent now deals, his predecessor
around 1800 was expected to carry out many of the duties which
today fall to other professional men; planners, architects, civil
engineers, surveyors and, in this case, to industrialists, publicity
agents and even market research experts for the new town.

A man of experience and sound judgement was badly needed;
preferably someone who had knowledge of both land reclamation and embanking and, above all, of the design and construction
of buildings, roads and harbours.

The country around Boston would provide a number of
candidates for such a job. Lincolnshire was both rich and pro-
gressive; estate and reclamation work flourished. A level-headed
Englishman who would energetically carry out his employer's
wilder schemes and at the same time bring to them the benefit
of his own practical experience would almost exactly answer.
But although Madocks had spent so much of his life in England
he was at heart a Welshman; he instinctively saw the futility of
bringing a clear-minded but undemonstrative Anglo-Saxon to
oversee the work on his Caernarvonshire estate. Language difficulties would certainly exist but difference in temperament would
be the real source of the misunderstandings which would inevitably arise. So he chose a very different man; young and inex-
perienced.

Not much is known of John Williams before this date. He

came down from Anglesey, where his father farmed,[19] probably as rumour spread of the big embankment that was to be built in the summer of 1800 when there was so much unemployment and hunger in the land. He was then rising twenty-two and had previously been employed as garden-boy at Plas Newydd[20] but he came to the Tan-yr-allt estate to find any work that was going. After the embankment was completed he was particularly useful in the new garden and nurseries but he had already shown less tangible assets which Madocks had not missed.

When, half a century later, John Williams died, the inscription that they put up in his memory described how 'endowed with a strong mind and equally strong affections, he secured the good opinion of the public and the deep regard of his friends. . . .' Perhaps these qualities, so much more important than any experience in estate management, were even at this early stage apparent to his employer. Not very long after the ex-garden boy's arrival, he was given charge of the whole estate.

Madocks was never a conventional employer. He had, for instance, recently engaged a stone-mason because the man was an outstanding harpist and had promoted a pig-boy because the lad had had the sense to run away rather than fight a duel in his employer's honour. Too often his own colleagues would turn out to be rogues: before he saw their true colours he found them entertaining company. But in the case of John Williams his seemingly haphazard methods of selection were rewarded a thousand-fold. At heart they were based on the sure foundation of mutual liking and respect.

Their partnership, for that is what it in essence became, was eventually only broken by Madocks' death and Williams continued to serve the district for the rest of his life. The ultimate success of the venture was as much due to one man as the other. When it began each had little to offer beyond his own enthusiasm; the young M.P., who was so full of ideas which had not yet been put to the test, had barely enough money to pay his steward's salary; Williams had nothing to offer but character, understanding and staying power. Both fortunately seem to have had a rare gift for inspiring affection in others; they had few other assets. Madocks, who was five years the senior, was a quick-witted man of the world. Warm-hearted and impetuous, he expected his schemes to be completed almost before the ink was dry. Plans for the property poured forth and all his powers of persuasion were to be needed to continue to raise money for his many projects. Williams, who was beginning to know the district as well as his native Anglesey, was both thorough and practical but not without that imagination which made him the staunchest of Madocks' supporters. He shared that sense of drama and occasion which Madocks enjoyed so much and this, which might otherwise have been a source of irritation, was an additional bond between them. Above all Williams was honest and utterly trusted.

In later years, when he had proved his exceptional ability, there must have been many occasions when he was to be tempted by a higher and a more certain salary to work elsewhere. That he should devote his whole life to what must so often have seemed a despairing cause is the highest tribute that could be paid both to himself and his employer and it is clear from quite early in their correspondence that William looked upon John Williams as a valued friend. This was probably the clue to their success: no formal relationship of employer and agent could have survived the stresses that were to come.

Madocks' political commitments and varied interests meant that even now he spent much of his time away in England: in the House of Commons or attending to his constituency or simply in the social round into which he still entered with customary relish. His absence threw great responsibility on John Williams and also meant that much of the estate business was dealt with by post. The bulk of the letters which survive from this correspondence were written by Madocks between 1805 and 1828 (unfortunately Williams' replies have not survived). Tantalising gaps occur, either because papers have been destroyed or because Madocks had come home and was settling things verbally, but even so an extraordinarily vivid picture emerges.

He must have been a stimulating if often exasperating employer. True to his eighteenth-century upbringing, his interests in various aspects of estate improvement were as boundless as his enthusiasm. Architectural details, new methods of farming, the mechanisation of the wool industry, or ideas about food and drink, seem to have been as avidly discussed in the coffee houses or clubs of St. James's, as politics, trade, and the progress of the war. 'Lord G tells me . . .', 'Mr. E is planting . . .' sprinkled the letters with ideas that must often have seemed curious to his Welsh agent.

These letters were usually written in sepia ink in clear, speedy, sloping handwriting although occasionally they would be dashed off 'in the Chaise with a pencil' with slight misgivings as to their legibility. They give a sense of breathless urgency. There are few paragraphs. Ideas follow pell-mell. Instructions are often supplemented 'I pray thee, attend to this immediately'. The letters flow on as if the writer were talking, and can seldom have been read through before posting: repetitions occur, particularly in the longer letters, and, although there is occasionally a summary at the end, it is usually left to John Williams to sort out the instructions as best he can. The mood in which they are written comes across vividly. Underlining is often vehement, and any success is marked by a cheerful flourish in the otherwise straightforward writing. If some of the letters were infuriating to the executive who received them (and it is hard to believe they were not), the relish with which they were dashed off is irresistible, and the optimism with which Madocks embarked on his schemes is extraordinarily infectious. They have that special quality, now not so common in business correspondence, of being written without one eye to the record—of how the correspondence might look in the files. Being intended only for his agent's eye, they have an ingenuous lack of guile. Unlike many men in his position, Madocks had no secretary. It is a mystery how he had time and energy to write so much (and this correspondence only represented one facet of his life.) Sometimes he would toss off two or three letters in a day. Occasionally they ran into twenty sides. Williams often must have wished to be left to get on with the job instead of being inundated by these closely written quarto sheets packed with instructions, impatience and enthusiasm.

1. William Alexander Madocks, aged 5, by James Scouler, 1778

2. Frances Madocks, William's mother, by R. Pio, 1747

3. William Alexander Madocks, aged 35. An engraving by H. W. Billington from the painting by James Ramsay, 1808. (A better-known engraving was made by G. Turner but its likeness to the portrait is not close)

Thomas Love Peacock, the novelist, spent the winter of 1811 in North Wales and knew both Madocks and his schemes. When reading Madocks' letters it is impossible not to be reminded in some respects of that impulsive squire of Peacock's creation: 'In all the thoughts, words, and actions of Squire Headlong, there was a remarkable alacrity of progression, which almost annihilated the interval between conception and execution. He was utterly regardless of obstacles, and seemed to have expunged their very name from his vocabulary . . . he saw no interval between the first step and the last, but pounced upon his object with the impetus of a mountain cataract.'[21]

Certainly few ventures can have been undertaken with more relish or fewer grounds for success. It was early in their correspondence that a letter from 5, Half Moon Street, Piccadilly, to Tan-y-Rallt, Carnarvon, finished: 'Wishing us both good luck, I remain

Your sincere friend

W. A. Madocks.'

Good luck in full measure was much needed.

4

The Town
1805 – 1811

In AUGUST 1805, Madocks had written to the Post-Master at Caernarvon asking him 'to send all letters directed for any persons at Pentre-Gwaelod in my bag. Pentre-Gwaelod is the name of some new houses I have built near Tan-y-Rallt on Traeth Mawr. Your future attention to this will much oblige.' This letter must have given him great pleasure, pronouncing as it did that his new town was firmly on the map. Now it at least boasted a name, although *Pentre Gwaelod* (bottom village) was hardly in tune with its founder's aspirations. But a name of any sort is better than nothing: it gives a place an identity and life of its own which can bring a special sort of satisfaction to its creator.

Even at the earliest stage, when the only new buildings on the estate consisted of a few cottages, there was already a town on the site in Madocks' imagination. No one had then had the brain-wave of calling it Trè Madoc, township or place of Madoc, by which happy coincidence the name could be attributed either to Prince Madoc or its founder, but a mayor and aldermen had already been appointed, and when the word 'village' was written in another letter at that time, it was firmly scratched out in favour of 'Borough'.

There can be little doubt that Madocks planned Tremadoc himself, probably with casual help from architecturally minded friends and the details given in the many architectural books which were then in circulation. From his correspondence it is evident that no master plan other than one in his own mind

82

existed. One or two thumbnail sketches of a very back-of-an envelope character have fortunately survived in his letters but otherwise there is nothing except a finely drawn but topographically irrelevant *Ideal Plan for Trè Madoc* which was published[1] some years later by John Claudius Loudon. Loudon, then in his early twenties, was to be well known for his numerous publications and projects in landscape design. He had recently written *An Observation on the laying out of Public Squares* and this may have caught Madocks' attention. Three years later he had a bad attack of rheumatic fever which disabled him for some time; such a plight would easily arouse Madocks' sympathy and may have been partly responsible for his invitation to Tan-yr-allt at Christmas 1806, but by then the town was under way. His report concentrated on the agricultural possibilities of the property and he was certainly consulted on this aspect rather than on architecture or town planning. Some of Loudon's later comments on landscaping in general, on the treatment of ruins and every imaginable aid to the picturesque, are reflected in various parts of the estate.

The miniature town was now beginning to take shape. Naturally enough it had much in common with its founder: its plan and the majority of the buildings belong directly to the classical tradition of the eighteenth century while, by contrast, its siting could hardly be more romantic. As might be expected, its choice shows rare sensitivity to the possibilities of the landscape.[2] (Map p. 136).

The idea of a town built on land reclaimed from the sea might in itself seem to be romantic; in fact it could well have been flat and dull. But the hub of Tremadoc, the Market Place (facing page 177), is built right under a great crag which once marked the Caernarvonshire edge of the estuary. That sheer wall of jagged rock towering a hundred feet above the modest range of the Town Hall and Inn, which were to make up the north wall of the square, gives a sense of enclosure and finality at the head of the main approach to the town that could not have been equalled by the most imposing and expensive wall of buildings and it provides the most dramatic backcloth to the orderly serenity of the Georgian architecture.

The exact site of the town had been carefully selected on practical grounds also. It was conveniently close to the spot where travellers crossing the Traeth arrived on the Caernarvonshire shore, and was therefore well situated both from the point of view of through traffic and as a local market centre. It would soon be connected to the river by the canal, and so to the anchorage at Ynys Cyngar which awaited conversion into a proper harbour.

The moving spirit behind Tremadoc was one of eighteenth-century improvement rather than nineteenth-century reform. Unlike Robert Owen,[3] for instance, to whom he has been compared, Madocks' agitation in that respect was channelled almost exclusively towards parliamentary reform. Town-planning was for him primarily an architectural matter which meant, in true eighteenth-century terms, that the appearance of the place was the first consideration. Its siting, the layout of the buildings and the design of the spaces they enclosed, as well as of the buildings themselves, all had to contribute visually to this end.

Tremadoc was to be first and foremost a sensible town, not some village ornée nor landowner's toy. From the beginning it was not to forget its *raison d'être*, and the two main streets were named London Street and Dublin Street. Those coy substitutes for the word street, now popular, would have been unthinkable. The plan was based on convenience combined with the best possible appearance which Madocks' limited resources could produce, whether this was in the layout of the town itself or the surrounding estate. What the place would look like and feel like to live in—those excellent eighteenth-century planning precepts since dismally often forgotten—mattered first and foremost.

Madocks certainly set out to provide decent living conditions, but he realised that such an attitude could not of itself produce a good town. The people who lived in Tremadoc, unlike Owen's workers, were to live as they chose. He believed that a man should be allowed to pray, work, educate his children, entertain himself, drink, gamble, garden, save or waste his money as he saw fit. A town should provide opportunities for such a variety of occupations: the idea was to attract people to build within the outlines of his plan and then let them get on with their own lives. His only stipulation was that any gentry who settled should be congenial company as neighbours. Solvent Chaotics were the ideal. Unfortunately, few could be persuaded to speculate in such a remote region so Madocks had to raise most of the money himself, hoping always that the rents would be forthcoming in time to satisfy his creditors.

In all his activities Madocks showed himself to be a superb showman, and this applied not least to his role as town planner. Every penny that was spent on Tremadoc was, in his eyes, wasted if it did not add to the effect of the town as a town; if it did not add to the urbanity of the 'borough'. It was no good spending money where it would not contribute to the increase of this effect and, in this microcosm of the world as contained in his estate, he saw to it that the scenery and props were always placed to their best advantage. His approach to architecture was so unlike ours, inevitably loaded as it is by precepts ranging from Ruskin to Le Corbusier and still reacting against the slums of the industrial revolution, that some might find it slightly frivolous. For instance: 'With respect to the Buildings behind Bartlett's and John Etheridge's houses. I have been thinking that whatever we build there *will be out of sight* and there will be a sum of money laid out without improving the apparent size of the town. . . . Four six or eight low cottages with no upstairs floor and *thatched* might soon be knocked off either under the rock opposite the present row or in a line with the Stables and Cow house. . . . At one or other of these places a neat row of small thatched cottages will look very well. I will *not* have them built near the Turnpike. . . .' Such humble dwellings were not to be under the gaze of travellers using the new road.

On the other hand the standard of the houses on London Street, or on the Tan-yr-allt approach to the town, was always considered to be of great importance: slate should be in sight and thatch out of sight. Tree-planting, follies and flag-poles received great attention as did the town privy (gothic); sewers, naturally enough, were non-existent. The chief public buildings were, very properly, given high priority. Madocks' list of immediate essentials, in addition to the houses, included a church and a nonconformist chapel; a town hall and theatre; a hotel and coach-houses for travellers and two inns for the local inhabitants; numerous shops; a factory; fulling and corn mills; and last, but by no means unimportant, a race-course. No school building was constructed but a school existed; probably classes were held in the Town Hall. There were also the roads, canal and harbour to be constructed. New farm buildings and cottages and many miles of new fencing and drainage ditches were also needed on the estate and the plantations and nurseries demanded constant attention. Most important of all, the 1800 embankment had to be kept under repair lest an exceptional tide should sink the whole concern.

Such an undertaking might have seemed formidable enough in the richer parts of England where an experienced labour force was available and materials were easily accessible. In the depths of Wales building projects on this scale were then rare. There were very few building contractors. Materials other than stone, slate and short lengths of oak timber had to be brought by coastal shipping to a still non-existent harbour. That England was going through one of the bleakest periods of the long Napoleonic Wars made matters no easier.

On the other hand the complete freedom from any kind of control, aesthetic or practical, considerably speeded matters. If a man then decided to build a town, he went ahead; the only restraint was lack of money. Building Acts such as the London Building Acts existed in the cities but in Caernarvonshire little was known of such things. More refreshing still must it have been to live at a time when the indigenous tradition of sound design meant that the local builder converted the haziest sketch into a sturdily proportioned straightforward building.

All in all Madocks perhaps had a clearer view of his objectives than many of his successors in this century. He set out to create a town, not a housing estate, nor a garden city, and he contrived to achieve this, despite his minimal funds, by always building where the main idea would be most effectively promoted. The commercial success of Portmadoc, which nipped Tremadoc in the bud, underlines this achievement. With fewer than a hundred houses Tremadoc has a sense of civilised urbanity often missed by towns of normal size (despite its diminutive size, it has been frequently studied by both architectural and town-planning students).

Scarcely a letter exists in Madocks' correspondence that does not urge the speeding of building operations; inevitably these seemed tediously slow, particularly at a distance from the site, and they often were. The fact that Madocks was so frequently away from home did tend to delay things further: '*Three* Months more are now elapsed, and yet nothing finished with respect to all these cottages etc–Covent Garden Theatre (burnt down in October) is nearly up again, & not above 200 persons at Work. Our Men must dawdle away their time terribly.'

The climate on the estuary was fairly mild and frost should not have slowed work as much as in England, where each winter thousands of men were laid off as a matter of course. The main problem at Tremadoc was to get contractors to concentrate men on a single job and to organise supplies so that they were at hand when needed. There was soon to be so much work, that few could resist taking on more than they could manage: 'I am paying heavily every week for Carpenters at the Town, and can not find any thing done. I have been absent from home nearly 2 months, & Robert Jones' Cottage is not even roofed. . . . What have the town carpenters been about? . . . Now do, once for all, attend to this *immediately and effectually*.' This plea has all our sympathy. Others pepper the letter more or less hopefully: 'Drive on the New Inn,' 'Is the Mayor's house begun?', 'Drive Griffith on with the Houses and *Steeple* to the Church. I must have the Steeple done *soon* . . .', 'When I know jobs are going on spiritedly I do not mind the money.' It seems to have been difficult to instil any sense of urgency into those small firms who contracted to build the town, some of whom had little or no experience, and at times Madocks' impatience outran common sense: for instance when, to speed the completion of the Town Hall, he suggested 'one great thing will be to begin the plaistering actually while they are putting on the roof'.

A letter written early in 1806 gives nice insight into the way the town was planned. It concerns the Market Place, Tremadoc's hub and architectural climax. Madocks and his brother John had had second thoughts about the plan for the hotel and had decided 'We think it better to stop, till we can give it further consideration on the spot. This delay furnishes you and me with excellent means to drive on the Town, & Mill etc. for Griffith having so many hands ready, he can knock off the Mill, and 5 or 6 New houses at the Market, besides finishing Dr Morris's house. I wish you would agree with him to finish the Mill and 6 houses by the *1st of July*. The Market place will be thus':

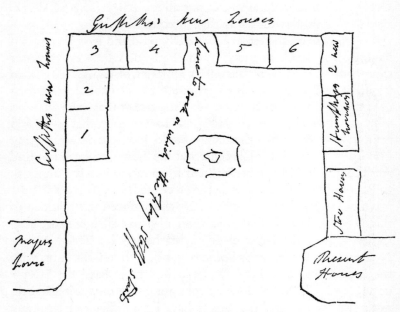

So much for carefully prepared drawings. (Had a master plan existed, the Town Hall which was to be the chief building in the Market Place would certainly have been marked across the bottom of this sketch. (See plan opposite; drawn the other way up.) Madocks continued 'I should like the 6 new houses to be nearly the same plan as those Humphrey is building. . . . You know, where the Mill is to be placed.' Numerous details unconnected with the town followed before the square was again taken up:

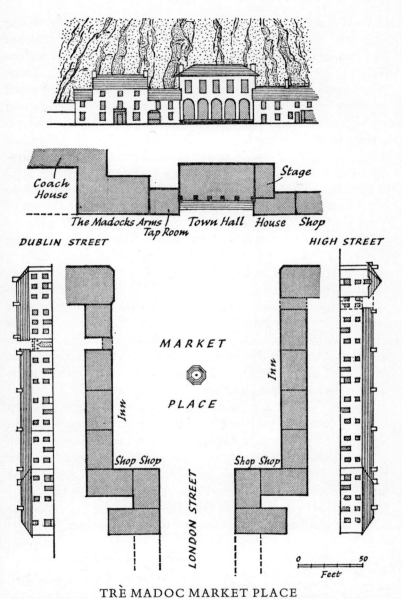

Coach
House

Stage

The Madocks Arms
Tap Room
Town Hall
House
Shop

DUBLIN STREET

HIGH STREET

MARKET

Inn

Inn

PLACE

Shop Shop

Shop Shop

LONDON STREET

0   50
Feet

TRÈ MADOC MARKET PLACE
Based on contemporary documents and on surveys made by Michael Dalby,
ARIBA, 1952, and by students of Liverpool University School of Architecture
under Dr. Quentin Hughes

'... and make the best bargain you can with John Griffiths, whose workmen and timber are so handy for that purpose. If Griffiths is likely to be dearer than Humphrey on the same plan, it will be necessary to make some trifling alteration to the plan, or Humphrey may grumble but I trust 100 guineas a house will be a full [?] price. I leave this entirely to your judgement.' These houses are straightforward and without fuss and John Williams, with no architectural pretensions but unselfconsciously working within a strong tradition of design which derived from nearly two hundred years of renaissance architecture integrated with the local vernacular, was considered to be quite competent to make 'trifling alterations' to the Market Place, the most important feature of Tremadoc.

Two years later, when the north range of the square consisting of the Madocks Arms (the hotel, here called 'Ongley's House') and the Town Hall, linked by the Tap Room, were under construction, its success did seem to be jeopardised by lack of dimensioned plans. Madocks wrote urgently: 'I wish much to receive an answer to my last letter about the Town Hall, and to have it described on paper with your pen, how the Angle fits into Ongley's house, & if the front of the Town Hall is exactly at right Angles to London street, and if it is strictly placed, where Slingsby & I put the stakes, and also if the Tap Room is right.'

Williams' reply cannot have been satisfactory for the next ten-page letter begins: 'Dear John, the Tap Room must *stop*, till I arrive, and a proportionate greater exertion made with the Town Hall immediately. There has been the greatest *Blunder* imaginable about the Tap Room.[4] It was never for a moment designed to be in the same line, with the Inn, but an Angle was to take place where it joined the Inn so that the Tap Room, the Town Hall, & Stage were All to range in the same direction, as thus:

The Angle was to have been at *A*. Not B. And the Tap, Town Hall & Stage quite at exact right Angles to London street, or to an imaginary line drawn through the Market Place from London Street. . . .' Three pages followed on possible ways out of this dilemma: '. . . Be it *Remembered* however Always, that I am supposing all the while, that the *Front* of the Town Hall is exactly at *right angles* to London Street, as Mr. Slingsby, You and I set it out with so much pains. I sadly fear that the stakes we so carefully put down to mark the Front of the Town Hall have been either buried in the Rubbish, or removed. If so, You will be all at Sea, and all will be wrong. . . .' But if it was right 'then we shall have to alter nothing but the front of the Tap Room, when I arrive'. (This letter surely has a familiar note; it is perhaps reminiscent of certain present-day telephone calls in site offices.)

It is rather surprising that they were not more often 'all at Sea', but a very creditable range of buildings emerged from this crisis. The lack of drawings did at least save them from the pitfalls of paper planning. Settling 'on the spot', as was Madocks' habit, meant that the three-dimensional form of the square, the heights of the surrounding buildings in proportion to its area, was most successfully handled. But having created this pleasant open space they seem to have been slightly nonplussed by its emptiness and a strange plan was produced for a Green Knowl planted with an odd mixture of trees: 'fine Planes, Black Italians & Birch. I fear Larch will not do. It will be too windy for them to grow straight. . . .' This was to be put in hand immediately and under it were to be 'clumps of Broom . . . and Furze. Mix these with Roses, Sweet Peas etc., & Red Beans which will look very well in the Summer'. How far the work had gone before the order was suddenly countermanded, is not on record.

The Town Hall[5] was probably not begun until 1807, but it must have been considered at an early stage since it is the focal point of the town. The immediate origin of this pleasant classical building is not known. Architecturally it is in the direct succession of the renaissance tradition that goes back to Inigo Jones' design for the piazza at Covent Garden, but the tradition of raising a building on piers to provide a covered market space underneath it was much older and was not unknown in Wales; Llanidloes, like Ledbury, is an unsophisticated timber example of a solution to the same problem.[6]

Market-halls were commonly built on island sites, either in a square or at a main cross-roads; this allowed for easy access all round. Tremadoc being at a T junction, it was logical to put the Town Hall, with its covered market space, across the top of the T. Equally important were those aesthetic considerations behind its siting which have already been discussed.

No drawings have survived but the design must have come either direct from an architect or his published work; it had obvious professional origins spiced by Madocks-worthy ingenuity. Basically it is beautifully simple; a market space at ground level whose open arcade supported a large room described as the 'Town Hall or Dancing Room' above. The façade to the square consists of five round-arched openings above which generously proportioned sliding-sash windows lit the first-floor room. Originally a flight of steps ran right across the building to form a plinth and its absence now slightly spoils the proportions of the lower floor. The roof is typical of the sort which Madocks most liked: slated and hipped with a shallow pitch and generous projecting eaves. (With typical economy the eaves are cut to the minimum behind the chimney stacks where the building cuts into the hill.)

The dancing-room is pleasantly proportioned and utterly simple. A fireplace at each end and a musicians' gallery in the long wall facing the windows (much more satisfactory than the traditional end-wall position) are its only features apart from the scale and rhythm given by the five great windows overlooking the square. The floor space was originally uninterrupted; since access was from the Tap Room of the Madocks Arms next door a stair in the Hall itself was not needed. This arrangement also had the practical advantage of separating the functions of the two floors; silk and lace did not have to negotiate market produce on the way up to the Ball.

The building's only decorations are the Coade stone keystones of the arches and simple medallions between. These keystones

THEATRE TRE-MADOC.

ON WEDNESDAY, AUG. 3d, 1808,

Will be presented Mr. SHERIDAN'S celebrated Comedy, called

THE RIVALS.

Sir Anthony Absolute,	......Mr. JOS. MADOCKS.
Captain Absolute,	Mr. DAWKINS
Acres,	Mr. SHEATH
Sir Lucius O'Trigger	Mr. ROOKWOOD
Faulkland,	Mr. FENTON
Fag,	Mr. JOHN MADOCKS
David,	Mr. BOYCOTT
Coachman,	Mr. FROST
Mrs. Maláprop,	Mrs. FENTON
Lydia Languish,	Mrs. W. FENTON
Julia,	Miss FENTON
Lucy,	Mrs. WELLMAN

After which will be performed the Interlude of

SYLVESTER DAGGERWOOD,

Sylvester Daggerwood,	Mr. DAWKINS
Fustian,	Mr. W. A. MADOCKS
Servant,	Mr. JNO. MADOCKS

THE WHOLE TO CONCLUDE WITH

THE PRIZE.

Dr. Lenitive,	Mr. DAWKINS
Mr. Caddy,	Mr. ROOKWOOD
Captain Hartwell,	Mr. SHEATH
Label,	Mr. W. A. MADOCKS
Juba,	MASTER FENTON
The Old Bonze,	Mr. JOS. MADOCKS
Young Bonze,	Mr. JOHN MADOCKS
Mrs. Caddy,	Mrs. WELLMAN
Caroline,	Mrs. W. FENTON

Tickets to be had of Mr. Fenton, or Mr. Morris, Market-square.

Boxes 3s. 6d. —— Gallery 1s. 6d.

To begin precisely at a Quarter before Seven o'Clock.

Playbill for Trè Madoc Theatre, 1808

give a clue to the third function of the building, now no longer
obvious. Each is decorated in low relief with the head of a
theatrical character. Madocks could not afford to build a theatre
for the short summer season so each August the market space in
the Town Hall was transformed into an auditorium. A pro-
scenium arch was built in the party wall (to the east) and a
permanent stage constructed behind the adjacent house; it was
in fact only the front half of a house although there was no hint
of this from the square. The economy of such dual purpose
planning is typical of the practical streak in its designer.

William tremendously enjoyed the Trè Madoc Theatre and
wrote for it stirring prologues (and at least one play[7]) which usually combined patriotism and topical comment in unabashed juxtaposition. His brothers were equally enthusiastic. John had been
an experienced amateur producer as well as actor and in England
had handled such diverse casts as the Duchess of Devonshire, the
Prince of Wales and the painter Reynolds in a single evening. Jo's
interpretation of Falstaff was renowned even in professional circles.

The rumour that Sheridan himself appeared in Tremadoc
Theatre in a production of *The Rivals* may well be true, but it is
more likely to have been his son Tom, who was a contemporary
of William's. Both families had known each other since the days
of the Wynnstay theatricals, if not before, and William had both
political and dramatic interests in common with R. B. Sheridan.
It was about this time that William had wanted his colleague, the
poet William Lisle Bowles, to meet the famous dramatist in his
rooms at Oxford. He called with some friends at Bowles' College,
only to find him out. Being without means of communication he
borrowed a piece of brown paper and a blacking brush from a
boot-boy who was working at the bottom of the staircase, to
write the invitation which began:

'Dear Bowles
Come to All Souls
To dine if you can
With Mr. Sheridan.'[8]

The Tap Room linked the Town Hall to the new Hotel, and

thus completed the range of buildings to the north of the square (see page 89 and facing page 113). The Madocks Arms was of the greatest importance to the success of the town. 'Depend on it, we can not make the Inn too good, too soon. I am shipping off plenty of good furniture . . . & will give Ongley [the publican] every Encouragement.' An inn sign–'very handsomely done indeed, looks beautifully and I think will have an excellent Effect' –was also shipped from London and its fixing in the most advantageous position was minutely discussed.

Inside, too, the hotel was certainly handsome and it seems to have been well appointed; but visions of the elegance of the day are brought realistically down to earth by the '12 Tin Spitting Boxes' which were provided. Besides the 'great room' (approximately a double square: 33' 0" × 16' 0") where the principal entertaining took place, it had twelve bedrooms and the Men's Attic and the Maid's Garret: the Attic was unexpectedly cosy being furnished with a four-post bed with check hangings and a Black-gammon box.[9]

The houses, many of which included shops, flanking the other three sides of the Market Place, could hardly be more straightforward. Their robust detailing and generous proportions make for a plainness which is thoroughly urban in character and sets off the other buildings to good advantage. The typical plan has a central doorway with a generous parlour or shop (16' 6" × 11' 0") on each side and two bedrooms above.[10] Behind is a scullery lean-to, also in stone, running the width of the house. Its design was not left to chance: 'Only let them be neat, like Tanyr Allt Colonade, as if it was enclosed. There will of course be good *looking Doors & Windows* in *each*. If a small projection in the wall, like a stone Pillar was introduced between each shed, or lean to as thus

. . . Let the Door & Windows *be a good size*.' (In his next letter Madocks introduced the term pilaster: he was always tactful about the use of English words.) A point was emphasised: 'The *Lean toos* at the back of the Houses at the *East End* of the Town, I should wish to be *smarter* than any of the others.' This was the Tan-yr-allt approach.

The houses, like most town houses of this period, open straight on to the square in the front. At the back there are gardens and some had cow-sheds. Tenants who wanted more land were allotted plots near by; some had orchards and everyone had the right to dig peat on the common turbary.

Two of these standard plans were modified for local inns. Because of the difficulty of digging a dry cellar on the newly reclaimed land, half the lean-to was built with stone vaulted roof to keep it at an even temperature. This vault led directly from the inn parlour and made that unusual but most congenial pub plan in which there is no bar. In each inn a bay window was substituted for one of the sliding parlour windows, and the numerous houses which were also shops had similar modifications.

Shops were rare in Welsh villages at this time so for Tremadoc to boast even one must have caused comment. Mr. Williams, the Mayor, had opened a general store to which one of the aldermen sent supplies from London. As early as 1805, John Williams was instructed 'Be looking out for a Shoemaker – a Tailor – a Butcher – and a Weaver. Robert Roberts will do no good as a Butcher, nor do I like to be treated as he treated me.' It seems that the new town was bringing, with the optimistic speculators, the inevitable collection of more dubious characters who were on the make and who would do their best to suck what they could. Madocks, as a tourist, might have been stung quite cheerfully, but as a landlord he was determined not to be fleeced. Only he knew how ill he could afford such treatment.

Several gentlemen's villas[11] were built in the vicinity and in varying degrees they are all stamped either with that peculiar charm of siting or the serenity of character which had been achieved so simply in the first extension to Tan-yr-allt. Those

4. Tan-yr-allt, water-colour by Kenneth Rowntree, 1941

5. Peniel Chapel, Trè Madoc. Water-colour by Kenneth Rowntree, 1941

shallow pitched slate roofs with big projecting eaves and hipped
ends which were the hallmark of the style were often repeated
very effectively (and economically) over single-storey parts of
the plan either as open verandahs or as Madocks' much favoured
'lean-to' rooms. A few gothic details were thrown in at whim
and he always preferred a coved or vaulted ceiling to a flat one.
The effect was simple and never pretentious.

Equal in architectural importance to the Town Hall, in
Madocks' eyes, was the Church. Tremadoc could hardly be a
town without it. Naturally enough it was originally intended to
be a parish church in its own right but, despite the geographical
logic of Madocks' case, consideration of tithes and other parish
matters proved too strong and only a chapel of ease was allowed.
Tremadoc, by some chance of boundaries, lay in the parish of
Ynyscynhaearn whose lone church lay two or three miles away,
remote from any building, on the edge of Ystumllyn marsh.
Penmorfa was nearer, but there was no certainty that services in
English would be conducted in either church. Nor was it to be
expected that the parishioners of Penmorfa, against whom
Madocks was cheerfully fighting a commercial battle over
markets, fairs and shopkeepers ('Wage constant war against the
Penmorva-ites!'), would welcome the citizens of Tremadoc in
their midst.

Madocks was not much in favour with the Bishop of Bangor.[12]
He had fallen from grace in the eyes of that dignitary by allowing, and probably encouraging, the Calvinistic Methodists to
build in the town. When the Bishop had inquired whether this
was true, Madocks is reported to have answered that it was so
and to have explained, with geological accuracy, that whereas the
new Church was to be built on rock, the Chapel was on sand.

The Church is romantically perched on what had once been a
low rocky islet in the Traeth and this siting gives some importance
to its not very high spire. Its picturesque withdrawal also makes a
nice contrast to the classic siting of the Town Hall on the square.
Changes in architectural taste long left the Church out of fashion.
By contrast, travellers in Madocks' time tended to ignore the

7

Town Hall (old hat to them) and to admire the Church's 'extremely neat gothic'[13] (high praise). It was one of the earliest gothic revival churches in Wales. Moses Griffith, Pennant's illustrator who had turned free-lance after his master's death, lovingly drew the Church and only included the Town Hall in a distant view of the Market Place. (More recently, Kenneth Rowntree chose to draw the Chapel; his water-colour is reproduced as Plate 5.) Fenton, as a classicist, was less enthusiastic and described the spire of the Church as 'very incongruously built of yellow freestone nicely wrought, perched on a stump of a tower, of grey granite, ill put together'.[14] It is, in fact, brick rendered with plaster; Madocks would have delighted in deceiving the eye of so keen an antiquarian.

Some years later Samuel Lewis's *Topographical Dictionary* described how 'Mr. Madocks has also built, at his own expense [£1,200] a handsome small church, in the later style of English architecture, with a lofty spire, which forms an interesting object to be seen from the coast: divine service is regularly performed in the English language, every Sunday, which is a great accommodation for families residing in the neighbourhood as there is no other Church within twenty miles, in which the service is performed in the English language.'

The building has now lost its box pews as well as the organ and stained glass which gave it warmth and colour. Just after its completion it was described enthusiastically as 'very beautiful . . . with 2 fine Pictures on each side of the Altar piece, the one of the Woman taken in Adultery, & the other of the Tribute Money shewn to Our Saviour, & a great deal of colour'd Glass in the windows'.[15] The entrance to the churchyard is unaltered and it is easy to understand Fenton's interest: 'The Gateway of Coad is composition, most superb and elegant, the ornaments uncommonly rich, and the whole not at all in accord with the other parts of the building,' he finished rather tartly. The business of shipping it from the factory in London, unloading it into small boats at Ynys Cyngar, and carting it to its site for erection without damage to the intricate perpendicular decoration of the plaster was a considerable feat.

If the Church seems withdrawn and austere and has for us little of the charm of the other buildings, the reason is partly unarchitectural. Besides endowing it with land, Madocks had set aside the surrounding ground as a graveyard. But it was never used for burials, perhaps because the building did not rank as the parish church, and therefore, instead of the finely carved slate headstones which usually press for space round Welsh parish churches, there is lush grass. That sense of continuity which grave-stones give between the living and the dead is sadly missing.

Peniel Chapel was one of the first buildings to be finished in the new town and it was one of the biggest. It probably caused pained astonishment among the North Wales gentry that Madocks, an anglican with a typical English upbringing, should not only have permitted but been enthusiastic about its erection. To those who knew him better this was less surprising. Freedom for the indi-vidual was the common thread that ran through all his political speeches; it even appeared in those light-weight prologues which he produced for theatrical entertainment. It followed then that religious toleration must not only be preached but be actively promoted in Tremadoc. ('In education and religion all ought to have fair play,' he was to write later when some trouble arose concerning the opinions of the schoolmaster.)

Nonconformists, at this period, were seldom architecturally minded.[16] Probably the long custom of open-air preaching and the material difficulties which obstructed them were as much at the root of this apparent indifference as any puritanical tradition. The few chapels which had been built had a moving simplicity, but usually they managed without specific buildings and so the tradition of chapel design was slow to develop.

At first, preachers visiting Tremadoc might use the coach-house of the Prince of Wales Inn or perhaps the shell of the unfinished Town Hall. In 1805 a Sunday School had been started in one of the houses[17] and a small congregation began to meet regularly. Then, unlike the majority of their faith, they decided to build (maybe at Madocks' suggestion?) and they were granted land on a ninety-nine year lease at a peppercorn rent. In 1808 they set to work on a vast building of unique design. Less than two and a half years later, services were being held in it.

If the very existence here of a chapel of any kind at this date is unexpected, its architecture is much more so. The focus of all nonconformist chapels is the pulpit, since the preaching of the word of God rather than the serving of the sacrament dominates the majority of the services. Therefore it was essential that as many people as possible should be seated so that the minister could be both heard and seen clearly. In a rectangular building this is achieved most easily if the pulpit is placed in the centre of one of the long sides rather than at the end and chapels at this date were planned on these lines (many have been altered internally since). Even in a large hall no one was then at any great distance from the minister; the pews were arranged in a three-sided hollow box round the raised pulpit, with the communion table immediately below it.

To accommodate the growing numbers, galleries became common. They proved to be both the most economical and, architecturally, the most effective way of providing additional seating. The sense of concentration on the pulpit given by galleries running round the three opposite walls can be intensely dramatic.

The reason for a radically different plan at Tremadoc, in which the pulpit is placed against a short end wall, was certainly not functional. It is more likely that the design, taken with very free interpretation from some classic copybook (provided by Madocks?), could only be treated in this way. In place of the usual simple exterior, Tremadoc blossoms forth with a bold stuccoed portico; two columns in antis support the pediment with a big circular window in the tympanum. Inevitably such an entrance had to be on an end wall and from this the internal arrangement naturally followed, with the pulpit opposite to the entrance.

For sheer dramatic quality Peniel Chapel would be hard to beat. Indeed it has at times been mistaken for Madocks' original theatre: he must often have longed to use it. To overcome any difficulties of seeing or hearing which might arise in so large a building the box pews were raked in plan and the floor is sloped towards the pulpit. This theatrical effect is further emphasised by the gallery.

The handful of Calvinistic Methodists who undertook this building showed extraordinary confidence. Even Madocks was taken aback when he saw its size: 'John, you will be like a needle in a haystack,' he told their leader John Jones, but the small congregation was not discouraged in the least. Money was borrowed on interest from as far away as Wrexham; £643 was raised in this way, while a further £263 1s. 5d. was actually given.[18] By far the greatest expense was the timber:[19] but this, considering the great span of the roof (46′ 0″), is hardly surprising. It was presumably constructed of imported Baltic scantlings. Stone, naturally enough, seems to have been free, and there is no mention of the iron columns with leafy capitals which support the galleries so they were probably a later modification.

Looking back it is easy to understand that, once it was decided that Capel Peniel should be something more than a simple traditional building, the classic rather than gothic style should have been chosen. It was not until well on in the nineteenth century that the nonconformists began to feel, as the anglicans were soon to believe, that pointed arches were synonymous with true religion. There was doubtless at this stage a strong reaction against anything which might be associated with the parish churches from which the methodists were escaping; since these were almost all medieval, a style of classic origin was the obvious solution.

Because he was not concerned with its building the Chapel is not mentioned in Madocks' letters, but one point does emerge which stands greatly to his credit. Although at the time when it was being built the Church was lagging badly, and the great Embankment was absorbing everyone's energy, it was never once suggested that labour or materials might be diverted from the Chapel. It was finished eighteen months ahead of the Church and the first service was held before a large and important congregation which included many eminent methodists and well-known preachers. Madocks and several members of his family were present; he sat with two or three of the ladies in the principal pew and, out of courtesy to these guests, the famous Thomas Charles of Bala, who took the service, read it in English. (He was still then a member of the anglican communion and only finally broke away the following year.) Twm o'r Nant, the equally famous bard and playwright, who had been working as a mason on the great Embankment was also present. Several people commented on the uniqueness of an occasion that brought such diverse celebrities under the same roof, and it may have been in retort to some busybody's jibe that Twm o'r Nant told the Reverend Thomas Charles: 'You look after the sheep and I will look after the goats.' He must have cut a strange figure in his dirty old cloak and immense hat (worn over two old nightcaps) but he was a character to Madocks' liking, and was often at Tan-yr-allt where his portrait hung in the drawing-room. In his day he had been known throughout the Principality for his 'interludes'; these were famed for their wit which tended to be too apt for everyone's comfort.'[20]

One of the earliest and by no means the least important buildings in Tremadoc was the Manufactory. It was one of the first woollen mills to be built in North Wales[21] (and probably in the Principality) where the use of water power was almost unknown except for the fulling of cloth. Inventions such as Cartwright's power loom and Arkwright's jenny which were to transform the industry were beginning to come into wider use in England, but it was not generally realised that, if the enormous Welsh woollen trade was to continue to compete with the production of the new factories in England and Scotland, it was essential that the new inventions should be introduced fast.

Welsh woollens were exported to all parts of the world[22] and were considered suitable in extremes of climate. Planters in South Carolina and the West Indies bought them for their slaves; the Spanish imported them in South America; they also went to North America and Russia. Merioneth webs[23] alone were believed to have a turnover of between £50,000 and £100,000 and this represented only one section of the trade. Montgomeryshire flannel was another and there was also the vast knitting industry centred on the Bala market.[24]

In spite of the scale of the trade, this output was achieved in farm houses and cottages. It was considered as part of the household routine like fruit-preserving or cheese-making; farm servants working with the family would get through phenomenal amounts of both wool and gossip. This was of little comfort to the really poor who could not afford to buy the raw wool, and there were many who would have been thankful for employment; but the foreign remoteness of much of the mountainous country damped the enthusiasm of other speculators, although unemployment and poverty would have provided a constant supply of labour.

Considered against this background, Madocks' idea to build a manufactory worked by water-power in Caernarvonshire in 1805, was revolutionary. Following the corn mill, a building which might be expected on any prosperous English estate (but not in North Wales where there was so little to grind), the factory was the earliest major project in the new town.

Its siting, although now once again in line with the latest planning principles of integration, is unexpected. Basically it depended on the availability of a good head of water to drive the water wheels, but this condition still gave wide latitude. To Madocks, the possibility of obtaining water-power close to Tan-yr-allt seemed most fortunate: the site chosen for the town's industry bordered his garden and lay between it and Tremadoc so that anyone visiting the house was likely to pass (and admire) the new corn mill, manufactory and fulling mill.[25] Satanic mills had then hardly begun to blacken other parts of the country and the idea that the owner should reside at a suitable distance, uncontaminated, had not come about.[26] The wheels at Tremadoc were, in any case, turned by the clean water straight off the mountain which flowed on to make green and pleasant the reclaimed marsh below.

The design of the factory was thoroughly functional and was based on the sequence of operations. It was built on the slope towards the foot of the hill so that the ground level was considerably higher at the back than the front. This meant that it could be entered on the middle floor, with two floors above and two below, and thus the vertical circulation, which was the basis of the manufacturing process, was greatly simplified.

The building is admirably plain and rugged with rubble walls and Madocks' favourite shallow pitched hipped slate roof. By July 1805 it was completed; and a memorandum instructed that it is to be *well yellowed* and the windows painted *dark* green. A dark brownish olive could look very smart with a light ochre lime-wash and the five-storey Trè Madoc Manufactory would be a building in which its owner could take justifiable pride. But it was to be at least another year before power was available. A big stone dam was built across a small valley in the hills directly above Tan-yr-allt. This formed the Llyn Cwm Bach, an enchant-ing small lake unexpectedly hidden among the high crags. A short distance below the dam, the stream, which dashed down through the steep oak woods, was diverted along the side of the hill to feed another small reservoir. This was constructed about a hundred and fifty feet above the factory and through a series of sluices fed both the mill and factory pools.

Madocks' great concern was that there should be ample reserves of water-power: 'Now for the Pool behind the Factory–remem-ber what height will do . . .' is a recurring theme in the 1806 letters. With such new techniques in mind he naturally feared that the full implications of the scheme might not be understood, and the necessity of sufficient reserves of water-power might be underrated. Two engines were already on their way by sea, and would be useless until power was available. This anxiety drew from Madocks one of his more dramatic but far-fetched analogies (written a few months after Trafalgar):

'Dear John,

When Lord Nelson, the greatest Hero of the World, attacked the French in Egypt his Plan was one of the simplest, though not the less wise and praiseworthy on that account. When the French Fleet was moved so close to the shore, that they thought nothing could come between them and the shore, Lord Nelson was of a different opinion and thought thus–If the French Fleet, that is if each French ship, can swing round, there must be sufficiently deep water for an English Man of War to go between the French line and the shore. So it proved to be, and he won, perhaps the greatest Battle that ever was fought at sea, unless we except the action in which he so gloriously fell. – *Thus* it is with our Factory. If there be *water* enough to turn *one* carding engine constantly, there be enough to turn a dozen in succession, or as many as the fall will permit, one below the other. . . .' He went on to explain that at this stage water was only needed for carding, as the other operations would be done by manual labour 'unless we can here-after accomplish weaving by water'. (Woollen cloth was com-monly woven by hand in England for some time to come.) The letter continued: 'Therefore do not despair about the Factory, which, if we can bring it to perfection, will much improve our Town and Valley. I hope to hear the Fulling Mill is at work, for *Remember* if any link in the Chain is wanting the next is *Useless*, waste, and loss of Money, time and labour. I am however much pleased with the disposition You, and Mr. Fanshawe [the Manager] shew to draw together to press *forward* the *Factory* concern with all *the Spirit & Zeal possible*. But the first of All things are the *Pools*, and for Heaven Sake Make the Pool at the back of the Factory on the *Grandest Scale* possible. You have my full instructions & Confidence to make this pool in the grandest *style*. Pay Mr. Fanshawe the compliment of *consulting him*, but I must leave the construction of the Pools to *you*. . . . Think, Think, Think, Act. . . .' (This exortation to action was repeated nine times.)

Mr. Fanshawe did not give satisfaction, despite compliments. Madocks feared he was 'too fond of pleasure' and 'Not up early enough the Morning' with the result that John Williams' work was extended into the field of industrial management. 'I approve all your observations about the Factory,' Madocks was to write. 'They are very sensible. But we have never yet hit on the right proportion between the warp and weft and the weaving. Nor is the oil or carding exactly proportional to the work. These propor-tions ought to be exactly hit on now that when we have a fair opportunity to extend the business we may be prepared by *Experience* and *habit* and *use* to carry it on to the best effect and advantage. We ought now to learn the business that we may practise it right in due season.'

They had soon to go deeper into the technicalities of the manu-facture of cloth. 'The Gentleman who is beginning a connection with me, as Army Clothier for the Webs, is very anxious to have the thread *spun finer* a great deal. The quality of the wool will do vastly well . . . he wants it to be well fulled & thickened & the pieces reduced to 27 Inches and when well fulled to be raised on the coating. If We can manufacture to suit him, he will take regularly from us without further trouble.' The snippet of dark indigo cloth which was sent as a pattern brings the whole enter-prise back to life: 'The enclosed Blue sells in London 6s. 6d. a yard, *6 Quarters wide.*' The jenny operators probably muttered over it, blaming the wool they were given to spin for the fact that Tremadoc cloth was coarser, but the deal was apparently clinched for Williams was to 'hasten the *Blue & Scarlet* dyes from Garn as they will be much wanted' and it seems that cloth from the factory was used by Wellington's men; this would appeal greatly to Madocks' sense of patriotism. But when his neighbour, the infamous Colonel Wardle became a partner in the enterprise the connection proved embarrassing. In Parliament, Wardle attacked the clothiers for racketeering and, since a third partner in the Trè Madoc Manufactory was himself in that business the pamphleteers were quick to take up the matter: Wardle was using the floor of the Commons to attack his partner's competitors. He was a colourful character to whom gossip clung, probably with justi-fication.[27] It was even rumoured that he was responsible for the export of cloth to France during the war, but suffered a severe set-back when one of the ships was seized, together with its cargo, by the British Navy.[28] No record of this has been found, nor of Madocks' name being linked with it, and the whole story may have been a wartime scare.

Both the export of cloth to London and import of wool had to be organised and an arrangement was made with one of the Ffestiniog Slate Quarries to share cargo space. 'It happens that the Liberty, Captn. Pritchard, is the very thing. She is about 100 tons built at Traeth Bach, & Pritchard is a native of our port, so that he may become a *constant Trader*. Slates & Webs to go together to Town and have back wool just as we please.'

Some years later (1810) when it was decided to sell the Factory, the advertisement in the *North Wales Gazette* was only slightly stretching the truth when it boasted that it was the only manufactory of its kind in the whole Principality. It went on to claim that it 'possesses excellent water-power, and that of the softest and best quality; and is situated near Carnarvon in the centre of the greatest sheep-walk in North Wales' and that it contained 'machineries of the most improved construction calculated to make and finish fit for any market, mixed and medley cloths, kersey-meres, woollen cords, coatings, flannels, and woollen goods of every description'.

5

Estate Affairs and House Parties
1805 – 1811

WILLIAM MADOCKS' LETTERS to John Williams give a livelier idea of the day-to-day work on the estate than could any orderly account of the business but, when reading these detailed instructions, it is easy to forget that they represent only one facet of Williams' work. The building of the town and the construction of roads and harbours were already taking up a great deal of time, and preliminary work on the immense new Embankment which they were shortly to be planning might in itself have been considered to be a full-time job. In Westminster, Madocks was as busy as ever with private bills and constituency matters and he was soon to be swept into a new phase in the battle for parliamentary reform. For the sake of clarity these events are described in separate chapters, although a truer picture might have emerged if they had not been unravelled from the domestic dramas in which they were enmeshed. The urgency of the instructions in Madocks' letters and the incongruous juxtaposition of subjects focus the everyday life of that distant estuary into a series of sharp stills which turn into a moving picture as the pages flick by. For instance, a stream of questions and injunctions might end a long letter which dealt with quite different topics:

'Are the mayor's things arrived and with them some wine for me? Has anything been heard of the *Elizabeth*? The Road to Morva Bychan? How are the Markets? What do the Permorvites say in consequence of their Victory? Is their Market revived in consequence? Drive on the New Inn . . . No *Greyhounds* at Robert

Jones's. Preserve the Hares most scrupulously. What is Payne doing? and how going on? Clear the Car-Dyke by Mill field & Avenue. How does the Grass spring. Wheat? Oats? Is there a good appearance for hay? 20 good whethers for the autumn to be very *fat*. I should like to kill *Beef* in August, & September. Can you contrive to have *two* or *three* nice Runts to be fat by that time? . . . The harder we work *now*, the sooner our Labour will be over, and the pleasure arrive of seeing things in Perfection.'

Closely woven into the estate business come instructions about the management of domestic affairs at Tan-yr-allt and the preparations for the house-parties with their attendant theatricals and race-meetings. Often, with such functions imminent, the buildings to be occupied were unfinished. While possibly giving the contractors extra incentive for completion, such crises complicated Williams' already exacting job. Shortage of funds was to be a constant anxiety, particularly since it was at the same time vital that confidence in the whole concern should be spread abroad; a nice balance between economy and apparent financial well-being had somehow to be held.

The second addition was now being made to Tan-yr-allt, and a fair idea of what was involved in furnishing both it and the Madocks Arms is given by the cargo lists which were sent. Madocks was inclined to be vague as to what had been shipped and this cannot have simplified its receipt. 'As far as I can recollect there was sent by the Swan and the John . . .' might head a long and detailed list. It is surprising more freight was not lost: 'Mind you measure the goods that come from London, the captains will impose if they can,' he warned and, sure enough, the following week it turned out that a large light blue carpet, red curtain, brass rod and gold mirror were missing. It would have seemed more likely that cargoes bound for the new inn or Madocks' own wine cellar might go astray but barrels of ale, reputed to be 'as good as Meux's' and cheaper, arrived intact. Another cargo of furniture brought numerous beds (including four-posters), boxes of books and pictures and a billiard table for Tanny, the kitchen range and smoke-jack for the inn, and twenty fenders and grates. For outdoor entertainment 'a nice Green Whiskey with new

Harness' and a 'Handsome Boat for the Canal with a large Green Awning to keep off the Sun and Curtains to draw round it' complete with 'oars, skulls and a punting stick' were sent. So were gothic window frames, artificial stone-work (Coade?) in the form of fountains and figures and, for civic occasions, a small box of alderman's insignia and a pair of gold candlesticks for the Town Hall. John Williams was instructed to take good care of 'a beautiful tall figure of Bacchus to put in the *Nich* in the Hall and from his [??] a handsome Lamp which I hope is unpacked safe . . . I mean where my Father's Bust stands in the Hall' and, before Madocks' arrival, 'a cleverish Understanding Man' was to be found in Caernarvon to help with the sorting and fixing of the furniture.

Such cargoes were fairly straightforward, if fragile. More complicated from Williams' point of view was the storage of 'the vast quantity of scenes, very valuable ones indeed. All of them from our theatre in Kent'. It was essential that they should be kept where they would be 'perfectly *dry*, and not likely to be injured by Rats or Vermin'. The big barn on the home farm was suggested, but first a lock must be got and the hay cleared out.

Rats from the marsh were a constant problem; they burrowed into the new bank and invaded the houses. Williams was 'to wage incessant war with them. . . . Their *Stink* is as bad as their Noise. I hope therefore you will do nothing by which they can lye & dye behind the battening of the rooms. *Cats in the roof* & all over the house, are one of the best preventitives, & remedies.' But the rats were not to be beaten, and to help in this 'furious war' a man who had been 'employed in killing millions of rabbits which inflict my Brother's Place in Kent' had, with Pied Piper confidence, 'engaged to kill all the Rats at Tany Rallt'. He was coming slowly, to spare the mare and young foal which he was bringing north; a reminder of pre-railway methods of transport which makes the popularity of the Tremadoc Races the more surprising.

The Races were to be one of the chief attractions of the Tremadoc season but, being remote both from any other meeting and from the stables of Madocks' colleagues (Shropshire and Denbighshire were far enough, let alone Lincolnshire), all his powers of persuasion were needed if horses were to be entered. His letters reflected natural anxiety: 'The Race Ground, Take most particular care of it. All the World are coming to the Races. The Inn Stables. Build a Coach House in the Middle, as you describe. This must be driven on with all speed. I have sent Griffiths bank Notes by this Post . . .

'My Brother & Nephew are going to send immediately to Trè Madoc Horses and Training Grooms etc—We must afford the Racing Gentlemen every accommodation, or if we displease them this year we shall ruin our Races for ever. . . .' But a few days later: '[if] I understand right the Stables at the New Inn is not yet *begun*! It is now nearly May! Good God! What is to be done. Hundreds of my Friends were coming this Summer and the *Races* will be in July. . . .' Worse complications soon followed. The 1800 embankment had again been damaged and the obvious place to take turf for its repair was from the dunes at Morfa Bychan where the Course was planned. 'I hope: I trust: I rely, I depend on No Injury being done to the Race Course, in consequence of the Unfortunate damage to the Bank. For goodness-sake do not let a sod be cut. . . .' This meant further delay so the Boston friends were again persuaded to postpone their arrival which had been planned for mid-June. 'I am sorry because the 17th is my Birth Day,' wrote Madocks, rising thirty-four but ever grateful for the excuse for a party.

Such house-parties always caused urgent preparations, but in the summer of 1807 there was the additional worry that the new addition to the house was not finished. Madocks wrote from London about the completion of the kitchen offices: 'I shall be in despair [if they are not ready] . . . and as to the Bed Rooms, if Every exertion is used, and a due foresight is exerted, in having laths and plaisterers ready, the Bed Rooms might be done in time to have them dry by the Races 7th August. The Plaister soon dries this warm fine weather. But much *foresight & exertion* must be used. *Not to wait to order & prepare a thing, till it is wanted, but to order it beforehand, and have it ready at the moment it is wanted.* . . . In short—It must be done

It *must* be *done* [repeated 5 times]

'The Old Kitchen must be ready as a Laundry & wash house, and Remember Above all things, that the present Butler's Pantry is turned into a Complete Water Closet. This is indispensable. In short my Dear John, you must work night and Day, till the *28th of this Month* when I shall be with you. . . . You must get the Workmen to work double Tides and pay them accordingly. Additional wages will make them work 4 or 6 hours every day more than they do now, which will get through a deal of work. By Heavens, till the 28th you should sleep as little as possible. I can assure you I am hard at Work about my two Bills, & with other business, have hardly a moment for Sleep. I wish every moment I could be with you. It would be most satisfactory for me to enjoy Tanyr Allt this fine weather. My Boston Friends are all cockahoop at the idea of seeing my works. . . .

'I approve your arrangement about stables for the Races. They must be well provided for. But *thousands* of stalls must be provided also for other Horses. You have no idea what crowds are coming of Gentlefolks, I mean with good carriage & saddle horses that must be taken care of. Some field should be well li[m]ed for Ongley to turn Carriage [?] Horses into for Grass. That would be a great relief.—Indeed you must have all your wits about you, and be as active as a prime Minister or we shall be ruined for Ever. But with enormous Exertion, we shall gain Everlasting Credit.

Yours sincere friend
W. A. Madocks

'No hay in the Barn [i.e. with the Scenery].'

In spite of these alarms, the *North Wales Gazette* was eventually able to give the meeting an enthusiastic press stating that 'few races in the Kingdom can excel them in company or amusement' and reporting 'most excellent running by very capital Racers, amidst a numerous company of the first consequence and respectability in the Principality'. Sir Watkin Williams Wynn and Sir Thomas Mostyn were Stewards; it was highly gratifying that they should give their support to this untried meeting. They presented a plate worth £ 50 and Madocks gave a cup for another race. As well as the usual events there were exciting individual matches when one owner challenged another to race his horse across the dunes.

But not everyone was so pleased. Nimrod later described how 'horses of repute were brought thither, much to the dissatisfaction of their grooms who complained of Welsh stables and Welsh forage for horses, perhaps heavily engaged further on in the year'[1] and, on rather different grounds, others thought 'the attractions . . .' to be of 'a more dubious nature, for however the imagination may be for a while excited and bribed by the sight of high-blooded horses, gay equipages and fashionable company upon a bleak and sandy flat long untrodden by any but a native's foot, the judgement must, I fear, ultimately decide that in the train of such sports and amusements comes idleness, profligacy and debauchery'.[2]

The majority of the visitors to Tan-yr-allt had interests in addition to racing. Landowning friends and Welsh cousins naturally came to see what Madocks was about and, like his parliamentary colleagues, were keen to inspect his schemes for improving the property. Theatrically minded friends enjoyed the plays, and impromptu concerts were a great attraction. Elizabeth Billington, the prima donna of international repute and sister-in-law of William's friend Horace Billington the landscape painter, was a frequent visitor. She was most helpful in listing the linen at Tanny. She is described by the nineteenth-century contributor to the *Dictionary of National Biography* as 'the greatest singer England has ever known' and it is nice to think that Chester, where she sang in the Cathedral in a charity concert, and Tan-yr-allt had a chance to share with Milan and Naples 'the melting delicacy of her turns'.[3]

Michael Kelly was another professional singer who joined these parties (he had a high opinion of the Madocks brothers' amateur skill). One of his most memorable experiences had been to rehearse under Mozart himself for the first performance of the *Marriage of Figaro*. Kelly would tell his fellow-guests how the orchestra had halted rehearsals by their own tumultuous applause after playing through parts of the opera for the first time.[4]

Such individuals further leavened the already lively gathering

8

but it did not meet with universal approval in the neighbourhood. Madocks was described as 'having at all times a House full
of visitors, chiefly English friends, so making Tremadoc an attractive Spot for the gay and Idle and others who hoped to benefit by
the money then being squandered. Beddgelert which had previously been the Mart for the Vendors of Welsh stockings,
Wigs and Chrystals, was now nearly deserted and the barelegged
Children of the Mountains flocked to Tremadoc, in hopes of
drawing larger sums from the English there'.[5]

It is tantalising to read of the detailed preparations for the
house-parties, since the correspondence inevitably breaks off just
as they begin. Newspaper reports bridge some of the gaps, but
they can only go part of the way. A few surviving pages from an
immense tome[6] help to fill in the framework which the correspondence provides. It contains both the constitution of an exuberant drinking club composed of Madocks' friends and the
proceedings of the meetings of the Mayor and Aldermen of
Tremadoc. These records give as cheerful and bawdy a picture
as any of that time. (Presumably Madocks belonged to both club
and corporation but his name does not happen to be mentioned.)

The skilfully drawn title page (Joseph's handiwork?) consists
of lettering composed of corkscrews, wine glasses, bottles of
Burgundy and claret, new moons and revellers. It reads:

'THE
NOCTUARY
of the
ΠΟΛΥΦΙΛΤΑΤΟΙ [7]
Anglicè
The Polu-fill-full-tatics
instituted at the 63rd Glass
after sunset on the 17th night
of the 6th moon in the year
after the invention of
CLARET
υπο της Αρχης
της Υυναι κυς Βασιλικης
ΚΑΡΟΛΕΙΝΗΣΗ [8]

The club's drinking song follows: thirteen verses devoted to its godparents, Apollo (who 'brought up the Salt that was Attic'), Bacchus and Venus, which end:

'Be Love our Philosophy, Drinking our Pratique
And Wisdom shall envy the Polu-fool-tatic.'

The minutes of Corporation meetings suggest that their activities were largely social, and that is perhaps why women were included in its membership. Occasionally there are serious reports on the market and factory but these are rare. The record of Jo Madocks' election to the Corporation is more typical. It is recorded that he promised to dine the Corporation and, whenever they should visit him, 'he is directed on no account to make any of them drunk, only to be sure they make themselves so.' At another meeting, when the question of the population of the Borough was considered, it was suggested that 'The best method of increasing it will be the cultivation of Cockles. . . .' Victorian historians have taken this to indicate an interest in the shell-fish industry; it would seem to make more sense if the contemporary addiction to punning is taken into account.

Tan-yr-allt was run on a small staff so additional servants had to be found before the arrival of a house-party. Their engagement often fell on John Williams, or on Madocks himself, since there was no permanent housekeeper. The butler was versatile but not always sober, so at least one responsible woman would be indispensable. Madocks, realising the limitations of a cook he had found, wrote cautiously of the new housemaid whom Williams had engaged: 'I hope she is a steady woman, for, as I said before, the Cook I send, *is only a Cook.*' The housemaid promised well and was speedily promoted to oversee the establishment. With a bachelor's optimism, Madocks expected the rest of the staff to be found with little trouble. Only three days before his arrival a letter devoted to business affairs ended: 'I forgot to say that it will be absolutely necessary for you to have some more maids. . . . I trust Mary has got a good washer woman from Carnarvon. I can not spare Mary for any work but to superintend the House Keeper's Room & Bed Rooms to see that all is clean, and nice every day for the Gentlemen. Towels, water, Beds made, etc. This superintendence will not allow her to do much work. Therefore we must have 2 Housemaids, a Dairy Maid and a washerwoman besides a Kitchen Maid to help the Cook, until the Middle of September when we shall be a small family again.' And as a postscript: 'we shall be 10 persons at least besides servants. . . . You must have plenty of Beef ready by the 1st. I hope the Larder is in good order.'

Poultry and meat were procured in heroic quantities against the arrival of a party. Fresh salmon came from Aberglaslyn where Madocks owned the Fishery (but it was also very popular locally: to overcome this difficulty, Williams was instructed to let the fishing 'with permission to draw as I choose. Let a good active Poacher & bold Fellow have it, at once with the Cottage').

The food at Tanny was certainly delicious; even the potatoes were particularly recommended. Occasionally, when something new had been specially to his taste, detailed instructions would come from England: 'I send Peggy Jones a Receipt for an excellent sauce which I wish she would learn to make. The principle ingredient is Horse-Raddish, of which I hope you have plenty in the garden. . . .'

Naturally enough, the Tanny staff did not always give complete satisfaction. The new cook for instance, true to the tradition of good cooks, was thought to be extravagant, especially in the winter when the household was small. 'I am extremely sorry to think that the Cook seems satisfied in her mind that 2lb & $\frac{1}{2}$ of sugar per Day is a quantity that ought to be consumed . . .', Madocks wrote critically during one of those bouts of domestic economy which inflicted him when bills came in.

Peggy Jones seems to have been replaced and relegated to the pantry; perhaps the horseradish sauce and other new receipts were not a success. But she did not give satisfaction there either. 'Peggy I hold to be perfectly useless,' Madocks wrote. 'The quantity of things *broke* (and she washes up Dishes & Tea things) is quite shocking. Only examine the Teapot. . . .' He badly needed a wife to look after his domestic affairs.

One of John Williams' less usual jobs was that of encouraging local trade. First there were the markets to set up in face of those already established each Friday at Penmorfa. Tremadoc's first market was held on a Tuesday and this did not please Madocks, to whom the Merionethshire trade was vital. 'Who was it a-set it going on a Tuesday? No friend I suspect. . . . The Merionethshire people are accustomed to come to *our side* to Market on a Friday. I suspect it to be a trick of the Penmorva people, but don't let them know that you suspect it . . .', and with such neighbourly sentiments a cheerful trade battle ensued. Tremadoc had the great advantage of being nearer to the crossing over the Traeth so, as a lure, sacks of oatmeal were displayed in the Market Place where the Merionethshire people would pass. They were also enticed by the dinner provided by the local inns and the provision of newspapers (rarely seen in those parts): 'Let me know how the ordinary[9] at the Markets goes on. . . . Mind the Newspapers are well displayed at the Market *on a Friday*. Mr. Pitt is *dead*.' This event would be of obvious local as well as national importance since it would almost certainly bring Madocks' Whig colleagues into office in both Westminster and Dublin; no comment was therefore considered necessary, and the letter immediately continued with a question about 'the proper way to spell *Easter Monday* in *Welch*'.

A bill for the first Fair, a great event in the life of the new Borough, was about to be printed in London. Soon after this, when the Ministry of Talents had been formed, a long letter about the houses in the Market Place ended: 'Fox is Minister with Lord Grenville. London is in a great stir. I long to return to you.' Since there were few things that Madocks enjoyed more than 'a stir', it can only be guessed that he was trying to convey that Tremadoc was in no way a backwater. He was soon able to write: 'There is a very good chance of your seeing Mr and Mrs Fox at Tanny on their return from Ireland. The famous Charles Fox, the Champion of the liberties of Mankind, is the first person in the World I should like to show Tanny to. . . . Get plenty of Chickens in the Neighbourhood, Geese & Ducks, and keep the Fishermen in full employ. . . .' (Disappointingly this visit never materialised, for Fox died a few months later.)

As the time of the Fair approached, urgent instructions came about the ale to be available at Robert Jones' Inn. Equally important was to be the display of stock: '*above all we* must make a shew of *Cattle*, though we do not sell any. Recollect it is the *first* Cattle Fair, and every exertion must be made to give it effect. . . .' Sad to relate, this first fair on which such hopes were staked seems to have been a flop. Although even the household supplies at Tanny were used to augment those at the Inn, they ran out of ale. Madocks was bitterly disappointed: 'That the whole should be destroyed by the langour and idleness of Robert Jones. Not but what we are to blame for almost a year ago I contrived an improvement to his brew house & Cellar, which might have been done in a very short time and we did not see it done. . . .'

Publicity was always considered and Madocks had a shrewd eye for the placing of his advertisements: 'I hope there will be grand doings on Easter Monday. I do not approve however of putting anything in the North Wales Gazette about it. That paper does not go to a class or description of people, whom we want at the Fair. The right thing is to *cry* it at all the Markets & Fairs in the Neighbourhood.'

London journals were now taking notice of their work and Madocks delighted in posting copies to his agent. 'I send you in another letter a Paragraph & Print cut out of the European Magazine. There is also another Account of our doings at Trè Madoc in a publication called the Atheneaum, which is circulated very generally, and sets us off to great advantage. So you see we already make a noise in the World. . . .' It was gratifying, too, that Madocks' friends now referred to the enterprise as 'the Wonder of Wales' (aware, no doubt, of the established claimants to this distinction), but he also knew only too well how much needed to be done before they would 'stand high and a *tip-toe* with the County and our Neighbours'.

Scientific farming was then almost unknown in Caernarvonshire but, from the time of the completion of the 1800 bank, continual experiments both in sowing and fencing had been tried on the reclaimed land. Enclosure was itself an expensive item and fences of marron rope (acres of marron grass grew on the dunes) woven with osiers were tried. Furze and broom were also used on the traditional turf banks; gates were made of local oak and numerous small stone bridges over the canals had to be constructed.

Madocks entered into the problems of agricultural economy with typical enthusiasm: '*Mow the Rushes*,' he wrote. 'But indeed you ought to have the farmyard shaped, as I directed, directly, as there is a sad waste of urine etc. The ground ought to fall from the pond from all sides to the middle so ⌇⌇⌇⌇⌇⌇⌇⌇ do this I beg. . . . But do not begin to strew the Rushes till it is shaped.'

The affair of the grass seed was characteristic of his no-half-measure methods. He believed a certain seed to be of great value and had offered samples to his friends. 'It should be got together by hand (the children can pick it, I think) and get as many sacks of it pure, and unmixed with any other seed as you can.' This was vital, and Williams was to watch carefully that the children did not mix any. But a few days later he was told: 'Fortunately I have made plenty of inquiries in time about the nature of the grass, that grew in the Avenue. Destroy it all immediately and don't let a seed escape if possible. It is the worst grass that grows next to couch grass. It is called Holens Lannatus[?], and is proverbially bad.'

A great variety of seed and roots were tried out on the new ground: 'In the New Turnip Field to try some Butts of Lucerne, Carrots, Parsnips, Rape and Clover, red and white mixed and separate.' In the nursery, too, many species of hardwood were to be sown as well as Scotch fir and larch, themselves an innovation in a district where indigenous oak on the hillsides and clumps of sycamore protecting the windswept farmsteads were the rule. 'The fame of our Nursery is gone abroad everywhere: Every body admires it, and it has as yet done us more credit than anything. I do not think with the assistance of Hugh It will take up much of your precious time.' (Hugh, besides making the garden at Tan-yr-allt, was busily employed in the cellar bottling brandy, gin and whisky). The picturesque was not to be forgotten and

Williams was also to 'Sprinkle a few large larches in the High Rocks between the North Sluice and Pentre Nelly'. Immediate effect was still wanted; fortunately it seems that he used his own judgement when interpreting such instructions.

In this respect Madocks found the Welsh tradition of colour-washing buildings more satisfactory than tree planting. Like so many of his contemporaries he regarded his estate not only as a place for agricultural experiment: to him it was an immense painting, or a gallery of landscapes, each of which produced a problem in composition, form and colour. Even the smoke from a cottage chimney, or a boat on a river, was to be considered. In a country where it was customary to colour-wash a cottage at each spring cleaning, the most humble building could be of great importance. The rough stone walls on which the lime-wash was painted year after year could be sparkling white, pink, yellow or apricot as a result of a morning's work. In this bare country they stood out boldly against the grey and green back-cloth, never looking garish. This was partly because the buildings themselves were small and so provided occasional bright patches on the grey-green, and partly because of the unostentatious simplicity of the vernacular design. The rough stone surface of the wall also meant that the surface was interrupted by minute shadows, giving it a texture in sympathy with the landscape itself. The list of buildings for which 'yellow okre is to be bespoke' sounds like the chorus of a song: 'Ynys y Madoc, Ynys Towyn, Pen Clogwyn, Tyddyn Llyn, Llytty Lanarrch, Ynys Hir. . . .' The shed on Ynys Hir opposite Tan-yr-allt was particularly noted; no doubt with the view from the windows in mind. Colour schemes were not confined to buildings. Sandwiched between two rather prosaic entries in the Memorandum Book concerning complaints about stray oxen and the fitting of cupboards in Tan-yr-allt comes the brief instruction: 'The tenant of Llyty to have a Green Coat and a Red Waistcoat.' And very smart he must have looked as he opened the new turnpike gate at the entrance to the town.

To give full effect to the scene gothic follies were constructed at strategic points. Architectural detail was left to Williams' imagination but he was given the rough outline: 'Mind you introduce in the Tower on every side Loopholes, as thus, very large & if you can a tall narrow Gothic window Blank. I should like this to be knocked off.'

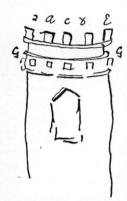

'G's should be alike

Such towers might be expected on rocky islands in the Traeth and other vantage-points, but it comes as a surprise to find that the town privy was to receive similar treatment. 'I hope all the houses in the ~~village~~ Borough will have their Cow Houses behind them. . . . The Public Necessary for them I wish also, *most anxiously wish*, should be finished. I wish you could get it executed in the shape of an old broken Tower, like the Necessary at the South end of Dolly. It would have a good effect in the neighbourhood of the Borough. . . . There should be free access to it from every part. The original spot we fixed on the South West corner of the Market Place, *over* the *ditch* in which the manure will fall, and if plenty of Straw, Fern or Rushes is put there, *fine* manure may be made.' A nice combination of the absurd and the practical, typical of its originator.

Bridges, plain and rustic, were also to be knocked off from Madocks' thumbnail sketches: 'And let the wall on each side take this shape, & the arch as thus:' and the siting of flag-poles was considered with great care. A brave show of flags and salutes of cannon were indispensable to any Madocks-inspired event. 'Get leave from the Tenant of

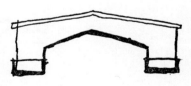

Pant Evan, I believe [that] is the Farm up on the Rocks, for leave to fix a high Pole for a Weathercock. I mean the furthest point, as you see from the Bow Window of the Drawing room.

I am sure you know where I mean, and there is a nice Fir Stick

lying by the Saw Pit which will do exactly, there is no occasion for planing it, or anything, but *put it up as it is,* with a Vane to it, the same as there is to the Main Mast of a Ship.'

Ships and boats were always given high priority, both for their scenic value as focal points in the landscape and because they always gave 'a grand Idea of the Business, and capability of the Town'. A 'Bason' was to be excavated off the canal in Tremadoc itself, for as Madocks so rightly said: 'Nothing will give the Town a more favourable and inviting appearance. . . . With respect to the Bason I should have preferred it oblong rather than an exact Octagon

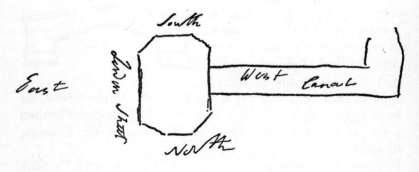

But it is not very material.' What mattered was that the new Boat with the Green Awning should always lie 'by the Town in sight' and not, as had been practically suggested, in a Boat House by the Sluice. But, above all, everything must be ready against the arrival of his friends.

By now the two projects nearest to Madocks' heart were under way: in Tremadoc the great new Embankment; in Westminster the next stage in the struggle for parliamentary reform. With both in full swing Madocks found time to write almost daily and, usually, Williams found time to read his epistles:

> 'I send you by this post Bank Notes
> value   120
> sent before   30
>   ,,   ,,   100
>   ———
>   250
> By this post 2 bills   1. 20
>   1. 30—50
>   £300
>   ———

to pay all the Bank Men & Workmen up to last Saturday in full, & not have one shilling in arrears.

'Drive on the *Town Hall*, and the *Canal full* and put all the Boats in the Bason, and the *Green Boat*. Have all the Bed Rooms in the Market Place ready for Beds. *Millions of people* are coming to the Races the 2nd, 3rd, 4th, & 5th of August.

'Drive all on. Make the Clerk of the Bank send me the exact account of the Workmen paid the last Fortnight. [P S] Get Tanny into *Exquisite Beauty*. The Colonade & all the walks & Roads cleaned. Get the leaden pipes mended to the Water Urn by the Billiard Room.'

The bedrooms in the Market Place were to be fit for 'Gentle folks' to sleep in. 'I have no objection to Pace's [the butler's] wife cooking if she can do it *well*. Has Pace given over drinking or he will never do at the Races. . . . Get the Cutter in trim. . . . I wish the large Green, Wooden, & Wire room which came from London last year, to be unpacked & put together & put up in the Back Yard of Tanyr Allt Ucha against I come. It will either make a charming Dairy or larder for the races. . . .

'Have the harper at Tanny on the 17th
1. The Windows mended
2. The Cutter repaired etc.
3. Green dairy put up
4. The Harper
5. The Canal & Bason filled
6. The flags flying
7. The Market Place pointed
8. Oxen, sheep etc for the Races.
9. The Racing Stables & Barn
10. The Green Boats floating on the Bason on the 17th.
11. The Office in order & no more plaistering.
12. Everything ready for 17th & All the Windows *Mended*.'

6

Parliamentary Reform
1808-1812

THIS BOOK concentrates mainly on Madocks' work in Wales, but since he spent such a large proportion of his time in London and Westminster a distorted picture would emerge if his political activities were not given a brief glance. The cause of parliamentary reform which he so enthusiastically and loyally supported had been largely forsaken by the time he entered Parliament in 1802 although it had been keenly advocated by men like Charles Grey (who forty years later became Lord Grey of the Reform Bill) in the seventeen-eighties. Even the short-lived Whig ministry was to show little enthusiasm for an issue which might have been expected to be very close to its heart. The aftermath of the French Revolution had shaken even radically minded Englishmen and had changed the current of political opinion. Societies which had been formed to promote what would seem the most common-sense reforms were treated with extreme suspicion and soon declared illegal. Set-backs in the prosecution of the war had caused otherwise progressively minded men to shelve the whole matter until victory was secure. It was considered unpatriotic to fuss about domestic matters when so much else was at stake.

But a few saw things differently, and Madocks, passionately believing in the cause and enormously enjoying the political drama that surrounded it, was one of these select few. To the entrenched tories they were hotheaded radicals. To us, now so accustomed to take for granted all they strove for, they seem mildly reasonable and clear-minded, if not in some instances cautiously conservative. They were among the small minority already aware of the inexorably changing social structure of England in the industrial revolution. In 1809 few sensed the strong undercurrents which still caused scarcely a ripple on the surface of the eighteenth-century pattern of society: the Framebreakers and the Luddites were as yet unknown. The argument of the Reformers was simple: that the House of Commons was no longer representative of the people.

Constituencies were then of two kinds, county and borough. In the county constituencies all freeholders of land worth forty shillings a year were entitled to vote: still a fair enough system before both the agricultural and industrial revolutions began to effect the distribution of population and land ownership so radically that the pattern of English life was to be irrevocably altered. The smaller independent farm was being fast swallowed up in the big estates where modern methods of farming and land enclosure were practised. With it went those who had qualified for the forty shilling franchise. At the same time vast new centres of population were springing up in the industrial midlands and north where the landless workers had no vote at all.

That other type of constituency, the borough, varied. There were open boroughs like Westminster, and seats like Boston so proudly held by Madocks himself, which resembled the county constituencies in their franchise. On the other hand there were the infamous pocket or rotten boroughs which were held by various individuals who could sell the seat to the highest bidder and who then could bind the member to their own political views. The biggest holder of these pocket boroughs was the Crown. By 1793, the situation had been reached where over half the members of the House of Commons were actually appointed by one hundred and fifty-four individuals who could thus control a majority in the House. After the Act of Union the coming of the Irish members to Westminster considerably increased this proportion. But however unrepresentative the elected body might be, by and large it consisted of men experienced in managing affairs and capable of producing a government to run the country. The majority of M.P.s, on both sides of the House, did not want a workable system which produced results, whatever its basis, to be altered at that difficult time. (Most of them, anyway, were in Parliament as a result of that system.)

The reform movement within the Commons had almost ceased to exist but it was not quite dormant; agitation by a handful of M.P.s was slowly gathering strength. Its leader was Madocks' colleague Sir Francis Burdett. It was he who had summed up the *laissez-faire* attitude which generally prevailed when he told the House that 'there were some who thought there were two improper seasons for reform – a time of peace and a time of war. In peace it was a pity to disturb the general tranquility, in war the nation had a great deal of other business on its hands.'[1] Burdett and Madocks had much in common besides having been close neighbours when Burdett took John Madocks' house, Vale Mascall. Both enormously enjoyed the drama of political life but combined it with a sense of the absurd rather than weighty pomposity. (They were to be together during the spectacular 'Burdett Riots' of 1810.[2]) Burdett would be a thoroughly congenial companion and colleague. Hazlitt was later to write of his speeches in the Commons: 'He could not have uttered what he often did there, if . . . he had not been a very honest, a very good tempered, and a very good-looking man' while Thomas Moore found 'something particularly attaching in his manner; his gentleness, almost bashfulness, forming such a contrast to his public career'. In temperament as well as outlook it seems that the two M.P.s had much in common.

Of the twenty or so other members who supported reform, the lawyer, Sir Samuel Romilly, had one of the keenest brains and one which he was always ready to use for the rights of the underdog. He was already renowned for his attempts to reform the penal code, having proved during his investigation into capital punishment that it was too harsh to be effective.[3] Another reformer, Samuel Whitbread, founder of the famous brewery, brought a business-like mind and the sympathy of the City to the cause. (A less well known but possibly even greater proof of his business acumen which would appeal to Madocks was the fact that he had contrived to make Drury Lane Theatre pay its way.) He was an orthodox politician and never dissociated himself from the Whig party. By contrast, by far the most colourful and least respectable of the reform party was Madocks' Penmorfa neighbour, Colonel Wardle, who by the spring of 1809 had become a national figure.

The previous autumn the *Independent Whig* had printed an article headed 'Corruption and undue influence in the promotion of military officers the source of a national disgrace', and in January Wardle had crystallised this general attack by his accusation that the Duke of York, who had had command of the British troops in the Peninsula, had connived at the receipt of large sums of money by his mistress, one Mrs. Clarke, which she was said to receive for her influence in procuring commissions and promotions through her connection with him. The leading Whigs were suspicious of Wardle, whose own reputation was not spotless. But the more radical members of the party, including Madocks, rallied; William Cobbett, the political writer who was one of the most staunch supporters of reform outside the House, was soon able to note with approval that certain of the older Whigs were coming round.

The excitement both in Parliament and in the press reached a climax when Wardle, seconded by Burdett, moved that the Commons should investigate the charges against the Commander-in-Chief. The hearing, which would have been manna to the press of any age, went on for most of February (during which such homely matters as the Traeth Bach–Barmouth Road Bill were also petitioned). In the end, although Parliament did not support the case against the Duke, public opinion did and he was forced to resign his command. Far more important, the discrepancy between the decision of Parliament and the feeling of the country gave life to the reform party. The surge of support the case had excited from all parts of the kingdom suggested to even the most cautious Whigs that the feelings of the people were no longer represented by the Commons. Thus the acquittal of the Duke of York inadvertently triggered off a new phase in the long battle for parliamentary reform. It was now channelled into two main streams: electoral reform and a drive against corruption in the trafficking of seats and holding of sinecures.

In May a tumultuous meeting was held at the Crown and Anchor in the Strand. Under the Chairmanship of Burdett fourteen resolutions concerning electoral reform and corruption were proposed. They were again substantiated by Grey's calculation of 1793, that 307 English M.P.s were appointed by 154 individuals, and it was stressed that the People were therefore not represented although they were taxed £70 million a year. In another attack on corruption it was stated that 78 of the present M.P.s were in regular receipt from the Crown of £178,944 per annum.

All the resolutions were carried before the diners cheerfully dispersed.[4] Madocks, who had seconded the motion, believed heart and soul in the cause and revelled in the jollification; his speech was gustily interrupted with cries of Bravo! Bravo!

Less to his taste was the task allotted him in the Commons at the end of the week. It had been decided that a generalised attack on corruption would get nowhere so, fired by their success in the case of the Duke of York, the reformers decided to bring the matter to the notice of the government front bench by direct attack on the Treasury control of seats in the Commons. During the hearing of the Duke of York's case a certain Mr. Dick, who had held one of the rotten borough seats at the disposal of the Exchequer, had been informed that he was expected to vote with the government or to resign; he chose the latter alternative. It fell to Madocks to bring this to the notice of the House by the impeachment of Spencer Perceval, then the Chancellor of the Exchequer, and Lord Castlereagh. It was thoroughly distasteful to Madocks to attack his colleagues even though neither can have been characters very sympathetic to him. Perceval's chief attribute is said to have been his efficient legal mind. Castlereagh's sterling qualities were well masked by his cold manner, boring speech and poor command of the King's English.

If he had to make an attack on ministers, it was at least fortunate for a man of Madocks' temperament that those chosen were among the most eminent and best able to defend themselves and that he was unlikely to see much of them outside the House. As he told the Commons: '. . . The task he had undertaken was most ungracious and unpleasant; and nothing but a strong sense of public duty should have induced him to place himself in a position of becoming the accuser of any man . . .' and he did his best to make the accusation as impersonal as possible.[5] After discussion concerning procedure this debate ran into various side issues but the Speaker ruled that Madocks should bring his case before the House again a few days later.

Then in a speech[6] which gained strength from both its logic and the sense of history in relation to which the impeachment was finally made, Madocks outlined the situation prevailing in the rotten boroughs, pointing out the stranglehold that the Treasury, as the largest holder of such seats, could have on the country through their control of the Commons. He began by moving that a Resolution which the House had made back in 1779 be read. In this it was stated that it was 'highly criminal for any minister or ministers, or any other servant of the Crown in Great Britain, directly or indirectly, to make use of the power of his office, in order to influence the election of members of parliament. . . .' Again he underlined that there was nothing personal in his charges: He 'entirely overlooked the men in the system, a system which seemed to say, that corruption was necessary to govern Englishmen . . . that the English constitution was inadequate without the aid of corruption. . . .' He denied 'in the name of the constitution, the necessity of such a system, and thought that any attempt to argue its necessity was one of the strongest proofs of its dangerous and fatal tendency. . . .' He reminded the government benches that they too had recently stated that it was the duty of the House to bring cases of corruption to light and he 'trusted that the indignation they seemed to express at the theory of corruption would not be allayed by an exposition of the practice'. He asked for 'the restoration, in their original purity, of all the good and sound old principles of the constitution'. His charge was one 'that the moment it was heard might be rebutted by an innocent man, unless it would be contended that there were degrees of corruption now so sanctioned by prescription, that that house

must necessarily connive them'. He was 'of an opposite opinion.
. . . In the whole course of the history of England he nowhere
found that Sinecure Places and Offices, and Rotten Boroughs,
were to be considered and venerated as comprising the palladium
of England'. He read nowhere 'that the constitution was only to
be preserved by the preservation of its abuses' but he warned:
'if the Treasury governed that house, the popular part of the
constitution was gone for ever. . . .' Figures were given of the
salaries of those who held the interest of several rotten boroughs
which were in the hands of men owing their positions to the
government. He then returned to the specific charge concerning
the seat which Mr. Dick had been asked to vacate when his
political views did not accord with those of the Treasury.

Madocks' diversion into the necessity for reform which was
the real reason behind the impeachment was seized upon by the
Chancellor of the Exchequer. Before retiring Perceval made no
attempt to deny the charges against him but pointed out that 'they
lived in a time in which the popular appetite fed upon attacks on
public men. The favourite doctrine was, that public men must be
necessarily corrupt; and they were the purest patriots who prose-
cuted most charges against them. . . .' He thus played on the fears
of many respectable members implying that a mass of other charges
might be brought if this particular case were allowed. He added:
'This, it seemed, was to be a first step to a general Reform. . . .
Perhaps they would feel it their indispensable duty not to establish
a precedent that would introduce a system of inquisitorial proceedings, fraught with the most violent inroads upon all species of
private and social confidence.' Such alarms were not to pass unchallenged. Another member sensibly pointed out that he 'would
not think one jot the worse of either of the rt. hon. gentlemen
accused, or that they were in any degree more criminal than all
former governments. The evil ought, however, to cease, and any
prospective remedy should have his support.'

Burdett questioned the reluctance of the Opposition to go into
the matter. 'Was it from a dread of French principles? Why this
was the very way to avoid the danger . . .' but when a member
speculated on the reactions of posterity to a House of Commons

which justified the existence of corruption in it there were calls to withdraw and a violent uproar.

It is difficult to understand upon what grounds the ministerial benches could so loudly oppose any suggestions that the case was one of high importance. 'If the fact be not so, why not inquire?' repeated another of Madocks' supporters '. . . and if you refuse to inquire, the country will not fail to form its own decision.'

Although the motion was eventually defeated by a majority of 225, 85 votes were cast in its favour, a much higher number than many expected. Wilberforce (whose efforts to abolish the slave trade had at last succeeded) was one of Madocks' supporters on this occasion. In the debate he had said that 'if they [the members] would but for a moment consider the question before them with a moral eye, there could be no doubt about their decision'.

Romilly was another sympathiser, and if Madocks had read the note that distinguished lawyer had made in his diary, he would have felt that his anxiety and trouble had been worth while. 'The decision of this night, coupled with some which have lately taken place, will do more towards disposing the nation in favour of a Parliamentary reform than all the speeches that have been or will be made in any popular assemblies.'[7]

But another member, Charles William Wynn, described Madocks' presentation of his case as having been brought forward 'with less ability than those who rate him lowest could have expected'.[8] It is probable that parts of Madocks' speech read with greater conviction than they came across live in the House, for it is unlikely that he would have been at his best in the role of impeacher, and Wynn, as a Whig whose opinions were too far to the right to stomach such policies, could have had little sympathy with those radical ideas which lay behind the impeachment.

The *Morning Post*, on the other hand, denounced the Commons for their acquittal and William Cobbett in the *Political Register*[9] was exuberant in his praise. Those who rated Madocks' abilities highest could not have dreamt of such an enthusiastic press: '. . . at last Mr. Madocks has brought the thing to a point, indeed to an issue, aye to a clear and unequivocal decision. This Debate, therefore, is the most important I ever had knowledge of. Will I hope be read by every man that can read, in this whole kingdom. Those who take in papers containing it, should *lend* them to their neighbours who do not. It should, if possible, be got by heart, and reported once every week, in every family in the kingdom. Boys at school should have it to read, in preference to every other thing.

'A concise statement of the charge and decision should have a place in all *Almanacks*; all the printed *Memorandum Books*; in the Court Kalenders; books of Roads; and I see no harm in it having a spare leaf in the *Books of Common Prayer*. It should be framed and glazed; and hung up in Inns, Town Halls, Courts of Justice, Market Places, and, in short, the eye of every human creature should be, if possible constantly fixed on it.–I mean merely the naked fact: the bare record, unaccompanied with any comment whatever . . .' he added with surprising reticence.

The matter of Treasury borough-mongering had now been thoroughly ventilated within the Commons and the debate had also helped to prepare the way for several other measures for reform during the summer, including Burdett's Reform Bill. Madocks seconded the motion in this debate. His speech cited examples now common in school books. (Old Sarum had become the classic example of a rotten borough returning two members to represent its near non-existent population. The secession of the American colonies was still fresh enough to most members for the cry of no taxation without representation to seem ominously familiar.)

Although this and other bills came to nothing they were not debated in vain. This period had been described as 'the seed-time of nineteenth century Reform'[10] and as such it was a vital prelude to the first reformed parliament of 1832. But that was a long way ahead; in 1811 when there was still a great rift between the moderate reformers, and Burdett and his colleagues, Madocks stood between the two factions and the following year when the Hampden Club achieved a degree of union between them he was among its founder members.[11]

As a private member he was also active both in the direct interests of his constituents and in matters concerning Wales.

Chief among the latter was the prosaic sounding but extremely important business of duties on coal transported by coastal shipping; so long as it went by land it was duty free, and thus absurd anomalies arose in its cost.

Walter Davies had described how 'Half starved cottagers on the sea-coasts of North Wales, far remote from any other fuel, cannot have coal under from 26s. to 29s. per ton of 32 Winchester bushels – while baronets and peers in inland parts may have it duty-free. . . .'[12]

Feelings were further incensed because the tax had recently been abolished in Scotland but not in England and Wales. It not only caused hardship (most cottagers would burn turf or wood besides coal), but it had a bad effect on agriculture since the prohibitive cost prevented all but the richer farmers from burning lime. (Numerous ruined limekilns still found beside small creeks and harbours around the coast show how important lime-burning was to become once the tax was lifted.) Industrialists, too, claimed that much that was now manufactured in England might be made in Wales if only coal were cheaper. Madocks introduced his Bill for the abolition of the tax in 1808 and it was rapidly passed by the Commons only to be defeated by the Lords.[13] Despite continued agitation the tax was not finally repealed until 1830, two years after his death.

His other political activities will be touched on as they occur, as a background to his activities in Caernarvonshire.

7

Building the Great Embankment[1]
1808 – 1811

WITH HIS many commitments both in Wales and London it
would be reasonable to suppose that William Madocks had had
enough to think about during the decade which followed his
acquisition of the Tan-yr-allt estate; his financial resources were
stretched to the limit and he had little enough time to enjoy
Tremadoc itself. During the winter of 1806 he had also been
working on further enclosure schemes and had outlined in
lengthy letters to Williams his ideas for a new embankment. This
would take in a further three hundred acres of the Traeth immediately outside the 1800 bank which had not turned out to be as
tempest-proof as had been hoped.

But Madocks was all the time thinking on a much grander
scale: 'You must know I have always encouraged in my mind the
great idea of sometime or other embanking the whole Traeth
either opposite Ynys y Towyn or lower down,' he wrote to
Williams in February. 'I tell you this *in confidence*, but it will be
necessary to have an Act of Parliament, and several very important steps taken beforehand that will require much more time
than I can afford in the present instance. . . .' With the newly
formed Ministry of Talents in power, William was agog with
activity. The Porthdinllaen Harbour Bill,[2] of even greater personal importance since some of his friends now had appointments
in Dublin, was about to be petitioned. But chief among those
'important steps' to which William had referred was the finding
of that very large sum of money which every engineer who had

135

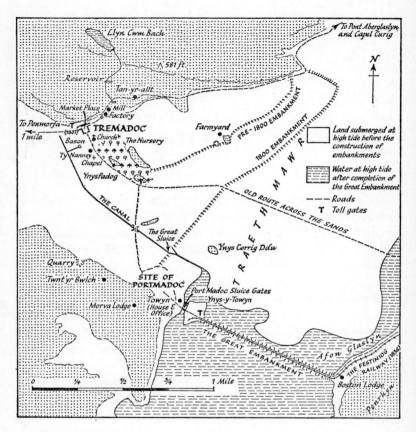

Trè Madoc and Port Madoc, 1824 (the line of the Festiniog Railway, 1836, is also marked)

cast an eye over the Traeth had considered essential to any such project. Such an embankment was an utterly different proposition to those which encircled parcels of marsh up the sides of an estuary. This would be a dam, close on a mile long, right across the entrance, and as such would have to bear both the full brunt of the storms of the Irish Sea on one face and the floods of the Glaslyn on the other. It was no do-it-yourself venture as the 1800 bank and scores of others up and down the country had been. It is little wonder that time was needed before such a scheme could be launched.

Suddenly, within a matter of days, the whole picture seems to have changed and the plans which had been outlined for years ahead were to come before Parliament within a few weeks. Money must have been unexpectedly forthcoming. It is very probable that John Madocks, who took a keen interest both in Tremadoc itself and in William's plans for the whole region, had been working to persuade his trustees to invest part of his father's legacy in the scheme, or he may have been negotiating a loan with his estates as security. At all events on 7 March (1806) Madocks presented a petition to the Commons on behalf of James Creassy, the engineer of the 1800 Bank, to enclose the estuary of Traeth Mawr by a great embankment across its mouth. With Creassy's professional skill backed by financial support everything seemed set fair.

But the situation was to change yet again with equal rapidity. In less than three weeks John Madocks was dead. William had seen, to his great anxiety, that his brother, with whom he was spending so much time discussing the project, was becoming gravely ill. He was only in his early forties but the surgeon diagnosed that the severe gout which afflicted him was beginning to affect his brain, causing attacks of delirium. Just as the brothers were about to set out for Tremadoc for the Easter holiday, he suffered another attack during which, it was reported in the *Gentleman's Magazine*,[3] he 'put a period to his existence'. William, who was with him to the end, was probably too grieved to care much when Creassy's Bill foundered in its committee stage shortly afterwards. Whether local opposition had proved too strong, or whether John Madocks' death caused loss of financial confidence, is not known. His son (also John) was still a minor so it is unlikely that his trustees would be enthusiastic about what they might legitimately consider to be an engineering gamble. Any doubts that may have lingered in their minds would have been settled by Creassy's death a few months later.

It was plain that with neither an engineer nor financial support the scheme must be shelved. But with intrepid persistence or amateurish obstinacy Madocks saw things differently. He was determined to go on and, if necessary, he and John Williams would do so alone. Less than a year after his brother's death, with neither an engineer to advise him nor any evidence of financial support, Madocks was himself petitioning for a Traeth Mawr Bill. That he should launch such a scheme without professional help is indeed astonishing. He had great admiration for the engineers of the industrial revolution and having read the opinions of their predecessors on the difficulties of building such a dam he could be under no illusions about the undertaking. It is possible that no engineer of suitable calibre was available; some of the best brains of the day were concentrating on the development of iron in bridges and aqueducts rather than on earthworks. The undertaking would be a great responsibility and expense and the lack of visible funds may well have caused sensible men to steer clear of it.

The decision to go ahead without outside help is even more audacious when it is remembered that John Williams played only a minor part, if any at all, in the building of the 1800 bank. Madocks was well aware of Williams' lack of experience; they had in fact planned the 1806 bank (which was not built because of Creassy's petition) largely for practice in bank construction. Their only professional advice, if it can rank as such, came from a surveyor, Renny Harrison, who was engaged primarily to give evidence before the parliamentary committees. It is clear he played no part in the design and Madocks had little faith in his judgement ('old Harrison is a fool in most things' he was to write later). Nor, despite many reports from Victorian times and later, is there any evidence that Thomas Payne, the Dolmelynllyn agent, was in any way engaged on the work.[4]

The young landscape architect, John Loudon, was to make a report on the possibilities of an embankment when he was in Tremadoc at the end of the year but this only dealt in a most general way with methods of construction; the line it might take does not seem to have been discussed. Loudon stated that no other embankment of similar dimensions had been made in Britain; this was probably an exaggeration but it did stress the size of the

Traeth Mawr project which was to enclose 3,042 acres by a 21-foot high embankment, 1,600 yards long.

February 1807 saw Madocks with three bills before Parliament: the Traeth Mawr Bill which was now petitioned in his own name; the Ynys Cyngar Bill; and a bill concerning his constituency, the Boston Small Debts Bill. As was to be expected there was considerable opposition in committee from local landowners to the Welsh bills. The surveyor's evidence was vital but he had disappeared: 'If Harrison is at Traeth bach or anywhere in the Neighbourhood, send off to him the moment you receive this, and tell him he must instantly set off for London, and not to loose a moment in coming as quickly as possible, as he is wanted before the Houses of Lords & Commons, and we cannot go on with my Acts of Parliament, for particular Reasons. . . .' Maybe he arrived too late for both these bills, along with various others, foundered in committee. Undeterred, Madocks immediately petitioned yet again. Again, too, the elusive Harrison was missing and was wanted 'every hour' but at long last at this its third attempt the Traeth Mawr Bill was successful and, a few weeks later, received the Royal Assent[5] just before Parliament rose for the summer recess. In its final wording[6] it was not materially different from its predecessors. Madocks was to undertake the Embankment at his own expense and in return the reclaimed sands were to be vested in him and his heirs. He was also to receive one-fifth of the annual rent of the marshlands (as against sands) which would be drained. Various estimates[7] were made of the cost of the undertaking but it was generally agreed that the Embankment itself would cost around £23,500 to which had to be added the cost of drainage, irrigation and sowing. (It turned out to cost over £60,000[8] – a guinea an inch.[9]) The ultimate object was to provide grazing, particularly early bite for the hill farms (as well as the permanently dry road from Caernarvonshire to Merioneth).

The period following the passing of the Bill happened to coincide with a time when Madocks was particularly active politically and his letters should be read against a background of renewed agitation for parliamentary reform: of those boisterous radical meetings and turbulent scenes in the House of Commons already mentioned.

For John Williams, too, there was much besides the Embankment demanding attention. Besides full responsibility for its construction there was the building of the town to supervise, the factory and estate affairs to manage and, not least time-consuming, those elaborate preparations for house-parties and race-meetings to arrange. It is easy to forget this more humdrum side of his work. But quickly scribbled notes bring the background to life: 'The moment you receive this send off to *Capel Curig* a light cart to bring some Boxes of small Seedling Larch, Scotch & Spanish Chestnut *which must be put in the ground immediately.*' A pencilled list below in John Williams' hand gives a clearer idea of what is involved:

'90,000 Larch
10,000 Scotch
10,000 Spanish Chestnut.'

Such instructions might distract from the organisation of a labour force of several hundred men and the solving of all the day-to-day technical problems which arose in the course of this major engineering project.

He still had no proper office; never much interested in paper work, this does not seem to have bothered him. It was Madocks who was ever urging a better arrangement: 'Without an office, and a Room completely retired for yourself it is impossible you can give that calm, cool, deliberate, and uninterrupted attention to my concerns, which the importance and magnitude of them require. This often occurs to my mind with some degree of alarm . . . and shows me the Absolute necessity there is for you to have a fixed, quiet, and Roomy Office, where all your *papers* can be properly arranged, and you can lay your hand upon them at any time you want in one Minute.'

It may have been slightly disconcerting to John Williams, now fully informed both of the project and his responsibilities as site engineer, to read at the end of a long letter which dealt with estate matters 'If John Evans [Caernarvon's most prominent attorney, who may have been acting in the capacity of under-sheriff] sends over to take an inventory of the Goods etc, at Tanyr Allt etc. and leaves a Man in possession at the House, *Do not be alarmed.* I am indebted in a large sum to a Gentleman, who is obliged to take this step to secure himself against malice. Do not be alarmed. We shall triumph at last.'

Whatever John Williams may have felt, he appeared unmoved; for the twentieth-century reader it is rather alarming to read of the bailiffs closing in just at the moment when Madocks' financial resources were to be strained to the utmost, and perhaps distressing to think of them in possession of the newly decorated house with its elegant but none too robust modern furniture. Further, general building expenses were still very high. The church was not yet roofed and its steeple only existed in the minds of the readers of the *European Magazine* where Tremadoc had recently been given an enthusiastic press. The Town Hall group was not yet complete. Porthdinllaen was progressing slowly but was already doomed by the government's growing preference for Holyhead. Ynys Cyngar Harbour had scarcely begun. The factory was barely paying its way. It did not seem to be an entirely auspicious moment to start this most difficult and expensive engineering project.

The approximate line which the Embankment should take had already been worked out and Madocks, who was never slow to delegate responsibility, left it to Williams to settle on its precise line, only stressing 'that it is a question of such great importance that every possible investigation and measurement ought to be made before we determine. . . .' Indeed it was. The point where the Embankment should leave the Caernarvonshire shore was fixed by the rocky outcrop of Ynys Towyn which projected into the Traeth; this was to form a bastion from which the Embankment sprang. Madocks' plan was to cut a channel through the neck of the outcrop and divert the river through sluice gates in it. The natural rock walls would hold the force of the water where expensive masonry might fail and the rock cut out in forming the channel could then be used in the Embankment itself. But the point where it should join the Merionethshire shore (somewhere near the farm of Penrhyn Isaf) was still to be fixed by the accessibility to it of the stone and gravel which would be needed for the bank. 'I think the question ought not to be decided till you have most fully examined the nature of the materials, and the Ease with which can get them . . .' he wrote.

The provision and transport of materials continued to be a major problem. Although the thousands of tons of stone were quarried virtually 'on the site' they still had to be transported from the quarries to the Embankment itself, a distance which increased to well over half a mile towards the end of the job. The iron railway lines were cast in the famous Brymbo works near Wrexham in which Madocks had a holding. From the foundry they were taken by road and canal to Chester where they had to wait for a coastal vessel bound for Caernarvon or Pwllheli whose captain would sail on to Ynys Cyngar. Waggons were made by the estate carpenters; wheels came from South Wales where the collieries were creating a steady demand. Gunpowder for blasting came mostly from Liverpool or London, as did baulks of Baltic timber for the scaffolding, and nails (and building materials for the town). The frequent cargo lists which occur in the letters and their reference to the wind and weather bring this business to life: a note that the *Dryader* had just sailed from London with 'the finest timber you ever beheld—

100 fine pieces none less than 30 feet, & some 50 [?] feet.
Likewise 50 barrels of Powder
8000 Bricks
6 large crates of Glass. Paints. Oils etc.
If the wind continues at the East she will be at the Traeths as soon as I am' (this estimate works out at six days for her passage). Two weeks later the *Atholia* was noted to be bringing 15,000 spikes 7″ long, and 6 bags from 9″ to 10″ as well as more powder and timber. Smaller goods came by carrier but they had to be fetched from Capel Curig, thirty miles up the unfinished road through the mountains. Valuable packages containing goods such as surveying instruments would then be carried by pack horse: 'A level is lying at Capel Curig for you addressed to Griffith. Send for it. It is a very fine one.'

Quarries had been opened up on each side of the Traeth during the winter and Williams negotiated to buy a ship. Construction was started at each end. The track was carried out on a platform constructed on scaffolding which was built out into the Traeth (the 'stilts' which are frequently referred to in the correspondence); as the Embankment grew these were thrust out ahead of it further and further from each shore. With the gradual narrowing of the gap the work naturally became more difficult, since the brunt of the tides was concentrated into an ever smaller channel in the middle, while the river, which had not yet been turned into its new course which would take it direct to the sluice gates, continued to pour through the central gap. The 'bold design' was described in some detail by a contemporary writer; '. . . a vast dike is forming. This embankment, which is to be twelve yards in breadth at the top, and proportionately wide at its base, is composed of rock and soil brought in small waggons on rail-ways from the land at each extremity. . . . The great body of water, which flows from an extensive range of the mountains of Snowdonia, is to be discharged by means of five floodgates, each fifteen feet in height. The piers to which they are attached, are calculated to support a bridge, and in their side towards the river are grooves to admit drop floodgates for the purpose of warping or irrigating the recovered lands. . . . A road, connecting the two counties is to be carried along the eastern side of the embankment, which will not only prove a most useful means of communication, but prevent the frequent loss of lives occasioned by the dangerous passage of the Traeth Mawr. Mr. Maddocks' charming place of residence, Tan-yr-allt seated on a rock, high above the town, amidst flourishing plantations marks his taste, as the gigantic works below do his bold and enterprising spirit. May he meet the success he so amply merits in an undertaking which combines so much energy, contrivance, and well-applied patriotism!'[10]

By the end of the summer (1808) work was well under way but it was already clear that this was to be a battle not only against the tides of the Irish Sea and the flood waters which the Glaslyn brought down from Snowdonia, but also against time and debt.

Financial affairs were again in a parlous state: the sums of ready money which Madocks was able to muster were pathetically small when compared with the scale of the operation. For instance, a letter of 3 November 1808 enclosed £90 with the note: 'The last fortnight will not come to more than £60 so there will be £30 over with which you can pay the Blacksmith and the small Bill of £8 to the Captain. . . . You shall never want money for men at the bank.' A cynic could read in this only Madocks' determination to keep together his labour force but, whatever his motives, despite constant financial anxiety throughout the project, his first concern was that the men should be paid.

The only hope for success lay in speedy construction. Confidence in the Embankment's early completion should stay the creditors' demands: as soon as it was finished the newly enclosed land could be irrigated and let at a good rental and tolls might be taken on the now dry roads across the sands as well as on that on the Embankment itself.[11]

At this stage Madocks was, as so often, optimistic about their progress. He hoped to find 'the platform 500 yards in length & the Bank advanced a great way beyond the Gulph. . . . The Bank will not take so much materials or time as I thought,' he added cheerfully, and on this basis he calculated that both the Bank and Sluice might be finished by the following May (1809). This vein of optimism, probably based on the fast progress of four yards a day which John Williams considered possible at this early stage, antedated its completion by over two years.

Problems soon arose which money alone, even had it been available, could not entirely solve. Labour was not as easy as it had been in 1800. The armed forces had skimmed off many of the hungry unemployed who flocked thankfully to work at the turn of the century and the campaign in the Peninsula would soon take more men. Other landowners were embanking land, not on Madocks' present scale but in parcels similar to the 1800 scheme, and this created further competition for an already reduced labour force. Trained masons were particularly scarce and a higher rate was sometimes paid to induce them to work at Tremadoc.

In spite of all the difficulties, a force of two to three hundred was soon on the job, but this itself created further problems. Many of these men came from far afield and all available lodgings were soon taken up. Barracks to house them were to be built on both sides of the Traeth (at Towyn and Boston Lodge) but it was some time before they could be ready; meanwhile Madocks suggested 'Put the Englishmen from Portsmouth at the excavation *Under the Stage*, and Welch's Tap-room will hold a good many for the present.' Workshops and smithies also had to be set up; and two cottages, which should have been already occupied had things gone according to plan, were to be available at each end of the bank for John Williams to use both for lodging and office.

Food for this large body of hungry men also presented difficulties and butter and cheese were sent from London, and later casks of pickled pork, beef and herrings considerably eased matters, but the distribution of these victuals took up more of Williams' valuable time. Certainly there were many days when, hard pressed by seemingly endless practical problems, he wished that Madocks was with him on the job. In reply to one such plea Madocks wrote firmly: 'Undoubtedly I wish very much to be with you. I need no urging. My whole heart & soul is with you. But the execution rests with you, and only stick to the Plan Laid down. . . .'

At the end of 1808 Williams still had no site office and Madocks found both the accounts and reports of the work were far behind: 'Whoever is your Clerk, he should do nothing else but write from 7 in the Morning till you go to Bed, and if the office at Penrhyn & the small House at Towyn by the Timber Yard *had been* finished, you might have had your Books & Clerks always on the spot by Your Elbow, and you might sleep on *either side* of the Traeth as the immediate Business of the place or the state of the Reports & accounts required. Your attention at the Town & the House would be required only, as much as a Horse would carry you occasionally to perform. *Now* how much *time is lost* by going backwards & forwards. . . . *Live on the Spot* as Creassy & I did the last Embankment. . . . Now Penrhyn side is going on so well & you have got men at work at Towyn, wheel 60 waggon loads an hour at Ynys y Towyn side as well as Penrhyn & let the *Two Ends Approach each other as fast as possible.*' Boats were to be used for filling in the deep hole at the end of Ynys Towyn; Harrison was to be in charge: 'If he is ever to be any use he would be most so in superintending the boating'–not a flattering comment on the capabilities of a surveyor. 'From the Sentiments in your last letter *we appear perfectly agreed upon all these important Points.* The only thing is to get these Plans executed with as much spirit as possible, & with as little loss of time & Money as possible. . . . In fact this letter you will find contains my general sentiments on everything, and you should keep it, & Read it often.' Another time-consuming occupation: twenty-one pages of this letter have survived and it is incomplete. The appointment of a clerk was also discussed: 'If Pace the butler undertakes it, He must be always regularly Sober. He must not *pretend to do anything else,* or be running to the town.'

A few days later Madocks had to postpone a visit to the Traeth: 'I have had an attack ever since last Wednesday, but don't be alarmed I am getting much better having taken it in time. . . . My doctor says it is only rheumatic no Gout & that I shall soon be able to set out.' When reading these long, energetic letters it is difficult to remember that Madocks was often laid low by such attacks. So frequently did they occur they were only mentioned when they actually caused some change of plan, which meant special arrangements had to be made: 'Have the curricle ready–I am still very lame,' he scribbled cheerfully at the end of a letter written when the burdens of debt and anxiety about non-completion would have been enough to depress most men in good health. There were to be times when he could scarcely write for swollen finger joints but between such bouts he was as mobile as ever: 'On meeting my letters at Bethgellert on Saturday I found I am obliged to run up to Town for a couple of days, about some important business. I shall return in the Mail to-morrow Evening & Trust I shall reach Tan y Rallt safe on Friday Eve or Saturday morning at latest. . . .' Life then was perhaps less leisurely than is often imagined.

For sake of speed Penrhyn Cottage had not been plastered before John Williams moved in. 'I trust if the outside is well pointed, that no cold will get in, and the scenes, or any fitting up will do very well, so as it is but warm.' The picture of John Williams, site engineer, with Pace at his elbow struggling with their books, surrounded by the sets from Tremadoc theatre has a nice touch of surrealism. 'I hope the Fire Place is large, which is seldom the case in our New Buildings which is a great fault. I approve you having a maid there who can cook, and who is *very cleanly.* . . . Why do you not put more Miners in the Excavation? Surely 75 is much too few. . . . This will never do. See to this immediately. The Expense, Carriage and Delay of an Engine to raise the water, *I think,* is a bad scheme. Why not stick to the Pumps. The Expense only lasts till the Excavation is finished. I never would change my plan without absolute necessity.'

Nor was work on the Bank itself anything like fast enough. 'We have not yet got sufficiently regular in conveying the waggons—not a moment of the day but a waggon ought always to be unloading.' Shortage of horses was partly responsible (by 1810 there were 104 at work). Even the precious curricle mares were to be used and Madocks also suggested 'My wall-eyed pony might go to the waggons. He will never be of any other use and it would be cruelty to sell him broken winded.'

After such pressure it is a relief to read 'Where is the Harper? *You must be sure* to get him by Good Friday, so that I may be sure of him on *Easter* day. Send fifty *Messengers* all over the County for him. Write also to Mrs Edwards, or some body to lend me their Harper. I must have *two*, if not *three* Harpers on Easter Sunday & Monday. Send two fidlers.' Distracting instructions indeed–but this zest for festivities, and the determination to see that they went with as much verve as the practical works, unconsciously forged the bond between men and management which might be lauded by today's efficiency experts.

When the Embankment had been building for about a year (and the Reform Bill agitation was at its height) progress seemed to be at a standstill. As fast as the stones were tipped into the

Traeth so they disappeared into the shifting sands. Once clear of the edges of the estuary the new Bank was subject to the brunt of both the tide and the river. Added to this difficulty the estuary bottom itself was there far less stable, so the stones, so laboriously quarried and carted, tended to wash away on the shifting bottom or to sink fast into it. Madocks was 'much disheartened at the Bank going so slow.' It was then suggested that mats of rushes should be sunk on the sands as a foundation and staked or weighted temporarily in position until the whole bulk of the Embankment was in place; its own immense dead weight would hold it firm. It was a method in use in other parts of the country (and still is today in Lincolnshire) but perhaps was less common in Wales[12] where few banks of this sort were built.

The rush matting proved itself and things went better. A thousand yards were completed by the end of the summer and work went on whenever weather would permit throughout the winter, but it became clear that the dam would only hold so long as the gap was fairly wide. By spring a short length in the middle and another over the Hog's Back (a natural bank in the Traeth where it might reasonably have been expected that construction would be easier) were still open. Again they seemed defeated.

Fortunately the lull in the agitations for parliamentary reform allowed Madocks to give full attention to his Welsh affairs. It was decided that the only way of closing would be to build stone piers at intervals on the Hog's Back in place of the stilts which were also constantly washed away by the force of the tide; the piers would buttress and reinforce the Bank that was to be built between them. This scheme was soon under way: 'Be sure you thicken the piers and make them strong enough against a stormy day,' Madocks wrote anxiously. More boats were to be used to dump stone between the two ends (tradition has it that one or two were sunk in position to help form the dam). By midsummer Williams was able to write more confidently and Madocks replied with enthusiasm: 'The progress & effect of the Boats is delightful. The success of the Piers very satisfactory. I sincerely hope the present High Tides will not damage them, as I presume they can hardly be sufficiently strengthened yet. But I rely on your not omitting to thicken and strengthen them. .... How happy I shall be to hear you can walk *across at Low Water*, which I hope to *hear* before I see it. At last our Church Bill is safe through,[13] and the whole explained to the House of Lords, who admire what we are doing with true patriotic feelings. Lord Walshingham compliments me very much. Only let us *persevere* ardently the next six weeks.'

The turning of the River Glaslyn into its new course was now urgent. It still flowed down the middle of the estuary so, on meeting the new Bank, it had to work its way along its back to its new outlet at the sluice gates at Ynys Towyn. This meant that it was constantly eating into the back of the Embankment as it tried to find its way to the sea. Loudon had mentioned, but not stressed, that the river should be turned before the Embankment was completed. In retrospect it is clear that this should have been done immediately the new cutting at Towyn was ready and before the construction of the bank itself was begun. It would obviously be a big job. Upstream a temporary dam would have to be thrown across the river bed to force it to take a new course and this would have to be done quickly between tides, so extra labour would be needed: 'Appy to Turner and all Mines & Quarries in the Neighbourhood, *in my name* in this Emergency to get a sufficient Gang to *turn the River* with all possible Expedition. .... ' This done, Madocks fully expected to finish by the end of the summer; but again he was over optimistic. There seemed to be no hope of either turning the river (lack of co-operation from neighbouring landlords seems to have been the cause) or of closing. Other aspects were equally depressing. Richard Fenton stopped in Tremadoc in early August (he just missed seeing Madocks who had waited in London to celebrate, with his friend Burdett, the latter's release from the Tower). 'After Dinner,' Fenton wrote in his diary, 'walked down to see the new embankment a gigantick undertaking, which would have appalled any other genius than that of the Gentleman to whose enterprising spirit we owe it.' But he was less enthusiastic about the plantations which he thought to be badly in need of thinning and about the state of the land: 'I never saw such abundance of Toads, which must ever be the case where there is so much stagnate water and foul Air engendered. . . . The only reason that can be assigned for this neglect of Mr. Maddocks's is that his main object, the new embankment, where he has so much at stake, occupies his whole thought, for his present motto with respect to that may be *totus in hoc sum.*'14

It was a very anxious autumn. Although, after two and a half years' toil, they had now achieved all but a hundred yards of the mile-long Embankment and could walk across the gap at low water, the tides and the river continued to defy all efforts to close. Winter gales would soon be upon them and then the floods of melting snows in early spring. Prospects were very bleak. The autumn winds tore the last leaves from the trees and whipped up the grey waves which battered and sucked at the still unconsolidated stones always taking some to scatter uselessly in the wide shallows of the estuary, while the relentless rise and fall of the tides continuously exposed different levels of the dam to the brunt of the attack.

For over three years Madocks had been striving to spread confidence among his creditors with promises of an early completion. Those who were not already sceptical were fast losing faith. If only his brother John had been alive, he could have borrowed easily using the family estates as security. Or, if Creassy had not died, the creditors would have trusted an experienced engineer when assured that all would be well given time; but an amateur's word was hardly good enough for the canny merchants and money-lenders.

The fact that the mood of the country was then against initiative and speculation added to these difficulties. 1810 was a year of gloom over England. The good old king was said to have gone mad and matters in the Peninsula were so bad that some were demanding the recall of Wellington and the abandonment of the war. Madocks' personal money worries were only part of a national financial crisis. It was particularly tough luck that the enormous practical difficulties of finishing the Embankment should have coincided with a period when the finances of the country were in such chaos. War expenditure was now on an immense scale. Our foreign trade was all but strangled by a combination of the Orders in Council and the Continental System. Gold was draining out of England at a serious rate. Wellington's demands for specie were one cause; the necessity of paying for imports in gold was another. The result was that most transactions within the country were made in inconvertible paper which was now the basis of British currency. The Bank of England then had no monopoly of the issue of notes so the hundreds of country banks which sprang up each issued its own. (Seven hundred had started business between 1797 and the end of the Napoleonic Wars when one-third of these stopped payment.) By 1810 25 million pound notes were in circulation; the guinea was worth 28 shillings and the gold value of a £5 note had fallen to £3 10s.[15]

Against this background it is perhaps surprising that Madocks' creditors were not more impatient. He had wisely taken the precaution of having a second report made on the prospects of the land reclamation and both this and that which Loudon had made in 1807 were no doubt widely quoted.[16] J. P. Kennel, who was responsible for the new report,[17] forecast that the land would be worth forty shillings per acre and gave an optimistic account of the whole concern. In these hungry years the fast-growing population was in sore need of any productive land, but at this stage the creditors could only see the project as a great tidal estuary into which a couple of long fingers of Embankment projected like jetties into the sea.

Even Madocks' old friend Horace Billington depicted the Traeth like this when he made the delightful drawing which was to be engraved and published to commemorate the completion of the work (see Plate 8).[18] His sketches were made in the autumn of 1810 when the tips of the fingers nearly met but the estuary was still covered by the tide. Once drained it would inevitably lose its magic; everyone admitted this. It would be utterly different, though not without character. Level green pasture, beautifully watered, would spread like an oasis between the rocky hills.

The flooded Traeth was also described by Peacock in his novel

Headlong Hall. He was then living at Maentwrog in the Vale of Ffestiniog.

'The tide was now ebbing; it had filled the vast basin within, forming a lake about five miles in length and more than one in breadth. As they looked upwards with their backs to the open sea, they beheld a scene which no other in this country can parallel, and which the admirers of the magnificence of nature will ever remember with regret, whatever consolation may be derived from the probable utility of the works which have excluded the waters from their ancient receptacle. Vast rocks and precipices, intersected with little torrents, formed the barrier on the left: on the right, the triple summit of Moelwyn reared its majestic boundary: in the depth was that sea of mountains, the wild and stormy outline of the Snowdonian chain, with the giant Wyddfa towering in the midst. The mountain-frame remains unchanged, unchangeable: but the liquid mirror it enclosed is gone.

'The tide ebbed with rapidity: the waters within, retained by the embankment, poured through its two points in an impetuous cataract, curling and boiling in innumerable eddies, and making a tumultous melody admirably in unison with the surrounding scene. The three philosophers looked on in silence: and at length unwillingly turned away, and proceeded to the little town of Tremadoc, which is built on land recovered in a similar manner from the sea. After inspecting the manufactories, and refreshing themselves at the inn on a cold saddle of mutton and a bottle of sherry, they retraced their steps towards Headlong Hall, commenting as they went on the various objects they had seen.'[19]

But it was all very well for outsiders to admire or regret. Madocks had to get on. If he was to allow weather, labour problems or financial straits to bring things even temporarily to a halt, the whole enterprise would sink in dismal failure. It was imperative that some method of closing be found before the creditors' dwindling confidence finally evaporated.

During the winter an inclined plane was laid down from the Embankment which was now considerably higher than the platform at the end. The idea was to unload vast quantities of material on each tip to hurl into the gap in the shortest time possible while

as many boats as could be chartered were to be loaded with stone
which would be jettisoned into the gap at the same moment.

At the end of February (1811) Madocks wrote cheerfully from
Boston (where he found himself 'triumphantly strong') to say
that he would be down the following week with '. . . Money to
buy all the Boats you can engage . . .' but the postscript contained
yet another warning: 'It is not impossible that John Ellis may
plague you for a day or two in the beginning of next week. But
do not let that, or any thing dishearten you: on my return to
London, I shall settle it, if it is so, in a moment & then off for
Wales to put all into Action.'

Money was tighter than ever. Only very small amounts could
be sent but Madocks was still managing to instil confidence:
'Never mind these Fellows [the creditors]. We will conquer
them,' he wrote, '– Only on all occasions be sure you give me the
name of the *party right*, who sues, because if it requires to be settled
in Town, I can do so the sooner.'

In early April he was back, very lame, but once on the Traeth
he stirred everyone to even greater activity. Unless they closed
this summer, the game would be up. A month later he was
writing from various stops on the coach route to London: 'My
whole soul is now entirely bent on closing the Bank. . . . Great
works are achieved by the Conductors being alive while others
are asleep. Every *Evening* & night should be employed in preparing to go to work next day. The precious hours in the morning
should be made the most of by the workmen . . .' and a day or two
later: 'Make a bargain with yourself not to think of anything till
the Bank is done' (an injunction quickly negated by other instructions concerning the town). There was to be a refinement to speed
construction in the last gap: formwork was to be set up into
which the stones could be poured; more baulk was coming for the
horizontals (the verticals were of local oak). They must practise
unloading at the rate of a load a minute. These and many other
measures were urged. Ideas followed pell-mell: 'We are not
nearly in full force with the boats. . . . Is the Boat Mender actually
in his house at No. 10?' Why was there a shortage of horses on the
Penryhn side? Had their owners not been paid? They should have

been given part of his last remittance of £250. 'I have written to Mr. R. Williams the Surveyor about his Men coming to take away ours to the Harlech Embankment. . . . We must get into the system of working at night. . . .' (But the Bank, as usual, was not Williams' only worry. The letter ended with a list: 'Settle Packham, Service at Church, School regular, John Morgan? Masons jobs rising up giving an Effect, the entrance to the Town from Ynys y Madoc neat and green and growing. . . . To conclude your last letter I repeat gave me great satisfaction as to your Zeal and Eagerness.')

Madocks was now organising the last cargoes of materials to be shipped to Wales; it was not easy to satisfy the merchants and captains that they would receive payment. He was also busy 'silencing John Ellis'. More money was forthcoming but it was not to go to the creditors: 'Be sure you do not apply one shilling of Mr. Oakden's £500 to John Ellis or John Evans his solicitor but pay up the Men with it. *Devote* it to the *Men.*'

By midsummer they were almost ready for the last all-out effort. To their intense relief a combination of the system of formwork with that for unloading at top speed was showing results and the gap was visibly narrowing. They battled on, day and night. In July, after three years' struggle, final closing was very near. During the third week they made a last mighty effort and the gap was closed.

The tremendous jubilation and impromptu festivity which followed was reported in most satisfactory terms in the *North Wales Gazette* under the headline COMPLETION OF THE EMBANKMENT AT TRE-MADOC: 'To attempt to enter into the merits of the individual gentelman (W. A. Madocks Esq.) who has finished the great work, amidst difficulties incalculable to the common mind, we feel ourselves inadequate to the task' it began, and went on to rank him with 'New River MYDDLETON'. After the actual closing when he returned to inspect the great work: '. . . the lower orders immediately with the native ardour of their ancestors, on Mr. Madocks' approach, took his horses from his carriage and triumphantly drew him over the embankment, which was, comparatively speaking, the work of his own hands.'[20]

8

Jubilation

1811

PARLIAMENT WAS PROROGUED at the end of the month and Madocks 'popped down to Boston' to report, as was his habit, on the progress of the session; there can be little doubt that his constituents would hear a good deal about Tremadoc too. He can seldom have met them with such confidence, and, living as they did in that flat, dike-dependent land, few would be better able than they to assess his achievement. Before returning to Wales he went up to the Humber to inspect 4,000 acres of particularly well irrigated land which had recently been reclaimed; drainage and warping were to be the next big job on the Traeth and as usual he was rearing to be on with it. He wrote to Williams from Gainsborough: 'The Improvement of Warping is most astonishing. I shall however reserve full particulars till I see you.' But preparations for the grand celebrations which were to mark the completion of the Embankment had now to be rushed through. Scores of guests were expected. 'I write this *principally* to Urge you, and to press on you the propriety of having the Addition to the House ready by the 28th of this Month so that all workmen may be *out* and all cleared away behind, and all neat. I am aware that the Bed Room plaister will not be ready for use for some days though we must use every artificial means of drying them by the Races which I have postponed principally on that account till the 9th, 10 & 11th September. . . . For Goodness Sake, Loose not a moment. The time gets every hour more precious. . . .' The letter ended with entreaties that all should be ready against the arrival of his Boston friends. 'On the 28th. the 28th. the 28th. Let us Shew off!' ran the postscript.

He wrote next from London: 'Your letter of the 9th which I have just met with on my return from Boston gives me sincere pleasure. I long to hear though the particulars of the High Tide running through the Sluice, & if it was above the domes [?].' After detailing various jobs, he continued: 'I long to be with you for the remainder of the Season. All the world will attend our Jubilee. Stick the Hand Bills all over the Country.'

Trè-Madoc
Embankment Jubilee.

An OX will be roasted upon the Middle of the Embankment

at 12 o'Clock on TUESDAY the 17th of SEPTEMBER, 1811.

The RACES will follow, and continue the 18th and 19th.

An EISTEDDFOD will likewise be held, when a Silver Cup will be given to the best Welch Poet, and another to the best Welch Harper.

There will be an Ordinary at the two Inns at four o'Clock on Monday the 16th, and the three following Days.

Also Plays, Balls, &c. in the Evening.

Printed by COX, SON, and BAYLIS, 75, Great Queen Street, Lincoln's-Inn-Fields, London.

Trè Madoc Jubilee Poster, 1811

But after this came an ominous note which shows that the bank, though complete, was still not entirely firm: 'Let us get the Sluice finished and the front of the Bank strengthened by the Jubilee, to have it well done. . . . We cannot do better than apply all our strength to the *Centre* of the Bank. Get the Double Rail Road laid, and set all hands to heap as much stone etc. as possible in the front.' After finishing the Sluice, Huggins was to point the Church with Parker's Cement, all round; a Weather Cock for the top of the spire was coming (it had reached the Lion Inn, Shrewsbury). Such crowning touches were symbolic of the jubilant mood which prevailed. In the excitement it seems to have been forgotten that the river still ran in its old course towards the sluice gates; or it may have been reckoned that the silt it brought down would be deposited and strengthen the back of the Embankment.

Other letters dealt with the Race Course; Humphrey Owen was coming 'actually to make the course' and holes in Morfa Bychan itself were to be filled 'so as to permit Carriages to drive about and Gentlemen to ride about during the Races'. What a fine sight it would be, out on the rabbit-nibbled turf by the edge of the strand looking south over Cardigan Bay. To this letter was added a long postscript concerning a Mr. Newberry who was not to paint the Billiard Room after all; instead 'He had better look over the Scenes and mend any that are damaged and he might run a pretty Border with his painting Brush round the Great Room at the Inn and decorate that prettily, over the Door etc with figures or any thing that will not take long in doing. Explain this to him. I enclose a Note for him.' Instructions concerning decoration were, as ever, delightfully vague; doubtless the long tradition in which the craftsmen had been trained produced charming results.

Remembering the preparations that took place before an ordinary house-party, it is not difficult to imagine the excitement and fuss now prevailing at Tremadoc. Last-minute delays caused the festivities to be postponed yet another few days but in the event they surpassed William's wildest dreams. This gala week marked the culmination not only of the strenuous years spent on the great Embankment itself but the whole establishment of the 'infant colony'. The *Trè Madoc Jubilee* could hardly have been better deserved or more enjoyed by citizens and visitors alike. The name must have come from the jubilees which had been held all over the country the previous year to commemorate the fifty years' reign of King George III.[1] Thus in one grand celebration Tremadoc could mark both its patriotism and achievement. Nobody was going to quibble about the slight delay in this show of loyalty when the works themselves spoke so plainly for the sentiments of both Tremadoc's founder and her citizens.

Considering Madocks' financial straits, the splendid confidence with which he now spent money is slightly awe-inspiring. Throughout the year, numerous orders to distrain his goods had reached the Sheriff in Caernarvon, but these were now forgotten in the display of well-being which marked the Jubilee. It could be regarded as a way of quelling any qualms which may have lingered in the minds of the creditors but it is doubtful if he considered it in this light. He simply revelled in the excuse for a grand party which gave every incentive to indulge his sense of drama and pageantry.

Friends came from all over the Principality and the Border country, from Lincolnshire and the south of England. Neighbouring landowners, parliamentary colleagues, theatrical friends and racing men crowded in. Tan-yr-allt, and all available houses and inns, overflowed with guests. In addition the surrounding country people, together with the strolling players, harpists, pedlars, tipsters and tinkers who flocked to the race-meetings and great fairs up and down the country, swarmed into Tremadoc. There was to be entertainment for everyone. The Plays, Races and Eisteddfod would be interspersed with impromptu recitals by the bards and singing of the crowds as they gathered in the Market Place between the advertised events. The square was to become a great outdoor room and the acoustic effect of the singing reverberating from the high crags above would be spectacular. The only entertainment which was by invitation only was the great Ball in the Town Hall: limitation of space made this necessary. But the crowds in the Market Place below had an excellent view through the tall windows of the brightly lit Dancing-room and, as the gentry in all their finery gavotted above, the square below doubtless became an extension of the dance-floor.

A full account of the more formal proceedings was given in the press.[2] They began on Monday, 16 September, when 'a numerous, and most respectable assemblage of persons of the first rank and distinction . . . met at the Madock Arms Tavern, where an Ordinary was served up at 5 o'clock in the afternoon. About six, the same evening, a fine fat ox, slaughtered that morning, was spitted whole, and continued roasting until 12 o'clock the following day. The evening concluded with a performance at the theatre, which was well attended. On the following morning, Tuesday, the new Church (a most superb building), which was opened for divine service at 10 o'clock was instantly filled by persons of higher rank, to the total exclusion of some hundreds, who, in vain, attempted to gain admission. The prayers were read by the Rev. Martin Sheath of Boston, who also delivered an appropriate sermon on the occasion; and the solemnity was rendered particularly impressive by the addition of Choral Service, performed under the direction of Dr. Pring, of Bangor. After prayers, about 50 carriages formed in procession, headed by a band of music, and the rear was brought up by about 300 of the workmen employed in the embankment, uniformly clothed by the munificence of W. A. Madocks Esq. Thus arranged, the cavalcade moved on to the embankment, about a mile distant, where slices of the roasted ox were cut, and presented to the company present; after which they were invited by Mr. Madocks to a booth, prepared for the occasion, where a most sumptuous collation was provided by that gentleman, consisting of meat, wines etc. etc. of the choicest description; during which the ox was carved, and served to the workmen, who dined on a spot lately gained from the sea, by the effect of the new Embankment. From thence, the Company proceeded to the Race-Ground, which afforded excellent sport to the Gentlemen of the turf—for never was there seen better running. The Ordinary which followed, at the Madoc Arms, was crowded beyond all description: and the unremitting attention of Mr. Madocks, who would not be seated until he saw all the company comfortably employed, exceeds all panegyric. The Evening concluded with a ball, where "the light fantastic toe" moved on until Chanticleer gave notice to retire. On the following day, Wednesday, an *Eisteddfod* or meeting of the Bards, was held, when a valuable Cup, the Gift of W. A. Madocks Esq. was adjudged to Mr. David Owen, of Llanysdumdwy, for the best Welsh Poem on Agriculture. There were five other Poems recited, all of which possessed considerable merit. At the same meeting a Silver Cup was won by Hercules, the best Harper of four who played in competition; and a collection was afterwards made for the unsuccessful candidates amounting to about £10. The Races were this day, again renewed; and the evening closed with a performance at the Theatre. On Thursday the company began to move off, highly gratified with their entertainment, but the Races were nevertheless well attended.' This exhaustive account ends with a heart-warming eulogy: 'We congratulate the public at large on the *completion of a work* which stands unrivalled in the history of the world.–That a single individual should attempt, persevere in, and at last (after four years exertion) accomplish, so stupendous an undertaking appears truly astonishing! and it only requires occular demonstration to convince the incredulous of its superiority over every other work of the kind now extant. We felt particularly happy in witnessing so full an attendance of our Cambrian Nobility, Clergy, and Gentry; and we do not hesitate to predict–that future ages will hail the day that gave birth to the enterprising W. A. Madocks Esq. whose family motto has, by undaunted exertions, been so amply verified: NON MIHI SOLUM.'

Samuel Rogers, the diarist, who was on his way from Snowdonia happened to be at Tan-yr-allt for the Jubilee, and his caustic pen could find nothing more sarcastic to say of his host than 'He is a great Lord in his little city of Tre Madoc'. It was satisfactory that he should use the word city. A very different guest was a rather shy lady who arrived at the end of the week, when the celebrations were over and things had quietened down. Her diary[3] gives a nice picture of the everyday life of the household. After rather a hair-raising journey during which her postilion had fallen asleep on his horse coming along the edge of the Traeth, she 'thankfully got safe to Trè Madoc between 3 & 4 in the evening–was very kindly received and found 18 Gentlemen and 8 Laidies in the house (but don't remember their names) dined between 7 & 8 o'clock & went to bed about 3 in the Morning–Tany Rallt a most beautiful place–went with Miss Charlotte Madoc down to Tre Madoc to a great Shop & made some purchases–saw the Assembly Room, a very handsome one–

2 transparent Paintings in it—on one Prosperity to Mr. W. A. Madocks & Success to the Embankment. . . .' The next day Sunday, they went to Church, where the service was conducted and the organ played by guests from Tan-yr-allt and 'Mr. John and Mr. Joseph Madocks sang the bass & the Miss Madocks the treble of two Psalms . . . dined at 6 o'clock, went to bed between One & 2; A most tremendous storm in the night & the Gentlemen making such a noise in the room below that I got very little sleep.'

During the days that followed there was much local sightseeing. The Madockses apparently thought nothing of an afternoon stroll of five miles which the diarist found 'most charming' and on another outing she showed no dismay at returning 'Wet to the Skin'.

Besides Boston gentlemen and William's numerous North Wales connection, her fellow guests included his old friends the Haymans. There is no knowing whether the Miss Hayman who was now at Tan-yr-allt was the Dear Coz. of the Chaotic days. A Miss Hayman had become Privy Purse to the unfortunate wife of the Regent and the diarist reported that Mrs. Hayman 'read us a very humurous Letter from the Princess of Wales to her acknowleging to be the Author of a New Tragedy (wrote by a madman) called Rovanzzo's Heart, or the Unfair Marriage'. This she dismissed as 'the silliest thing I have ever read' but she was delighted to discover that 'Another Gentleman is Mr. Clemons[4][?], Sergeant at Arms, & who took Sir Frances Burdett to the Tower, & burst into his house—a very civil Gentlemanly man, & who treated me with some of the best Snuff I ever took, out of remarkably fine Gold Box', but now the party was beginning to break up and 'we dined only 16'. It is difficult to imagine how they crammed into such modest rooms.

Her stay at Tan-yr-allt had occurred just when everyone was exhausted by the Jubilee celebrations so none of the usual expeditions and excursions were made. These were amply provided for by the curricle, the gigs and new cart, and various ponies and horses in the stables. For special guests, there were three mares in

II

the Best Stable (Lilley, a grey, the Red mare, and Comitt a very valuable Pied). For outings on Cardigan Bay there were the three pleasure boats, and for picnics by the sea the Bathing Machine[5] and the Caravan. At home they could stroll in the garden, thick with late roses, and admire the silver pheasants and peacocks that paced the lawn or inspect the plantations and woodland. But even if it rained incessantly the house itself provided all that the guests could ask for. Tanny was certainly 'in exquisite beauty' that summer; it is tantalising to think that nothing there was of a later period than early Regency. An inventory[6] had recently been taken of the effects at the suit of one of William Madocks' creditors, so we know exactly how it was furnished.

The Drawing Room with its french windows leading onto that wide verandah was simply fitted out. The curtains were cotton lined with blue calico and on the floor was a 'green baize' carpet; the large sofa also had a cotton cover; the big mahogany arm chairs were upholstered in red morocco and the other chairs were rush bottomed. There was a mahogany card table and desk with a blue leather top. A Piano Forte, a weather glass, a telescope (with which to view the Embankment), a microscope, a quadrant, a thermometer and a 'very large Library' provided other diversions. There were a number of paintings and prints in gilt frames (one of the *Cambrian* of Boston beating a French privateer, and another a portrait of Twm o'r Nant) and a large screen ornamented with pictures. It sounds agreeably comfortable and informal. The Dining Parlour was rather richer in its furnishings and the Billiard Room boasted a 'Shandelier'. The bedrooms were furnished with dimity-curtained beds and in the best bedroom was a harpsichord. The inventories of the kitchen and housekeeper's room[7] suggest that no one was likely to lack creature comforts.

During the week of the Tremadoc Jubilee a comet was clearly seen tearing through the sky. It appeared for several nights in succession just before midnight and its course, as observed from an eminence in Snowdonia, was scientifically recorded. What it portended was another matter; but whether it was thought to be an omen of prosperity or disaster is immaterial. Both interpretations might be considered correct; it was simply to be a question of choosing the relevant timescale to foretell the evil days or the good.

Parliament did not reassemble until the New Year and this gave Madocks some breathing space in which he hoped to consolidate both his financial affairs and the Embankment itself. Now that it was complete the bulk of the large labour force could be paid off and it was reasonable to assume that given a few more months the creditors might be satisfied.

The next great work was to be the drainage and irrigation of the reclaimed land. During the winter various systems were closely considered and some of the conclusions reached were argued in a document[8] entitled THE QUESTION which had the sub-heading *'How can seven thousand acres of land – newly Embanked from the Sea – be best inclosed, Divided, Subdivided, Drained, Supplied with Water, Occupied and Cultivated considered and discussed In a Colloquy between the Proprietor and A Stranger.*

Dec 27 1811

Their argument clearly demonstrates the dilemma of an ardent admirer of Picturesque landscape when confronted with a scheme for agricultural improvement. At the start the Stranger pointed out that only adequate drainage could 'keep away the Demons of Disease that haunt the shores of Kent and Essex from the Marshes of Tre-Madoc'. He had evidently produced a plan[9] showing the land divided into plots, each of forty acres subdivided into eighty parcels, fenced by 'ditches of living water' each with its own road and drain at right angles to the main stream. The Proprietor recorded his reaction with engaging candour: 'an impulsive and involuntary distaste, ie. a prejudice to the Plan has taken possession of my mind – it bears some resemblance to Dutch Gardening where everything is Straight and equilateral – It raises images of things in my mind that it would seem hideous and sarcastic to describe.' But the scheme was not to be dismissed 'without hearing what you have to say in its explanation and defence' and so the argument unfolded. It is clear that Madocks the creator of the romantic landscape was to give way to Madocks the scientific improver. The ultimate aim was to provide grazing for the upland farms for which the proprietor already had applications; it was pointed out that such pasture would incidentally save 'the immense expense of building Farm houses and Farm Steads' but the Stranger avoided giving an estimate for the cost of his proposals with the unusual excuse that the calculations would be so simple that the work 'has too much of mere Drudgery in it to deserve my Labour or your attention'.

At the time when these future improvements were being planned the creditors were still giving considerable trouble. Their continued agitation probably was due largely to the general financial state of the country which made everyone restless and bothered about overdue loans. It is extremely difficult to disentangle Madocks' legal and financial affairs but it is clear that the bailiffs had now become very familiar with his Caernarvonshire property, so often was it put under distraint; but, by a combination of delaying action and Madocks' powers of persuasion, it had never actually come under the hammer. He personally enjoyed the privilege of a Member of Parliament which granted freedom from civil arrest both during a parliamentary session and for forty days before and after; thus a Member was generally immune from imprisonment for debt but occasionally, when Parliament was prorogued for an unusually long time, it would have been possible for an M.P. to find himself in the Fleet Prison. This Madocks managed to avoid despite both the long prorogation in the second half of 1811 and the ceaseless agitation of the many solicitors who wrote repeatedly to the office of the Under-Sheriff in Caernarvon demanding that his property should be impounded. They seem to have got little satisfaction and found it necessary to write again and again, their irate feelings prickling the formal legal language of the letters.

Briefly the position was as follows: the English creditors were impatiently writing to the Under-Sheriff demanding that Madocks' property should be impounded, not realising that much of it was already under distraint at the suit of Welsh creditors on the spot. They were unable to understand the Sheriff's dilatoriness and bitterly complained that matters were conducted very differently in England. At the same time Madocks was writing to his own solicitor, John Evans,[10] urging that the creditors should be delayed and the sequestrators be taken off; he only needed a little more time and all would be paid up.

Madocks of course knew, but at this stage the English solicitors were quite unaware, that all these letters were delivered to the same office in Caernarvon, for the Under-Sheriff in question was John Evans' Clerk: a nicely balanced state of affairs and one which, given a short breathing space, Madocks had every confidence would resolve itself satisfactorily.

Back in Westminster, Parliament had reassembled and Madocks was busy. At the end of January he launched the Boston Harbour Bill on its course through the House of Commons. The new town there was growing fast and the harbour, its original *raison d'être*, was badly in need of renovation and repair. The Bill provided an admirable opportunity for Madocks to prove that his interest in his constituents would never suffer through his devotion to Wales.

In Tremadoc things were relatively quiet. For the first time for years there was a chance to catch up and do some very necessary maintenance work before spring was heralded by a flurry of letters and plans from Half Moon Street.

Confidence in the Embankment itself was gradually established. To begin with it had been impossible to believe that this thin, mile-long line could possibly hold against the enormous winter seas. 'Tourists without numbers'[11] had come to gaze in wonder at the extraordinary achievement and the local inhabitants had described with pride just how the work had been done. In answer to those who were tactless enough to remark that it leaked like a colander it was pointed out patiently that the design allowed that the sea itself should help in the work by hurling shingle and sand against the mole and thus gradually filling the interstices between the larger stones. What appeared to the outsider to be neglect of detail simply showed ignorance of the scientific principles of its construction. The opportunity to expound was not wasted. Nor was the sheer poetry of a story which, if it could fire the English imagination, was certainly not lost on that of the Celt. With the telling and re-telling of its history the Embankment itself grew in strength and wonder.

But the tricky operation of turning the course of the river so that it did not eat into the back of the Bank still remained undone despite Madocks' urging during the previous summer. Throughout the autumn and early winter the river was a constant source of anxiety, as were the first autumn gales. After a rough night worried workmen would hurry down to see what damage had been done. John Williams would order the maintenance gang to pack in more stone or to dump another load in readiness and, as the sea piled up more shingle, the Bank grew gradually stronger. Keeping a careful watch on the tide table in his office, Williams would take a last turn up the Bank before going to bed. A strong wind behind a spring tide made him particularly anxious and in the early winter he would lie awake listening as a storm gathered its force. Even the long low house at Ynys Towyn, relatively sheltered by the rock, shuddered under the impact of the worst gusts. Then he would battle his way out into the wet chaos. The Bank itself looked only slightly blacker than the black water, but all along its outer edge the heaving surf gave a clear indication of its line. Only occasional waves would break right over the top and he would return, soused to the skin, to steam in front of the kitchen fire, bitterly cold but with an easier mind.

There was a particularly dreadful gale in early February. It was scarcely worth keeping watch during the night, so blinding was the sea-laden wind. In the morning it was found that, although the Bank had held, much damage had been done. Madocks wrote anxiously from London: 'I am very sorry to hear in your letter the Bank has suffered much. We must give a straight direction to the River towards the Sluice, & not let it work at the back of the Bank. I will write fully tomorrow.' Two days later he added: 'We may on my return to the Country determine on what is to be done about staunching the Bank as well as raising it,' and with that the matter was left since Madocks intended to be down in less than a week to see the problem for himself. The letter continued

with other pressing details. A house in the square was to be let
'to a *medical* man if you know a good one. . . . As to the Brick-
makers I do most particularly request that you give them *every*
encouragement. I must have 20,000 Bricks made. Why should you
reflect on them in your letter, because they come from Boston or
England. Trè Madoc will never flourish if there are any jealousies.
We ought to be liberal to all. That is the way great plans[?] have
become great. . . .'

Affairs in London delayed Madocks' visit but with John
Williams in charge there was no immediate urgency. The maintenance gang were set to work on repairs, more stone was packed
in where any danger of settlement seemed likely and everyone
slept rather more soundly; if the Bank could hold against the
onslaught of that last gale there was not much to fear.

9

Disaster

1812 – 1813

SUDDENLY, LESS THAN two weeks later, disaster overwhelmed them. The tides were again increasing towards high springs when a tremendous sea created by another south-westerly gale driving the incoming tide breached the Bank somewhere near the mid-point. It was scarcely possible for a man to stand even leaning his full weight against that wind and the roar of the water as it poured through the gap could hardly be heard above that of the sea, nor could the crash of the stones be distinguished as they were battered and sucked out of position by the surging tide. The shouts of the men were at once blown out with the spume; even from a few yards' distance they looked like characters in an early silent film gesticulating in the face of some gigantic tragedy. The whole of the central part of the Bank seemed to shudder and no one could tell how much more would go with the next tide. That night it was hopeless to hold a flare or a lamp in the raging gale and work had to be abandoned until the morning.

The dreadful news spread quickly and by first light more and more men hurried down from the town and the surrounding farms to gaze blankly at the havoc. As the wind eased temporarily and the tide ran right out, the fury of the storm seemed unbelievable; the gaping hole through which the river was again pouring with the remains of the ebb seemed a mockery. But the next few tides would grow in strength: unfortunately the wind strength-ened with them.

John Williams immediately set about organising all available hands into work gangs, but as a labour force to cope with work of this magnitude they were pathetically few. The great army of men who had built the Embankment had long dispersed. Quarrymen and miners were urgently needed to cut fresh stone but most of them were now working away in the hills or back in England. To make matters worse much of the iron railway had been lifted (presumably to be sold to satisfy some of the creditors), so all the material cut to fill the breach had to be laboriously moved in farm carts or by sledges.

Realising the hopelessness of this situation if they tried to cope alone, Williams at once sent messengers throughout the district asking for help: men with teams of horses were needed above all else. Meanwhile those neighbours who had already heard the bad news, or had seen the devastation for themselves as they looked down from their hill farms on to the flooded valley, sent off all the help they had. Things might be in a very bad way materially, but the disaster had changed the spirit of the neighbourhood overnight. Where there had once been hostility or apathy to Madocks' schemes among the local landowners and farmers, Williams now found spontaneous sympathy coupled with a generous acknowledgement of the Embankment's importance to the whole region.

In the Embankment Office, Pace (the ex-butler who had been found to be 'rather too fond of the bottle' and who was now John Williams' Clerk) wrote on and on making copies of the draft letter which were to be sent throughout the district asking both for help and for the news to be spread further. Replies poured in by return. The fascination of these letters lies in the way that everyone, facing a crisis and writing in a hurry, seems to come out in his true colours. There is a tremendously moving sincerity in those from the small farmers who, after mustering their entire resources, could send perhaps one man and one horse and found it even more difficult to put pen to paper; by contrast the more articulate sympathy of the gentry makes less impact, though it was none the less heart-felt. The fellow-feeling of some of the bigger landowners who perhaps had faced similar trouble themselves, if on a smaller scale, shows up the wordy pomposity of a very few characters who might always have been suspect as fair-weather friends.

For many it meant writing in a foreign language:
'Mr. J. Williams. Mr. Madock Aidgent. Tanyralld.
17 Febry 1812. from Mr. Cadr Owen, Dolbenmaen.
Kind Sr

it was to leat lasd nite to send the leters but Ive send my son with them be for day lite and before non of them was up: I am very sorry Ive only 2 hors. I hope son in Law can assissd me for one hors– your Berar didnot speak to me– wether he has been at Tyddun mawr Dolwgan Rwng y ddwurud & sow forth where is good Teams Ive nomor but wishing you sugsesfull and good faithful Nibaures in the disdress your sincear Humble sarvant and well wisher

CADR OWEN.'

A most heartening letter if ever there was one. Good, faithful neighbours were dearly needed. They came forward readily. Most wasted few words, answering the moment they heard the news and spreading it among local farmers. 'I have sent the Cart per bearer & have likewise had the promise of the Tinllan cart & my Uncle Jones's of Mynithednifed bach as soon as his Husbandmen returns for Carn. . . .'

Others did not immediately grasp the real gravity of the situation: '. . . would have sent you all the help I have this day had it not been for the badness of the day tomorrow morning if the day suits will send you a Team all that I have and Six Stout men . . . in case the stones should be large have sent a Sled in the Cart.' Similarly a Miss Williams of Plas Hen answered in her father's absence promising help and adding 'When the hurry you are in is a little over Will you be so good as to allow yr Gardener to send me cuttings of Virginian Creepers.' The Attorney-General for North Wales, David Ellis (later Ellis-Nanney),[1] and his wife who were near neighbours gave invaluable support. As her husband was engaged on professional matters Henrietta herself drove round the county enlisting help. More accustomed to letter-writing than most of John Williams' correspondents she sent long screeds of encouragement to report progress, her enthusiasm often

breaking through their formality. Quite apart from the practical
help given, it would greatly boost Williams' morale to have the
support of such influential and true friends. Whether or not he
had time to enjoy her lengthy epistles is another matter, but her
detailed accounts of the help to be expected must have been read
avidly. One such winds up '. . . – So that from Gwynfryn [the
Ellis estate] there will be next week from eighteen to twenty
Carts for three days each, *besides* Mr. Priestley's Tenants. . . . Mrs.
Ellis is happy to send Mr. Williams this Calculation, because the
expectation of further Supply will chear his Spirits . . .' and the
same day she penned another note assuring him that he 'may
rely on an application to every Soul who has a Horse or Man
to lend . . . so let Mr. Williams be of good heart, for fresh
Supplies will pour in next Week and before the high Tides
come on. . . .'

But a week later they were still in dire need when she reported
that Mr. Rice of the Crown, Pwllheli, was considering whether
he could help: 'she hopes he may send his Team but has not much
dependence on a Man who does not do so from the first warm
impulse of his Heart upon such an Occasion, and finds it necessary
to *think* of what he ought to do. . . .' However her letter ended
with a most cheering postscript: 'Mr. and Mrs. Ellis were informed
this Evening that the Support of 300 Men was arriving from Lady
Penrhyn's Quarries. They anxiously hope this Report is correct.'
Here was help on a scale to match the undertaking: so many of the
offers which John Williams had received, although they brought
the writer's entire resources, amounted, numerically, to pitifully
little. 'My Cart and horses are at your disposal. Command them
as your own' one small farmer had written with fine flourish, but
when compared to the magnitude of the problem one cart was
not very much to command.

Had the surrounding country been even half as rich as that of,
say, Kent or Lincolnshire, there would have been little difficulty
in mustering the teams and men that were needed. But in Caernarvonshire and Merioneth there was little arable land; many of the
small tenant farmers owned only a horse and a sled, a team with
a cart being a luxury. The great teams of shire horses who worked

the enclosed land of the Midlands and East Anglia were as foreign as a tractor might now seem in Tibet.

Fortunately some of the clergy were keen agriculturists and farmed on a slightly bigger scale: 'I have sent 4 Teams and 6 men, two of my Own and two I hired and paid for; I wish it had not been so busy Time with the Farmers that I might be able to have left them with you another Day. I am very sorry that such Disaster hath happend' wrote one such farming parson but another, Williams' kinsman, the Rector of Llanbedrog, was less able to help although certainly none the less willing. He had 'but one Cart Horse, the other being 25 years old or more, and Wm. Joseph my husbandman has been ill all this week. . . . Could I possibly command 100 Men or Horses, Mr. Madocks most certainly shd. have them all. As it is, I can only bewail this sad request, which I do from my heart and soul.' However he was not to be defeated and wrote again: 'I did every thing in my power to *hire* a Team to lend you all the little assistance I could, but it was impossible. I have, however made my old Horse and old Man rouse themselves, and have sent them to you with a Colt and Strong Mare for as long as you can make them useful. They are both old and invalids–and even for that reason, I know you'll take every care of them. . . .' To this was added as a postscript: 'Mine is literally *the Widow's mite*' and on the back: 'Pray let me know by ye Bearer that you have effectually secured ye Gap etc. etc. P.S. Be so good as to see that the sickly Bearer takes good care of the Cart and Horses, but *not so good* a care of Himself.'

John Williams had written right away to Doctor Morris (lately a tenant of one of the villas) who had taken a leading part in the earlier jollifications at Tremadoc. He was now living in Chester and might be influential there in raising money if not help. He was apparently smitten by the news, excessively wordy, but offered nothing: '. . . I feel and am worse in my health ever since. Good God that such an event should ever happen; what will become of my Dear Friend: however let the worse come I will never enjoy my bottle nor my Guinea but what I shall share them with him. I repeat to you again the shock has hurt me. . . .'

A few others were equally useless, but rather through stinginess than stupidity. 'I am very sorry that I cannot prevail on any of my men to go to Tremadoc–they would not go unless they were paid 2/6 per Day their board and Lodgings–which I consider so much out of the way that I declined to send them–' wrote a Mr. Samuel Worthington (who leased a quarry from Madocks, but never worked it). A very different response was that from Colonel Peacock in Anglesey who sent '7 Men & 2 Carts and Horses, to remain with you a week. . . I have given Money to my Husbandmen to subsist them: at two shillings a day each, and I allow the same pay, besides, as if they worked for me at Home–I mention this to you to prevent you giving them any money.'

The question of lodging was becoming increasingly difficult and the men had to have some sort of warmth during the long February nights. Miss Williams, Plas Hen, had written again: 'I am much concerned to say that having at this time a housefull of Company We have not a single blanket but what are in use but the enclosed letter to the Housekeeper at Corsygedol will I trust assist you. . . .' Another letter ran: 'I have sent herewith 6 men to be employed at the Embankment and I trust you will find them industrious People. I hope you will accommodate them with Beds.' An optimistic request. 'Pray find some Stable etc for my people,' wrote Hugh Reveley, the Merionethshire landowner, realistically. His exceptionally generous help came although (or perhaps partly because?) he was in similar straits himself: '. . . I wish I could do more, but my own Embankment opposite Barmouth has suffered terribly, and I am getting all the hands I can to Stop the Gaps before the next Tides.'

By contrast, the High Sheriff of Caernarvon was slow off the mark, writing to his agent a whole week after the break: 'Finding that Mr. Madocks' praiseworthy exertions for the benefit of this and the adjoining County has sustained considerable damage I think it a duty due from the publick to render every assistance in their power to repair the injury.' Yet after such laudable if pompous sentiments, instead of forging ahead to send off help without more ado, he continued: 'I therefore wish that you will lose no time in seeing Mr. Madocks's Agent Mr. John Williams and ask him how many carts with three horses in each would be acceptable–of my own I can only offer one as I have many mares in foal but I have the assurances of the assistance of my tenants in this quarter. . . .' Perhaps he was weary of Madocks' affairs, so often had the creditors from London demanded his deputy's action on their behalf.

William Madocks himself was expected hourly at Tremadoc. His apparent lack of action on hearing of the disaster is, at first sight at any rate, astonishing. He might have been expected to post immediately into Wales where, even if Williams now knew far more about the technicalities of bank construction and repair, his presence would have been invaluable both in restoring morale among the men and in giving confidence to the neighbouring landowners. The disaster was an enormous burden of responsibility for an agent to carry alone. At this distance from the events it is absurdly easy to be critical and even those alive at the time can have known only part of the story, so closely guarded did Madocks keep the secret of his financial crisis. John Williams, knowing better than anyone else the true gravity of the situation, would at least have been able to guess at the reasons behind his continued absence and have some idea what he was about.

The first news of the breach, written as it must have been under great pressure of events, does not seem to have given a very clear description of the extent of the damage. Williams may have tried to spare Madocks' feelings by not painting too black a picture. In any event, writing under such stress, he would not consider that his letter would be read in surroundings quite foreign to the circumstances under which it was written: the whole scene, so vividly in the foreground of his mind, would have to be filled in piece by piece like a jigsaw in the reader's imagination. Already burdened by other worries and pressed for time, Madocks might be slow to grasp the full impact of a new and more devastating problem. The Bank had been severely damaged before and yet had survived.

Whatever the reason, Madocks seems to have had no conception of the magnitude of the damage and he took the first news most sanguinely. He wrote by return of post but otherwise the letter shows less feeling of urgency than those that had been written after the storm at the beginning of the month: 'Although I am truley sorry for the accident, yet I have much consolation in the fidelity, zeal and activity expressed in your letter. . . .' He inquired what harm had been done to the wheat and optimistically relied on the damage being repaired by March when he was to bring colleagues down to see the estate. The letter concluded cheerfully enough: 'But it strikes me in one word that the front of the Bank slipped down into the hole, which will make the base stronger in future.'

As more news came through, Madocks realised the imperative necessity of raising further funds and this he could do only in London where no one yet knew of the disaster. It was also absolutely vital that he somehow kept his creditors' confidence, such as it was, for once this went they would close in like vultures and everything would be lost. His sudden absence from Westminster during the early stages of the Boston Harbour Bill would cause deep suspicion, particularly since the grave illness of his fellow member for Boston, Thomas Fydell, threw the whole responsibility for the Bill's passage onto Madocks. (Fydell's death in March and the impending by-election made matters even more difficult, besides depriving Madocks of a colleague with whom he had served for nearly all his parliamentary career.) It seems possible that with these very valid reasons for staying in London, and knowing that Williams was better able than anyone to cope with the practical repairs to the Bank, Madocks may not have been able to bring himself to face the overwhelming disaster which had literally sunk this his most cherished dream. Until he actually saw the devastation, he could make less of it in his mind.

But in Wales he was asked for daily; nobody, except perhaps Williams, could understand his absence. 'I am very anxious for the success of Mr. Maddocks' whole Plan,' wrote Colonel Peacock, 'and I hope it will be completed to his most sanguine wishes. I am sorry that He is not at Tre Madock, for his presence at this critical time, would be of Infinite use.' His sentiments were shared by many others. With no inkling of the financial crisis which was about to ruin both Madocks and his plans, they felt his cheering presence would do much for morale.

Circumstances could hardly have been less favourable for borrowing money and Madocks wrote ten days after the break in a chastened mood, but still without grasp of the true extent of the damage:

'*London. 24 Feb. 1812*

My dear John,

I am truly sorry, I am just returned from My [?] Bankers and all the Daventry [?] Notes they had were sent to Daventry [?] yesterday so that I cannot send off any more remittances till tomorrow Tuesday which will not reach you by the registered post till Friday. If you want supplies very much before you must send off again on Thursday to Carnarvon but probably you can wait till Friday. The Exertions of the County and our friends do them as much credit as they do us.

Your zeal and activity make me feel much more easy. If you can get it closed before the 11th of March² what a grand thing? The Experience of last year of course will prove of the greatest use, and give you much information and confidence in your present proceedings. I shall certainly *remit* by tomorrow's post.

Yrs very truly
My dear John
W.A.M.

Monday eve: Do not let any thing be written to England about it, but Let us repair it before it is known.'

This secrecy was abetted by a report in the *North Wales Gazette* on March 5 which tactfully ignored the disaster: 'Mr. Madocks, M.P., who has enclosed so large a tract of land from the sea at Tre-Madoc, in this country, is about to try a question of the greatest importance to the landed interest, viz, Whether land so inclosed is liable to the payment of tithe?' Such hypothetical arguments might seem less important on the flooded Traeth where John Williams had now reinforced his earlier appeals by sending out a printed letter which cast the net yet wider. It was a difficult letter to draft in his employer's absence, but he wrote directly to his fellow countrymen. The result has compelling sincerity.

in the shape of a Tower is nearly finished,
at the back of the Borough. — I am surprised
the Market sheds are not finished. Whose
fault is it. Remember the Gothic arch between
the Store-Houses & Humbug's two new houses

Somehow so, at the entrance of the Alley from
the Market & the back of the row of houses
across towards the Inn. Remember the
Meadows under the House (viz, Paynes Lodging)
that they are levelled sloped &c. and the
fences all made good. The Road under Pentyr
Bach may be postponed a little. Have you
let Pentyr Bach. Your sincere friend
W M

6. Extract from a letter from William Madocks to John Williams

7. Trẽ Madoc c. 1811. An engraved heading for writing paper

(CIRCULAR.)

Tan yr Allt.

February 26 1812.

Sir,

YOU have doubtless before now been made acquainted with the dreadful result of the late High Tides upon the TRÈ MADOC EMBANKMENT, which I am sorry to say has placed almost the whole Undertaking in a most perilous situation. . . .

Though you are distant from the spot where this catastrophe has taken place–and though I am unknown to you, and likewise my Friend and Employer, yet still I have that confidence, that any Friend to the country which has given him birth, will not accuse me in taking this liberty, which, I humbly confess, far exceeds the bounds of propriety: – My Employer is far from home and was, in course, unprepared to meet this event; and as it is totally beyond my power to collect one half the number of Men and Teams, that are really necessary to save the Concern, in so short a time as the nature of the accident requires, I have thus taken the liberty of soliciting your aid:– the support that can be effectual to us at this moment is comprised in Manual Labour, Horses, and Carts.

Should, therefore, this my solicitation have its desired effect, any time in the course of the ensuing week (or even the week following) will not be too late for you to lend us your assistance. . . . Such of our Friends as may be disposed to aid us, may rely upon their Servants and Horses being properly taken care of, in suitable food and provender, in case they should stay with us more than one day.

I am,

Sir,

Your most obedient humble Servant,

JOHN WILLIAMS.

(Agent to Mr. Madocks)[3]

Help continued to pour in. Teams came from Anglesey, Trawsfynydd and other agricultural districts. '3 excellent stone blasters, a description of Men I understand you most want' were sent from Bala with the advice, 'They promise to be steady & to work hard & I should be glad to hear that they did their duty.'

In the second week after the accident, 400 men, 222 horses and 67 carts were reported to have been at work,[4] and a note of John Williams', probably written a few weeks later, gives a total of 892 men and 737 horses sent voluntarily to work for six days successively. The big landowners had now rallied with the small farmers. Sir Thomas Mostyn, M.P., for instance, sent 151 men and 155 horses and Lord Bulkeley lent 50 men.

The scores who came for one or two days only, also had to be cared for; and the organisation, billeting and feeding of such a labour force would have daunted most men with adequate financial resources to draw upon. John Williams pressed on undeterred, improvising endlessly, never knowing what the next day would bring in men, horses, wind or weather. He only knew that the next spring tides were due on March 18 and, since they coincided so nearly with the spring equinoctial gales, conditions then would be even worse. Meanwhile they were just holding their own.

His efforts were tremendously appreciated in the neighbourhood. 'Indeed Mr. Madocks owes you a great deal, for your attention, and fidelity to his Interest; and He is that good Man, who I am sure will amply Reward you for it,' wrote an Anglesey landowner, little guessing that Williams well knew that financial recompense might never be forthcoming. (Madocks readily acknowledged his gratitude and appreciation for his agent's gigantic efforts and this may have gone some way towards compensating for tangible reward.)

Endless small problems arose which diverted Williams' energies from the main work. For instance, from a distracting and rather distracted note from Henrietta Ellis it is learnt that Lord Bulkeley's agent had met with an accident on the Embankment. She wrote at some length to inquire 'how the poor suffering Gentleman finds himself & whether there is anything at Gwynfryn which could in any way Contribute to his Comfort', while her husband, quite as fluent with a pen as his wife, sent a long letter in which he also explained that three of his mares 'have Colds, in a greater or a lesser degree', adding 'I was much surprized to hear that your Horse power was so far diminished.' Potato planting and spring sowing were bound to reduce the available teams; soon only those late farms on heavy wet soil would be able to spare their horses. Potential labour was also lost through a confused rumour which went around that 'many well-wishers have been returned for want of employment'.

Some inkling of the real financial straits must have been by now apparent to the North Wales gentry, for it was suggested to Williams that a subscription might be raised for the Embankment. This put Madocks in an awkward position: while he wanted and badly needed to accept, acceptance might amount to an admission of his perilous state. 'If you have had so many applications to this effect, as you state (which is so highly honourable to the country) [this was written above something that had been scribbled over with unusual care] and you really think it a proper thing to do, I will consent, if you think it can be done without anything appearing in the North Wales Gazette or other Newspapers, but I should particularly wish *that not* to be the case. . . .'

Meanwhile David Ellis had been trying to do something about the Welsh creditors, but he wrote to Williams to say he had proposed many plausible schemes in which they took no interest and he was beginning to despair: 'What can possibly be done with a set of people so obstinate & selfish?' Oddly enough it was Madocks himself who managed to cheer them: 'I thank you for Mr. Madocks' letter: poor fellow–it is a comfort to find a man who has such strong & various causes for depression of spirits a little sprightly and recovering.'

Sprightliness in Madocks was usually a symptom of some new plan. Action always raised his morale. The true peril of the situation was now clear to him. The breach which he had so optimistically hoped would be closed in a matter of days was, if anything, widening. Worse, his chief creditor, a lawyer named Samuel Girdlestone who had not pressed for money before, seemed to have got wind of the break. At the end of February Madocks had somehow managed to find money for half a dozen of the creditors who demanded small sums: only one of these ran into four figures, most were between £50 and £100; their very smallness now seems to make them the more irritating. The debt to Girdlestone amounted to £30,000.

It had become a matter of the utmost urgency to prevent the whole estate being seized and sold to pay off the debts. The only answer was to forestall the creditors by an arrangement through which none of it remained in Madocks' name. Complicated consultations were now in progress to produce a solution which, if acted upon quickly enough, could save something from the wreck. Girdlestone, for his part, reckoning that the creditors who had got in first with their writs were going to suck the estate dry, decided that he had better cut his losses and immediately buy out the whole of Madocks' personal estate at valuation. Personal estate is a dry description for all those things with which Tan-yr-allt had been so lovingly furnished: they were all to go, along with his books, harpsichord, and microscope, the horses (including his favourite grey mare) and the curricles, the new sets of harness, the boats (even that one with the green awning of which he was so proud), the bathing machine and caravan, the goods on the Embankment and the furnishings of the Madocks' Arms. Everything he possessed other than land or buildings was to be sold, but not a murmur of complaint or regret crept into one of his letters.

Most probably Girdlestone would have liked to lay hands on the real estate, too, but in this he did not succeed. It was to be made over to William's brother Joseph, and one Alexander Murray who back in the early 'nineties had been their father's Clerk in Lincoln's Inn, and Girdlestone was to become tenant of the property.

Speed and secrecy were obviously vital if these negotiations were to succeed. William himself had not read for the Bar for nothing and was perhaps able to participate and, in a detached way, almost to enjoy the moves and counter-moves in this involved game which was simultaneously to break up and preserve his estate. Such transfers could not be made overnight, and now the great question was whether his London lawyers could work fast enough (and the under-Sheriff of Caernarvon slow enough?) for the whole property to be conveyed in time to forestall the numerous other solicitors who were trying so hard to lay hands on it. Meanwhile all local debts were to be paid up.

Williams was now urgently needed in London to advise on the valuations. That he should have been called away when things on the Traeth were still in such a very bad way, must have come to him as a severe shock, and on the Traeth they were bewildered that he should leave at such a time. His absence was sorely felt. By sheer weight of character his presence had given confidence and kept rumour within bounds. Some weeks after his departure a contractor, writing to him on a business matter, summed up what many must have felt: '. . . indeed I am longing to see you as I never did for my Father.'

Those left in charge of the Embankment rallied to the occasion, but they knew as little of the legal negotiations as the men and were in no position to quell rumours. The Hon. Robert Leeson,[5] (who had opened up the quarry from which much of the Embankment stone had come) wrote to Williams to report progress: '. . . Another point of view which you need not mention to Mr M. as it might give him uneasiness under his present embarrassment, the whole of the goods are under keepers for some debt and it has made a very *great impression* on the minds of the people here that affairs are in a bad way & this day I have heard that Mr. Girdlestone is to be here to take possession of the property on the part of some of the [Creditors?], no man can contradict it & it has deaden'd the whole works, I hope you will watch to contradict it as soon as possible . . . money *must be got* as some people who never complained before are now clamarous . . . I think John it is madness feeding so many mouths if it could be dispensed with, as most of the men eat more than their work is worth.'

From Caernarvon John Evans now wrote to Madocks to tell him how busy he was on his behalf: 'Mr. Smith [Girdlestone's London solicitor] appoints a Mr. J. Jones of Beaumaris, a Brother-in-Law of Mr. Row^d Williams and a first Cousin of mine, his Deputy. I expect that one of my Clerks will be acting Deputy—indeed I have no doubt upon that Subject, I must make a Sacrifice of some Trouble, risque and Money to obtain the Management of the due Execution of the office—You may depend upon my Attention and exertions on your Behalf.' On March 24 Girdlestone got his warrant (to levy £14,500 on the £30,000 debt) and

Evans rode over to Tremadoc with his Clerk and a warrant directing Madocks' servants to act as special bailiffs to secure his effects. The business could hardly have been more complicated, and Smith, thoroughly bewildered and alarmed by happenings in Wales which were so unlike those in Lincoln's Inn, wrote to say that he intended to come down at once 'if it is possible to secure a place on this Night's Mail'. The coach turned out to be fully booked which was perhaps as well considering the number of lawyers, clerks and bailiffs who were already bearing down on the small town of Tremadoc. For at this point Rumsey Williams, the Caernarvon solicitor acting for the chief Welsh creditor, also proceeded with his bailiffs to take possession at Tan-yr-allt, disregarding or choosing not to believe that it was already under distraint. Evans set out once more for Tremadoc to set things right.

They had all arrived to stake their various claims on the same day and it naturally seemed that the worst rumours about Madocks' financial affairs were amply confirmed. The townspeople were appalled at this proof of his insolvency and their fears were easily fed by Rumsey Williams' faction who were quick to spread the tale that Madocks would never return nor would any of them ever see their money again. Fortunately the invaluable David Ellis made a point of being in the town that day and the presence of the Attorney-General did much to keep the situation in hand and to boost the rapidly dwindling morale of the neighbourhood; scores of local people swarmed in to hear the latest news and gossip as well as to attend business in the market.

Pace wrote to John Williams to tell him of the extraordinary tumult that reigned that day. He had been engaged with John Evans' Clerk to appraise the goods at Tan-yr-allt, where according to another writer there was 'nothing but dreadful confusion'. He reported tremendous scenes in the town when 'Sharpe [one of the bailiffs] stuck a paper on the pump in the eyes of all the market people and which I am afraid had a bad look with it. . . .' This,[6] under the heading *A Caution to the Public*, warned them not to buy, seize or take in possession any of Madocks' lands, goods, or chattels, because his personal and real estate had been seized and sequestered for his CONTEMPT to the King and Court of Great Session back in August 1811, in not putting an answer to the Supplemental Bill of Complaint filed against him by William Griffith, Farmer.

At the same time John Evans' Clerk was fixing his notice in a parlour window opposite and on the yard wall at the Embankment and in the dining-room window at Tan-yr-allt. This, in contradiction to Sharpe's, stated that the real estate was now in the possession of Joseph Madocks and Alexander Murray while Samuel Girdlestone now owned all Madocks' personal estate and was tenant of Tan-yr-allt. It certainly seemed that the town had seen the last of William Madocks. The usual gossip and barter of the market gave way to whispered rumours, sullen groups of discontented men opposing the few who remained staunchly loyal. The general despondency was broken only by the uproar which greeted the contradictory notices as they were posted about the property. Even David Ellis could do little to allay their fears in the face of so much printed evidence, all of which seemed to point to Madocks' downfall. The Tremadoc people were not to know that one faction of the distrainers were acting as life savers to the fast sinking concern.

A nice touch, which by contrast high-lights the scene, was given by the arrival of a gardener from Boston who happened to reach Tremadoc in the height of this confusion with 'vines and pines [pineapples] and a vast quantity of fruit trees' for which 'no ground had been prepared, nor a hot-house'. Since the news of Madocks' affairs had been kept so well from his constituency the unfortunate man must have been utterly bewildered by the intensely emotional drama which gripped the town. He might as well have found himself on the stage of an Italian opera house so little was he able to comprehend the Welsh chorus that filled the square. It would be with considerable relief that he found some sane fellow Lincolnshire men, the brick-makers. On this same day, with all Tremadoc in the throes of disillusionment and anguish, Harden, their foreman, reported laconically and sensibly to Madocks: 'We have dug good Clay & turn'd it once over which it is very good clay for the Purpose of Making Bricks that can be but now we are at a stand for we want two men.' He carefully explained their other needs before finishing. 'And concerning our money we are at a stand for it which I think it very unpleasant that we should not have our money as we ought to do. . . .' They were all feeling the pinch now and each expressed his difficulties in his own way: 'We are Willing to Work but we can not work without meat & we Can not get Meat without Money . . .' wrote one of the Welsh contractors with poetic logic.

However the lawyers' plan had worked: Madocks had lost all his personal property but none of the real estate could be swallowed by the creditors. The various sequestrations would soon be taken off and the creditors, other than Girdlestone, were once again frustrated. Though in practice bankrupt, technically Madocks was never declared so and as a Member of Parliament he would not be imprisoned for debt.

While this legal drama was unfolding, work on the Embankment had not stood still. The struggle had to go on; if they eased up for as little as a day, the tides would irrevocably get the upper hand. The various characters who had been left in charge of operations in John Williams' absence wrote to him at Madocks' rooms in Conduit Street where he was now staying. The gap had considerably widened and throughout the March high springs they had scarcely held their own but, now that the tides were slackening once more, it was hoped that things would be a bit easier. Because of the widening of the breach the whole business of erecting scaffolding (the stilts) and forming a bridge, which had caused such trouble the previous summer, had to be gone through again.

Pace reported from the Embankment Office at the Towyn end; in his beautiful copperplate hand the personal affairs of himself and the men were inextricably woven with those of the Bank. The voluntary help at the end of March had fallen to 66 men and 6 horses and he would like to take the 'paines of Glass' out of the lower part of his parlour window and to have instead 'wood paines . . . as every little Child about the place is liable to break them'. Cash was as short as ever and he reported such small amounts as one pound given to a man with a sick wife and two to the Brickmakers. The letter finished 'They put up one Stillt yesterday, a verry good one'; this was the kind of news that Williams so much wanted. Better still, the railway was being relaid.

A relative of Williams', one William Davies, had taken over at the Merionethshire end and seemed to have the situation more or less under control:

'*29 March 1812, 4 o'clock,*
Boston Lodge.

My dear Cousen.

. . . Saterday Evening Last she was mead a very strong and Rapided Tite with us and take away One of the stillts from Carnarvon side at 12 o'clock at Night. We have the stillt now in safe anchorage and I hope we can make that up very soon. Our stillt at Penrhyn side has stand against all this stormy Weath [*sic*] the Slipping Place was in the lowest side of the Bank near the Breach. The work that we have in hand now is Lay Down the Rail Road as fast as we Can we are now about half way to the Breach with the Round Rails.'

In a long letter which the unfortunate Pace did not finish until 5 o'clock in the morning, he told Williams that he had collected an abstract of the Workmen's Demands from October 21 1811. These added up to £1,094, a sum which many of Madocks' friends would have cheerfully gambled away in an evening but which represented a fortune to those concerned. Pace continued: 'if it had not been for receiving £7 from my Mother in Law out of Anglesea, within the last 6 weeks, my family must have starved.' This, coupled with the exhausting responsibility of keeping the work going without the pay he needed for the men must suddenly have become too much for him, for in the next sentence he gave in his notice (this was written before dawn broke on a cold March night). He finished in utter despondency: 'N.B. If the Amlwch Miners comes I don't know what will be done for provisioning.' Certainly not a letter to give Williams confidence.

Another of the men in the Embankment Office (Griffith Parry the Carpenter) told how the Bank was now wearing away on the sea side: 'Mr. Williams pray do not be discouraged by this disagreeable nuse,' he wrote. There were now no voluntary men:

'I believe our own men are dressing their gardens at home, for a day or two. We feel the want of assistance this morning. I hope sum will come by 12 o'clock . . . the more they say against Mr. Madocks, the more I feel myself engaged to stand in his defence, they say you never see him no more neither have a farthing of wages. . . .'

The Earl of Uxbridge[7] wrote to Madocks from Chelsea referring to 'the enterprising undertaking in which you are engaged' and saying that he was directing assistance from the Pary and Mona Mines. But in Anglesey things were not so simple: the Earl's agent had called the miners together and suggested that about twenty should go, but they inquired how and by whom they were to be paid, and got no satisfactory answer. The potato planting season was in full swing there, too, which made them even more reluctant to leave home. 'If you was to send a trusty man here to give them the satisfaction required he might be at liberty to engage whom and as many as he pleased,' came the reply. However hard his lot, the Welsh labourer had a wonderful freedom when it came to deciding where and for whom he would work, or whether he would take time off for his own affairs.

Williams' cousin, Davies, reported again from Boston Lodge that he had never before seen such high spring tides, but things seemed to be in hand and the men were working hard. They had got another stilt in place and rock was being blasted, but from Towyn, a few days later, Pace reported more trouble. On Saturday afternoon when Mr. Ellis was down on the Embankment 'one or two of the scabbed flock' swarmed round his gig and said they must have their complaint known. A reasonable enough request, it would seem, but Pace, who had so recently been in service, believed in each man keeping to his station. But late that evening a boy had arrived with £220 sent off by John Williams: 'On the Monday morning I began very early with the men to distribute the money, which raised their spirits very much, but when I told them (which I individually did) that you was loading a vessel with corn & provision of all sort, you cannot conceive how they appeared to be overjoyed. The markets here are very, very, high, so much so that the Hobed of Oatmeal was sold las

Friday for £*2.12.0.* but I see by the newspapers that that is the case all over the Kingdom.' No one was paid less than one pound, some thirty shillings. There had been very few voluntary men because of the fine weather and they were down to seventy-five regulars. Powder for the miners had run out so a man had been sent with ten pounds to buy some from Ffestiniog. But Pace was happier and he ended: '. . . Thanks be to you good sir in saying that I am giving both Mr. Madocks & yourself satisfaction which is more gratifying to me in this present emergency of times than anything else.' Williams had evidently written a swift and comforting reply to that letter in which his Clerk gave notice of his intention to quit.

In the midst of this tension and tumult one William Weaver was much concerned about the sale of cloth from the factory: 'If the book of patterns is left tomorrow morning at the Carolina I will show it to a gentleman who is shipping to Canada,' he wrote with touching loyalty to the fast sinking affairs of his employer. But the factory was soon to be added to the list of valuations and to be put up for sale.

There was another bad day at the end of April, not unlike that a few weeks earlier when the lawyers had arrived in strength. 'There is Bailiffs in the house now from both parties,' Pace reported, but this was only one of his worries. Money had again run out: 'the post bringing nothing, the Men struck at Noon & came to the Town where was both Counsellor and Mrs Ellis. . . . I tryed with Parry to [pacify them?]. They went back to work but stopped again at 3.0 pm and I am very much afraid will not return again till you come home, & they are thoroughly settled & paid, the times here are severe & very hard, their was a many crying & making their complaints known to Counsellor Ellis to-day concerning the Market, that villian Cadwaleder Evans of Maentwrog was fore-stalling the market, having purchased 4 Hobbeds of Oatmeal, & they were put in Rowland Thomas's house, but the scoundrel could not be found. The Counsellor went to the House but the old woman was very saucy but he said he would learn her better manners next time. I am very sorry to say it is no wonder the men should give up when such things are told & held out to them as their is, & that by people that ought to call themselves gentlemen & do before you & Mr Madocks pretend to be his friends. Names I shall not commit to paper.'

Pace went on to explain that rumours were being put about that 'they were working for who they did not know nor who would satisfy them their labour . . . & now Sir I must beg to inform you (however paintful it may be) that you must not by any means, make use of Mr. Madocks's name, in regard to any property of the smallest value, for it will be torn from him in an instant if you do. It is also quite requisite & necessary that you do by the *return of post* send down countermand orders respecting the Vessel that is coming, otherwise the goods will be seized immediately. . . . R. Williams is trying hourly to make Mr. M's out a Bankrupt, & ruin him if possible.' John Williams must write at once saying that 'the goods are . . . Mr. Girdlestone's or Mr. Joseph Madocks' or someone other's, anybody's excepting Mr. Madocks' . . .' and in a final appeal: 'N.B. if possible do pray keep sending as near as you can the men's weekly subsist until you come for their is amany of them actually starving—' (This state of affairs was unfortunately not unique. The failure of the last harvest meant that many of the poor in England were very hungry and bread riots had followed.)

Griffith Parry also wrote describing the strike: 'I feel unwilling to write this letter for I know how it will hurt your mind.' At four o'clock 'the men all struck and stood by the end of the office'. It was a lightning strike and Parry did his utmost to persuade them to work, but they only blamed him for previous promises that John Williams would soon return bringing the money. There was another rumour that they would never be paid 'but no one will confess who spread it' but a few were still working. It was 'Ten Thousand Pittys that such an Event took place as it is such fine weather to go on with the work. . . . On Thursday evening, we have put One more Stillt up 23 feet further forward. Now our Waggon's discharge over the very middle of the Gully. The distance at low water from the End of our platform is to the otherside 27 yds. the depth in the middle of the Gully from 20 to

22 & the Axact distance between the projected Balks is 19 yds and I was determined by the Blessing of God to put the Bridge over it by this day week.'

To add to his frustration the high spring tides were again coming. 'Send us a good deal of money little will not do the men are quite hard of promises they will not listen to what I can say—how sorry I am that things are so miserable amongst us.' The letter was not closed until the next morning when it reported only about a dozen men at work. 'We can do no good with so few.'

Most of the men returned but it seemed their work was doomed to fail. Again a strong south-westerly had driven in the spring tides. In his next letter Pace wrote: 'With heartfelt Sorrow I have to inform you of the loss of the Bridge [and] all but one Stillt. . . . A most immense high Tide it was yesterday morning . . . it was amost as high as the one that broke the Bank. The bridge went about $\frac{1}{2}$ past 7 in the morning, it went all at once & almost instantaneously, just before High water. Such a force of Tides, I never saw them so rapid & with such Vengeance, but once that was the second and third mornings after the Bank broke, and you will undoubtedly recollect how they were then.' He implored Williams to come if only to refute malicious gossip for it was now rumoured that he, too, would never return.

But things were not quite so bad as they had seemed. The tide had done no damage to the Bank itself and they had somehow managed to recover all the timber from the Stilts which had been lost. This, and a letter from Madocks, had combined to cheer David Ellis who had come down at once to inspect the damage. 'The Counsellor was in very high spirits,' Pace concluded. Spring must soon bring both better weather and new hope. Better still, with the legal business in London completed, it was to bring John Williams back to the Traeth; there could be no surer tonic than his return.

10

The Doldrum Years
1813 - 1817

AWAY FROM the cold realities of wind and tide Madocks now
had reason to be slightly more optimistic, and his lifelong habit
of instilling confidence, where others could see little reason for it,
had not been slow to reassert itself. A meeting had been held at
Lord Bulkeley's house in Mayfair to raise subscriptions for the
Embankment and, in a vote of thanks, Madocks was warmly
praised not only for its 'extensive utility, but for the exertions he
has made on all occasions, connected with the prosperity and
improvement of the Principality'.[1] Such sentiments must have
come as sorely needed balm after the continuous anxiety and
disappointment of the last few months.

Some weeks later, on his journey back to London after an
inspection of the work, he dashed off a spirited note to John
Williams which showed his old form: 'You may depend on my
attending most particularly on what we settled on parting. Let us
pluck up Courage and fight a bold and steady fight. Plenty of
Granite the next week will do the business, & *depend* on it, the
moment the Gap is closed all will mend. . . . Believe me my dear
John, I fully appreciate your anxious zeal.'

Madocks seems to have returned to spend much of the summer
on the Traeth and eventually the breach in the Embankment was
closed. But funds were pitifully low, so instead of being able to go
fast ahead with the very necessary reinforcement along its whole
length to make it secure before the autumn, the small work gangs
continued only piece-meal. The river, too, ran in its old course.

The months wore on. There was the sale of goods on the Embankment including the caravan and bathing-machine. The Madocks Arms then came under the hammer but Williams managed to postpone the sale at Tan-yr-allt, pointing out that the house would let more easily as it stood. It was advertised in the *North Wales Gazette*[2] in a style that may have surprised the local gentry:

'Romantic Residence in North Wales

TO BE LET

FOR A TERM OF YEARS, AND ENTERED UPON IMMEDIATLEY

Unfurnished, or the elegant furniture to be
taken at valuation'

It might catch the eye of some fanciful tourist from England, but after several unsuccessful weeks more bait had to be added: 'In view and near the sea, and adjoining excellent roads, within a convenient distance of good market towns, with any quantity of land from 20 to 500 acres.' Tan-yr-allt could hardly be made more tempting: romantic, elegant, conveniently sited and not too remote. But still no one showed any real interest and, to make matters gloomier, it was rumoured that now Girdlestone was not meeting his creditors and that more bills were piling up. Work on the Embankment consequently slowed as the men drifted away to find surer work.

Many went off to bring in the harvest in the small fields above the Traeth. The scale of their inconclusive battle with the tides regained proportion when measured against this age-old struggle in the upland meadows. As the small patches of oats turned to pale stubble they returned each evening to the empty farmsteads with a sense of achievement instead of the all too familiar frustration.

It was towards the end of this harvest that the whole district was to be appalled by the violent murder of a servant girl in the farmhouse just above the Penryhn end of the Bank.[3] It turned out that one of the men from the Pary Mines who was working on the Embankment had decided to steal from the house supposing everyone to be out in the fields. The girl had surprised his attempt and he had lost his head and killed her. In the days before an established police force the services of any likely citizen were enlisted, so life in Tremadoc revolved round the hunt until the murderer was eventually taken. Bills were posted and the search was widespread (the Tremadoc blacksmith was paid three guineas for searching as far away as Barmouth). The whole region was deeply shocked and not least Madocks himself.

A local murder cannot have made the letting of Tan-yr-allt any easier even if it had the opposite effect on the tourist trade. Travellers continued to come and gaze at the Traeth, and wonder at the great work that still had to be done. If Williams was about they offered a few sympathetic words before hurrying on to admire the salmon leap on the Glaslyn, always the next item on the Welsh Tour.

In September an unusual party put up at the Madocks Arms. Unlike other visitors, the young man showed enthusiastic interest in the Embankment and Williams took a liking to him and discussed the many difficulties that dogged the work. Little was known of the stranger except that he was acquainted with and greatly admired Madocks' colleague, Sir Francis Burdett; he might therefore be assumed to have radical leanings. He was also said to be a poet, a profession common enough in Wales, and to be the heir to a considerable fortune, a situation less usual. His sixteen-year-old wife charmed everybody; she was open, frank and cheerful and dressed with taste and simplicity.[4]

They had come up from Lynmouth where the poet's political leanings had caused too much local feeling for their stay to be prolonged. They were therefore house-hunting and, what was more important, were also searching for some cause to which he could give his whole-hearted support.

John Williams realised that he could provide both, and wrote quickly to Girdlestone. The lawyer replied, having made thorough investigations: 'With respect to Mr. Shelley, however good his connection may be, they do not seem at present much to avail him—He being himself under age [Shelley was nineteen], no security he can give, will be at all binding. . . . I am afraid that Mr. S would by no means prove the sort of Tenant that wd. be useful to us. A young man who has, I suspect, married beneath

8. The Embankment as it appeared in the autumn of 1810. Drawn by H. W. Billington and engraved by M. Dubourg, 1811

9. Portmadoc and the Festiniog Railway, probably *c.* 1840

him, & thereby offended his family. . . . You must take special care to not let Mr. Shelley into possession of the house or if he gets in, we may have great difficulties in getting him out again.'

Williams, however, was not to be put off and continued to press the case: any tenant would be better than none if only to keep Tan-yr-allt aired during the winter. A neighbour who would take an active interest in the Bank would be an immense asset. But there was now a matter of much greater importance in the wind for it seems that Shelley wanted to invest a considerable sum of money, as well as his time, in the Embankment: the great drawback was that he had not yet access to the estate which should eventually come to him.

Meanwhile he was already busy raising subscriptions and, less promisingly, being run in for debt in Caernarvon. However, he obtained bail and continued his good work by attending with John Williams a meeting of the Corporation of Beaumaris[5] where 'many gentlemen of respectability' were gathered with the object of raising subscriptions. Toasts were drunk in three times three and an excellent evening was enjoyed by all, one of its highlights being Shelley's impassioned speech for 'this great, this glorious cause'. The subscription list totalled £1,185 of which he promised £100.

Shelley and his party, accompanied by John Williams, now set off for London to convince Girdlestone and Madocks of the soundness of their new scheme, but meanwhile Girdlestone was writing: 'The intended dissolution of parliament which will probably take place in a day or so has very much disconcerted all my plans,—Mr. M must I believe go off for Boston tomorrow–I hope there is not to be any opposition there–I shall however think you will see me by ye end of this week, so don't you or Mr. Shelley come posting off to London in ye expectation of seeing me or Mr. M. as ye motions of both are at present wholly uncertain. . . .' But they were already on the road. Madocks, in the middle of his election campaign in Boston, also wrote with unusual caution: 'The interest Mr. Shelley takes in the Embankment and his proposals on the subject are very handsome. When I have considered the matter more fully in London I shall be better

able to express my feeling. . . . It requires some consideration
before I lay myself under so great obligations to a Gentleman to
whom I am a stranger. . . . Write to me by return of post.' But
he was soon to write in a more typical vein: 'My best compliments to Mr. Shelley & I hope in a very few days to be at
leisure to pay attention to his liberal and handsome proposition.'
Madocks was full of hope: if the claims of this obscure poet
matched his enthusiasm, his inheritance might be invested in the
Embankment and the land reclamation schemes at this most
critical stage, when some new source of money was desperately
needed. It was to be a bitter disappointment when it transpired
that Shelley's proposals had, at least temporarily, to be shelved,
but having looked into his more immediate expectations and
taken into account his undoubted enthusiasm for the progress of
Tremadoc's affairs (and perhaps the absence of any other prospective tenant), they agreed that he might lease Tan-yr-allt at an
annual rent of £100 with the option of paying when he came of
age.

John Williams, after concluding his business in London,
returned home (laden with Spanish stocking wool, new music and
other trifles of which Mrs. Ellis-Nanney had need). The Shelleys
stayed in the south dealing with publishing affairs, meeting Peacock (and doubtless hearing his poor opinion of their future
neighbours) and continuing to campaign for the Embankment.
Shelley wrote to Williams from St. James's Coffee-house to
report progress: it would be hard to imagine two men of more
different background and outlook united by such an unlikely
objective.

'I received your long and kind letter . . . I need not assure you
of the pleasure which I receive from the intelligence of the safety
and success of the embankment. . . .

'I see no hope of effecting, on my part, any grand or decisive
scheme until the expiration of my minority. In Sussex I met with
no encouragement. They are a parcel of cold selfish and calcu-
lating animals, who seem to have no other business, on earth, but
to eat, drink and sleep; but in the meanwhile my fervid hopes,
my ardent desires, my unremitting personal exertions (so far as

my health will allow) are all engaged in that cause, which I will desert *but with my life*. Can you hire me a trustworthy maid-servant as we shall require three in all? Believe me, I feel the attention of the Nanney family very deeply. . . .'[6]

The Shelleys arrived at Tremadoc in mid-November and found their new surroundings idyllic. 'The scenery is more strikingly grand in the way from Capel Curig to our house than I have ever beheld,' he wrote later and was to recommend that it should be seen from horseback rather than 'jumbled in a chaise'.[7] Tan-yr-allt he described as 'a cottage extensive and tasty enough for the villa of an Italian Prince'.[8] He spent much of his time in the Embankment Office writing for subscriptions or riding about the country collecting money. Books were sent from London and Harriet Shelley and Mrs. Ellis-Nanney exchanged music and played duets together, but otherwise they made few friends. Shelley's natural intolerance would already be biased by Pea-cock's opinions and after less than three weeks he declared that he found 'Welsh society is very stupid. . . . They are all aristocrats or saints.' Bigotry was universal and he found 'more philosophy in one square inch of any tradesman's counter than in the whole of Cambria'.[9] It is possible that Welsh society noticed a certain rigidity of outlook in their new neighbour who was for his part both a confirmed atheist and strict vegetarian.

By January the novelty of the Embankment was beginning to wear thin and reaction set in against Shelley's initial enthusiasm. It was only a few months since he had found in it 'the poetry of engineering' and Harriet had been equally enchanted by Tan-yr-allt. She was now beginning to feel she had been 'dreadfully deceived' in reports concerning Madocks. 'We are now living in his house where formerly nothing but folly and extravagance reigned,' she wrote, faithfully reflecting her husband's mood. 'Here they held midnight revels insulting the Spirit of Nature's sublime scenery. . . .'[10]

The bitter winter cannot have helped. 'This is Russian cold,' wrote Shelley incensed because some books he had ordered had not come: a particularly exasperating state of affairs when the freezing weather, by putting a stop to Embankment activities, gave him a chance to write. The constant interruption caused by these outside commitments was now a major frustration. Having embarked on that cause wholeheartedly with no writing on hand, he was now deep in *Queen Mab* and his one wish was to forge ahead: if it had not been for these interruptions, he felt, they would be completely happy.

But with the approach of spring he was already planning for his friends to come and share his undiminished appreciation of Snowdonia where, in congenial company, everything would take a different aspect. If any of this news reached Madocks, it gave every reason for hope that having weathered one winter the Shelleys might prove to be long-term tenants. In some respects they might almost class as 'Chaotics' and, if only their stay could be prolonged, the Embankment might indeed benefit from those earlier optimistic proposals about finance.

The next news from Tremadoc must have finished all such dreams. It was only a few days later that Shelley dashed off a not very illuminating note to his publisher:

Tan-yr-allt, March 3 1813,

Dear Sir,

I have just escaped an atrocious assassination. Oh send me £20 if you have it! You will perhaps hear of me no more!

Y our friend

PERCY SHELLEY.[11]

The attempted 'assassination' had taken place at Tan-yr-allt the night before.[12] Its story, whether real or imagined, has been examined[13] too often to be retold here but it seems likely that the first attack may have been a practical joke which went further than was intended, while the second could well have been an hallucination. The recent murder just across the Traeth could have added fire to Shelley's imagination and it is not impossible that that of the Prime Minister, Perceval[14] who had been shot in the Lobby of the Commons during the spring, could also have preyed on it. The whole nation had been deeply shocked by the assassination and Madocks' own portrait, in which he held a scroll reading 'Impeachment of Perceval and Castlereagh . . .', hung in the Town Hall. It could act as a sharp reminder of the unfortunate man. (In engravings made of this portrait the words were changed to 'Trè Madoc Embankment. . . .')

Madocks was very angry, believing it to be a ruse to get Shelley out of the district on account of his liberal principles: 'How could Shelley mind such a contemptible trick as has been played off on him?' he wrote to Williams. 'Whoever the parties are, it is a transportable offence if discovered.' From Tremadoc's point of view it made little difference why he had gone: the fact was that both the Shelleys and Tremadoc's hopes of his fortune were on the way to Dublin. Several years later David Ellis-Nanney was still sorting out the debts left behind by 'that ungrateful fellow'.

During the Shelleys' stay, the creditors had renewed their activity with increased vigour. The London mail coach can have made few journeys without carrying a missive from one or other of the creditors' solicitors who were by now utterly exasperated by methods of business they considered to be quite foreign. One wrote wearily: 'I do assure you that I have never had during 30 years practice a tenth part of the trouble as I have taken in this to get a Settlement of a Debt and Costs . . .' and another: 'Your conduct respecting this action astonishes us very much. All we want of you is that you discharge your duty as our agent. . . . We don't know whether the Sheriff may consider himself discharged but we do not consider him so.' They now had wind of the close connection between John Evans to whom they wrote as their agent (who was also Madocks' solicitor) and the unnamed under-sheriff whom they found to be so mysteriously dilatory in acting upon their writs. To be informed that Evans' Clerk had held the office at the time in question was not reassuring. 'I shall on the first day of the Term move the Court against The Sheriff . . . and especially against yourself,' wrote another London solicitor.

The financial and legal vicissitudes of the estate at this stage become impossible to disentangle. Girdlestone was himself now deeply in debt and is last heard of in the Fleet Prison. David Ellis-Nanney, who had handsomely agreed to indemnify the crafty Evans for the value of the goods seized by Girdlestone the previous summer, paid out to the tune of £2,000. Evans, having saved his own skin, turned his attention to the Traeth where the prospect was very bleak indeed. Various English speculators were encouraged to invest in the drainage of the marsh. One surveyor gave his opinion that a further £10,000 laid out (provided the Embankment were secured) should allow the estate to sell for £80,000. But no one showed real interest and the outlook seemed hopeless. 'Everything here wears the air of neglect and approaching ruin,'[15] wrote Fenton after a visit, '. . . with regret at the probable failure of this great plan we turned from it. . . .' Nearly everyone did the same. Few of those enthusiastic gentlemen who had revelled in the house-parties and race-meetings only two years before, now gave a thought to Tremadoc. To run into debt was a common enough occurrence and to be faced with bankruptcy certainly a misfortune, but it was best to avoid those who had such ill luck as if they were struck down by smallpox or cholera. Like his Cardiganshire colleague, Thomas Johnes, whose paradise at Hafod had exhausted even the Johneses' seemingly endless resources,[16] Madocks found that his friends were suddenly very thin on the ground. (Horace Billington, who would certainly have stood by him, died that winter). To a man of so warmhearted and naturally affectionate a disposition it was a particularly disillusioning experience. It was made so much worse for Madocks because he had no wife or family of his own for companionship and moral support. Financially this was a blessing but the inevitable loneliness was a high price to pay. Joseph had never been really interested in the Embankment or estate affairs and William had little in common with his nephew John, who seems to have been a rather conservative young man enjoying fox-hunting, public executions and the classical styles of architecture. It would hardly be surprising if he were rather embarrassed by the tastes of his radically minded, penniless uncle. At forty it was time this exuberant relative settled down. But this, despite every discouragement and disappointment, he showed no sign of doing. John Williams, who had gone up to London again in the summer to attempt to settle the business of the Welsh creditors, wrote to report on matters to David Ellis-Nanney and added without comment: 'I rather think Mr. Madocks has some new scheme in his head. What it is I do not know.'

Unlike so many of his contemporaries who ran into debt but managed, by selling property, to contrive a degree of comfort, which by our standards often seems to border on luxury, Madocks felt severely the pinch of his straitened circumstances. For a man who had boasted so recently that he had millions at his disposal it was a salutary experience to write to his agent: 'I want to return home sadly, but my pocket is dreadfully low. I wish you could somehow contrive to send me 10*l*. Even 5*l* would do, and I will contrive to return it in about a fortnight when Mr. John arrives in the country. . . . Direct me Post Office Chester.' But two days later and before the money had had time to reach him the irrepressible Madocks had arrived at Llangollen from where he wrote: 'Pray send over my Grey-mare to *Barmouth* early Thursday morning, and some sort of horse by the same man to take my portmanteau to Trè Madoc. . . .' This was indeed a comedown from the days of ordering his own curricle but he continued undaunted: 'You need not send the Money now to Chester, as I have borrowed enough to take me to Barmouth, or rather a Gentleman is giving me a lift.'

But back in London in the autumn for the new session of Parliament, Madocks was struck down by his 'old enemy'; he was laid low with gout and rheumatism and quite unable to attend the House. He wrote urgently to Williams for some small rents '. . . *by return of post*. I am wretchedly ill. Confined at the Coach Office Hotel, Hatchett's, Piccadilly, without a single comfort. I never never was so wretched. But do not let my sufferings be known. I will bear up & write next week, all I have done, am doing and hope to do. Deduct the 10*l* for Godsake send me up the Rents. Direct them to Albany, Piccadilly.

> Yrs my dear John
> Most miserably
> & in greatest pain
> W.A.M.'

It was a long lonely year and his indifference or hostility to any scheme whereby he might have cut his losses and perhaps gone to live in reasonable comfort on the continent, puzzled those who could only see the whole affair as a very red balance sheet. But the gloomy winter dragged out its course and was at last over. May 1814 found Madocks ill and poor as ever but the spring had given him new life. 'Still in Bed, but I live in hopes now the fine weather is come of getting durably well, and in June enjoying Salmons & Gooseberries & a good long ride with you everywhere in Snowdonia. Pray pack up *my watch* carefully and send it by Mail to Albany.' Presumably it was destined for some pawnbroker. No tradesman would now give credit; even his bookseller expected cash on delivery and Madocks, who was still a vociferous reader, sold up old books to pay for the new.

His morale was also to be boosted by the Friends to the Purity of the Election and the True Principles of the Constitution who held a dinner in his honour at the Red Cow Inn, Boston. There it was decided to hold an annual dinner to commemorate his first election as Member for the Borough. Madocks' own speech on this occasion was described as 'impressively eloquent' and he much enjoyed the expressions of enthusiasm on the part of the populace who had taken his horse from the carriage to draw it themselves in the traditional manner on his entry to the town. His life certainly had full measure of that contrast for which he yearned as a young man: one month in dire poverty hitch-hiking his way home; another, graciously disposing of carriage horses to satisfy the enthusiasm of constituents. He truly deserved this short break from the depressing atmosphere of lawyers' offices and importunate creditors. He was soon to have another.

With Napoleon safe on Elba, Europe was no longer at war and, having a little ready money in his pocket from the sale of some Denbighshire property, William took the opportunity to slip over to France to examine Cardinal Richelieu's great mole at La Rochelle. Most of his contemporaries would have been happy to stay there leading a relatively cheap and carefree life, but not Madocks. Foreign travel simply stimulated further ideas and on his return he was up at Tremadoc working them out. A planner to the marrow, he saw things as they might be and not only as they were, and as a whole made up of dependent parts. The miry swamp of the Traeth was already, in his eyes, well drained and scientifically farmed land; the Embankment stood firm against the tides and all the other improvements were forging ahead. After this winter visit he wrote summarising his ideas: 'I assure you I employ my mind incessantly in thinking how to compass those important objects necessary to complete the system of improvements in Snowdonia, any one of which wanting, the rest lose half their value. If I can only give them *birth, shape* and *substance* before I die, they will work their own way to posterity. . . .' But of the immediate future of the property he wrote: 'If it does not advance it will recede. It will not be stationary like the mountains around it.'

He went on to explain how necessary it was 'to complete the system in all its parts, and to reckon nothing done, till the harbour and the rail road, which includes the additions and repairs necessary to the perfect security of the bank are established, and the road to Harlech with the Traeth Bach Bridge opened, a line to Trawsfynydd following of course'. Nor would the scheme be completed until 'the clay-burning system is introduced generally –the very best means of improving the agriculture–nor until means are taken to attract sea-bathers, for which the steam-boats from Liverpool have made so good an opening'.[17] A contemporary writer had good reason to exclaim, 'Nothing seems to escape that Gentleman's reach of mind.'[18]

This new wave of energy was probably the result of the culmination of the legal negotiations which had been going on to decide the future of the estate. At about this time it was conveyed back to William, and Joseph also advanced a sum on mortgage which was to be secured by the Tremadoc property.[19] Nothing could have been better for his morale but, almost as if to counterbalance any undue optimism, his excruciating attacks of gout and rheumatism continued unabated. Now, however, although there was no evident reason for optimism, his spirits were not to be damped: 'Like sour small beer. But not small beer that's dead' was the way he described himself during one such bout. Correspondence was often difficult: 'I write now in a flannel glove having been last attacked in my elbow and right hand. I have been suffering sadly for more than two months but I hope the Enemy will soon be exhausted, and that I shall be able to get to Wales.' Most sufferers would have been complaining of utter weariness but he somehow managed to treat this affliction with remarkable detachment. A month later, still undefeated, he scrawled: 'Tho' still in Bed I am getting better. Though my hand is very weak from Leeches.' In spite of the frequency of these attacks Madocks did little to avert them. His prescription (written when laid up during a now rare theatrical house-party) hardly suggests sound medical practice:

> '. . . The morning long we count our ills
> And dolefully complain
> At dinner D—n all draughts and Pills
> Save draughts of brisk Champagne.
> Whats to be done, why eat and drink
> The thing is past all question.
> Let us do anything but think
> Of gout and indigestion.'

The turmoil and bleak prospect of Madocks' own affairs was a reflection of those of the country as a whole. The peace which followed Waterloo had brought with it acute post-war depression. The demobilisation of several hundred thousand men (400,000 from the Navy alone) flooded a labour market which, through the introduction of new machinery, was already uncertain. This meant mass unemployment and with it hunger and dreadful privation. The winter of 1815–16 was exceptionally bitter; it was followed by a complete failure of the harvest. Prosperous farmers, already suffering from the post-war slump in corn prices, now became parish paupers.

In Parliament Madocks and others were engaged in opposing the continuance of the Property Tax which originally had been imposed to raise money for the prosecution of the war. The farmers and landowners, worst hit by the slump and harvest, were also those to be most affected by any proposal to continue the wartime taxation. Madocks, in a period of respite from gout, entered into the fray with his old zest, finding relief in doing something positive again. He was active both in his constituency and the Commons[20] and his passionate concern for the freedom of the individual was to be yet further exercised the following year over the suspension of the Habeas Corpus Act.

The government, in its wish to retain the Property Tax, had little intention of using the income derived from it to relieve the appalling hardship then rife in the country. It seemed to be only aware of this misery in manifestations of social unrest, and to be curiously insulated from all that lay behind the activities of the Frame-Breakers and the mass-meetings of unemployed: it appeared to be unable to grasp the immense volume of suffering that had built up as a combined result of the post-war depression, the inventions of the industrial revolution and the famine price of bread. Most of the meetings were peaceful enough, but one or two ugly scenes, together with not always well-substantiated reports provided by the secret committees appointed to look into reports of revolution, decided the Cabinet to press for the suspension of the Habeas Corpus Act. Scores of petitions were sent up to the Commons in protest against what so many considered to be a gross infringement of civil liberty, and needless to say Madocks spoke strongly against the suspension, pointing out that it was almost unheard of in time of peace. He asked that the third reading of the Bill should be postponed so that Members then in the country might have time to return to Westminster having registered the feelings of their constituents. 'Would they allow the people to petition on a turnpike road that leads to a county town, and prohibit them from petitioning on a measure that leads to the county gaol, and that too on suspicion? And where was the road by which they were to return? Not through the avenues of justice, for they were closed, and the trial by jury denied them. And when? Who could predict the duration of their durance?'[21] Thus were repeated the age-old arguments against imprisonment without charge. In spite of strong opposition, Habeas Corpus was suspended. The country was in a sullen mood but a good harvest eased matters and the atmosphere was temporarily more relaxed. Madocks' fortunes, too, seemed about to take a better turn.

11

Marriage
1818 . . .

TOWARDS THE END of 1817 John Williams received a letter stamped with the postmark of Hay in Breconshire. Madocks' presence in this district was unusual enough to cause comment, and when it transpired that a young widow who happened to be co-heiress to a large fortune (admittedly in the hands of trustees) lived in that neighbourhood, the gossips were quick to speculate. It was rumoured that they had previously met in Bath, where they had appeared at the same assemblies and card parties. Earlier that year, at a meeting of the Board of Agriculture, a letter from Madocks had been read stating 'that he had accidentally lost the Gold Medal voted him some years ago by the Board for his Embankment at Tre-Madoc, North Wales, and requesting permission to have another struck'. This surprising and seemingly unnecessary expenditure suggested that there could be someone whom he particularly wished to impress.

The inevitable gossip which soon percolated most of the Principality irritated and worried him. He may have been the subject of such talk before for, although a *mariage de convenance* was never for him, his eye had been free to wander so long as matrimony was not his object. Now, when so much was at stake, it really hurt. His letter to John Williams inquired what rumours were being spread and, although he made a pretence not to care, it was transparently obvious that he minded very much indeed: '. . . if they busy themselves in thinking about me, I shall return the compliment by not thinking about them,' he declared uncon-

vincingly, and continued, 'Be that as it may I shall thank you just
to state the current reports. . . .'

Since both parties came from a background to whom the
maintenance of property was a first consideration, marriage would
not have been considered had Mrs. Roderick Gwynne (born
Eliza Anne Hughes) not possessed a considerable private fortune.
She was a practical young woman who could appreciate this fact,
but in her twelve years' widowhood there must have been many
more eligible suitors who had been turned away. Her first husband had died when she was twenty-one, and now in her early
thirties she was considering marriage to a penniless middle-aged
bachelor who was frequently laid low by gout and rheumatism.
He certainly had nothing to offer except his debts but Eliza evidently saw things differently. At forty-five William was otherwise in the prime of life, could be as amusing and companionable
as ever; and his enthusiasm for his future plans had remained
undimmed by the years of frustration. It also seems that he was
very much attracted to her.

Eliza had one daughter but no son by her first marriage, so
after her husband's death she had returned home to Tregunter
near Talgarth in Breconshire where, with her elder sister, she
helped to run the family estates. Apart from her short marriage,
life cannot have been easy. When she was still a child, her father,
two elder brothers and small sister had died, reducing the Hughes
family from seven, with every prospect of a continuing male line,
to a widowed mother and two daughters in the space of a couple
of years. But they were not the type to repine. Eliza's father,
Samuel Hughes, had come to Brecon as an agent and had married
into the remarkable family of Harris which had left its stamp on
eighteenth-century Wales and society far beyond in such markedly
different ways.

Joseph, Eliza's grandfather, was the eldest of the Harris brothers.
He was a mathematician and scientist and became Assay Master at
the Royal Mint. His property together with that of his wife went
to Eliza's mother, their only surviving child. Since Thomas, the
next brother, had no legitimate heir he also left the fortune made
as a master-tailor in London, together with the mansion-house of

Tregunter which he had rebuilt in the manner of the 1760s, to his niece.[1] Certainly Eliza was co-heiress to a considerable fortune and it is easy to see that there was plenty of scope for speculation when her name and William's were linked.

The youngest of the brothers, the famous Methodist leader and evangelist Howell Harris, left no fortune. His agricultural and industrial ideas were no doubt of great interest to the founder of Tremadoc. In the mid-eighteenth century he had founded the religious community of Trevecca in one of the family farms not far from Tregunter; here advanced methods of agriculture were also discussed and a woollen factory and printing-press set up, but it was the architecture of Trevecca which would have most intrigued William.

An astonished early nineteenth-century traveller had already described it in his *Tour*: 'Within a circle of five miles round London [is] a space which comprehends most of the architectural absurdities, and most of the horticultural deformities, to which a vitiated imagination has ever given birth,' wrote that worthy antiquarian. 'Yet does Trevecca seem, by combination, to have outdone them all. Here a Gothic arch! There a Corinthian capital! Towers, battlements and bastions! peacocks cut in box, and lions hacked in holly!'[2] The catholic taste of that mid-eighteenth-century preacher was indeed amazing.

As well as architectural extravagances the neighbourhood provided enthralling engineering works. William, true to his times, was fascinated and sensed that relatively small projects like the recently opened Brecon-Hay railway (1816) were minute foretastes of what was to come. There was also the Brecon Canal; not only was this romantically beautiful as it unwound its level ribbon of water through the leafy stands of young woodland and disappeared mysteriously into secret stone tunnels, but its aqueducts, bridges and locks were all of great interest to the owner of an unfinished canal in the north.

Rumours of a General Election put a temporary halt to this most pleasant interlude, for William had to hurry down to Boston once more to meet his constituents. His tenacious views on the rights of the individual citizen and the necessity for the lowering of taxation (to be made possible by economy in the exorbitant government spending on sinecures and placemen) received enthusiastic support. It was now nearly three years since the war had ended but the suspension of Habeas Corpus suggested that sections of the government were as fearful of the English working man as they had ever been of the enemy. Parliamentary reform might generally be forgotten but it was for the private Member to keep the public in a state of awareness of how they were governed.

William also reminded his electorate, since 'nine-tenths of the people have no vote, what responsibility devolves on the remaining tenth! A few men even, of independent principles in the House of Commons are of infinite service. They provoke discussion, prevent the doors of parliament from being closed on the people, and through the medium of the press inform the public mind. Thence arises public opinion, and it is the power of public opinion which is the only practical check left on the arbitrary measures of government.' And, after again condemning the suspension of Habeas Corpus, he told them: '. . . If men would do as much for their liberty, as they do for their property, they would save much of the latter by taking more care of the former.'[3] A salutary thought for the freemen of Boston.

He threw himself into the election campaign with gusto. In Boston the three parties were known by their colours, their political leanings being less clearly defined. The Pinks, oddly enough, backed the Tory government, while Madocks' Reform party was the Blues; the Orange, whose candidate was Madocks' colleague, Burrell, had Whig leanings.

Work in the borough came to a standstill as citizens, plied with ale and promises, stood around the Butter-cross waiting to cheer or heckle. No one got much sleep, for processions with blazing tar barrels (a practice which the authorities vainly tried to stop) patrolled the town each night. A long saga written in doggerel as a country lad's letter home nicely describes the 1818 campaign. It was probably typical of the times. The writer asks innocently:

'. . . What makes it worth while
For fine Gentlemen to cringe, bow and smile,
To take by the hand, and call their dear friend
An old drunken cobbler – and likewise to spend
Much money in treating the people with drink –'

He described with spirit the various parties and their candidates:

'There's the BLUES with their friend little BILLY MADOCKS
These are *nation* fine fellows as sturdy as rocks;
Oh Billy's a Briton, the Freemen adore him,
And they're firmly resolv'd there shall none be before him;
He's for PEACE and REFORM, to the poor he's a friend,
And Father believe me, to hear MADOCKS speak
I could stand without eating or drinking a week.
He's none of your mealy-mouth'd yea-and-nay men
But his language is strong and his argument plain.
There's certain great folks, who can't MADOCKS abide.
Because he is not on the Minister's side:
They call HIM hard names and HIS PARTY A MOB
But with all their base tricks they can't manage the job:
They may do what they will, for the "*damnation blues*"
As they call them, are resolute MADOCKS to chuse.'

The actual poll took place in the great medieval church and the
ballot was quite public, which was perhaps as well considering the
amount of money reputed to have been offered in bribes to
promising turncoats by the Pink candidate. The jingle continued:

'We rushed to the Church, helter-skelter pell-mell,
Where we got in good places and saw very well.
On a bench sat the Mayor, and the three Candidates,
And below them the man with the book of poor rates;
And men with great papers, upon which they note,
The names of the Freemen, and for whom they vote: –
They ask if you're rated, and live in the town,
And then who d'ye vote for – and then put it down . . .

About four o'Clock there came up to the Poll,
Of sturdy BLUE PLUMPERS a numerous shoal;–
The LADIES applauded, the PINKS stood aghast,
To see the blue voters keep *plumping* so fast;
Whilst us *Billinghay lads* rais'd a thund'ring huzza
Whenever a vote was given the right way. . . .'[4]

Numerous stirring verses were written to be sung to the tunes of popular songs and hymns. *Heart of Oak* was a favourite and to the National Anthem and *Derry Down* the Bostonians were also encouraged to return their radical member. These cheerful songs mocked at spies and informers, sinecures, job-men and Jacobin scares. They stood for tax-cuts, electoral reform and retrenchment in government spending.

The ladies of Boston had long given Madocks their support and during this campaign they presented him with an elegant flag on which was inscribed in gold letters 'May Patriotic virtue ever meet its reward'. It did. After these hilarious and exhausting weeks in which one of the electorate complained that he had been deliberately shot and another unfortunately lost his arm through the accidental explosion of a cannon, Burrell came top of the poll, to be closely followed by Madocks who was returned for the fifth time by faithful freemen.

The election of 1818 turned out to be the last time he stood for Boston. Geographically it had always been awkwardly inaccessible; from Tregunter the journey was to be even more difficult, and worse health coupled with his other commitments was to make the distance formidable. In the 1820 election Madocks stood for Chippenham in Wiltshire and was returned ('Are not the Chippenhamites fine fellows?' he was to write with evident satisfaction), but he was going to have less and less time for politics. However, like many of his colleagues, he was to be outraged by the behaviour of the new king, George IV, to his unfortunate if tactless and rather stupid wife Caroline. They had been separated for many years but since the death of their only daughter in childbirth there was no legitimate heir to the throne; the King wanted a divorce and his wife wanted to claim her place on the throne. A most unpleasant situation: whatever her behaviour in the intervening years when she had toured Europe with a strangely assorted retinue, her husband, the ex-Prince Regent, was scarcely in a position to criticise.

Madocks, whose habitual chivalry asserted itself, became Chamberlain to the Queen.[5] He was also much occupied in presenting petitions in Parliament from sympathisers in various counties although in his heart he may have shared the wish expressed in the popular rhyme:

> 'Most gracious Queen we thee implore
> Go away and sin no more
> If that effort prove too great
> Go away at any rate.'[6]

The unfortunate woman complied with this request, living only a few months after the King's case against her had failed; so Madocks' appointment did not last long.

1818 had been an anxious time for William torn between wooing his constituents in one part of the country and his widow in quite another, but the romance also prospered and at the end of March he was able to write, rather self-consciously, to John Williams from Tregunter: 'You will probably in a short time hear that I have altered my situation and concluded what the World has, I believe, been busy putting about for a long time–I am confident in your good wishes, and that your happiness will be proportional to any increase in mine. Give me a line to *Oxford*, & I will write you when you may fill a cup extra-ordinary to propitiate the Event . . .' and, as an afterthought, 'Mind the Gate House at T. have only one decent family in it.' Three days later they were married at Talgarth.

Marriage was to make a vast change in William's life. After so many years as a bachelor this was to be expected, but in wedding Eliza he took on not only a wife and step-child, but a sister-in-law who was also a permanent member of the household at Tregunter where they were to be based for a large part of each year. To form part of such a predominantly feminine family was change enough in itself but to William, who had for so long had to run his own domestic affairs, it must have seemed particularly strange to join a long-established household where, in a sense, he was almost a guest. But if it was an enormous relief to be at last looked after properly in both sickness and in health and to leave the problems of servants and the kitchen to others, it was even more important to have Eliza's companionship and intelligent interest in his many schemes. Of his sister-in-law, who was his exact contemporary, he was somewhat in awe; she was the co-heiress. But with eleven-year-old Eleanora he was on the easiest of terms. She was delighted to have acquired a step-father who was not only affectionate but entertaining, who would act, sing, impersonate their more pompous neighbours or some prominent member of the government, solely for her amusement, and could be trusted, however otherwise occupied, to remember that her bedroom was to be papered 'with the *White* ground Paper with Green & Pink Sprigs' directing his agent 'Pray Hurry it, as it is of much importance'.

Many of these subtle changes are discernible in a letter which William wrote shortly before that most crucial occasion when Eliza and the family were to visit Tremadoc for the first time. Although the old urge for pageantry and display was as strong as ever, private entertainment was to be on a reduced scale. Only a little wine was now to be ordered and a quiet dinner on arrival was to replace the customary uproarious parties. Even so, things were to be anything but dull; fireworks, balls and salutes of guns were as prominent in the arrangements as ever. William also had the assurance of being able to do business at a bank once more. Married life had many compensations.

'Gloucester

Wednesday Eve

My dear John,

I am all aground. I have arrived so late the Bank is shut up and the accomadation is hopeless till tomorrow morning, so I may as well take up my pen to reassure you, that we shall be at Tany

Bwlch, Thursday Evening, the 2^d of July, and make our Grand Entrée, as you propose, on Friday, into Trè Madoc. As you feel equally alive to it as myself, I need not enjoin you to prepare. Only let me Urge the removal of the Gravel Bank in front of Ynys Towyn. The Flag Staff. Borrow some *Flags* from Pwlhelly. Get 2 or 3 or 4 Harpers. A few bottles of White wine from Carnarvon. The Flag Staff at the North Sluice. The Cannons in the Rocks. You may depend on our being at Tany Bwlch the 2^d of July, Thursday, tomorrow week.

Do *not* ask Mr. Nanney or Miss Jones or anybody to break in on us at dinner the first day. Let the Dinner be Snug & we can repair after the Illuminations. All the rest of the plan holds good. The Dinner *at the Town*. Freeholders Ball in the Town Hall etc. Illuminations etc. You will hear from me again about the line of March from Tany Bwlch. I mean all the plan to remain as we settled except as to the Dinner at Ynys y Towyn, where we had rather that first day be alone among ourselves. That is 3 ladies and myself, as we can then stroll on the Bank after dinner etc., without interruption or form, before the Ball & the Illuminations.

Let the *Nursery* Walks etc. be swept & weeded.

I am sure, my dear John, you will do the best to give effect to a day which, if anything can restore Trè Madoc, *that will*–You may put Mrs. Madocks name down for 10^l a year to the School, which she will present that day. *All* the Children of the School *should join the procession*.

I know you will make a good thing & produce an effect, so I will leave all the rest to you, with the hints I have given. Borrow plenty of Flags from Pwlhelly & Carnarvon. *Detain* a Captain or two, & fill the Port.

Prepare a Horse or two to meet us at Dolgelly, if necessary. I summon you to that effect. We shall bring plate & Servants.

Relying on your Zeal to make a great day for Trè Madoc. Believe me

Yours Ever
Most sincerely
W.A.M.

Do *not* open any of my packages by the Vessel, till I arrive.'

A change is also reflected in William's attitude to the behaviour of certain of the tenants who rented Tan-yr-allt and the other villas. John Williams was instructed about re-letting:

'Neither you nor I shall have Trè Madoc comfortable, till that is done. . . . It is not possible for me to bring ~~Mrs. Madocks~~ Ladies to such a neighbourhood. Some sort of decency and respect must be kept up. . . . Respectability is of much consequence at Trè Madoc & the Colony as Rental. Depend on it the prosperity of the place depends upon it.'

This indeed was a change from Madock's bachelor days, but Williams would appreciate the sentiment for he had also heard that 'Mrs M's trustees can lay out several thousand Pounds in any part of the Principality of Wales. North or South'.

Joseph Madocks' unexpected death (1820) could have had a more immediate effect on William's finances. The *Gentleman's Magazine*[7] reported how 'This gentleman, who was well known as the gayest of the gay, he being the life of every circle, was only a few days since walking among his friends in St. James's Street.' William hurried up from Bath much shocked and saddened. It was inflammation of the lungs that had finished poor Jo, not gout as might have been expected from his easy-going love of good living. They buried him at North Cray in Kent where so long ago William had grown up in the company of those dashing elder brothers; with Jo went his last link with the old life, and those carefree days when there could be such genuine consternation over the loss of Falstaff's belly on the Shrewsbury Mail.

William should now have inherited £ 12,000 in consols which their father had left in trust for Joseph with the proviso that the capital should pass to William if he died without a wife or heir. Whether the trust had been broken is not clear. This capital could have made him comfortably independent of the Hughes' estate had he not already had plans for ever greater schemes in the north.

12

The Years of Speculation
1820 - 1826

THE PRINCIPAL OBJECT in Madocks' regional plan had always
been the improvement of communications and the opening up of
the interior; trade of all kinds was crippled by the difficulties of
export. Since the end of the eighteenth century there had been a
steady increase in slate production in North Wales and those
particularly inaccessible workings above Ffestiniog[1] in Merioneth
had proved to possess great possibilities. Quarry owners had built
a road down to Traeth Bach but the slate still had a three-stage
journey from the quarry face to the hold of the coaster which
was to take it to the English markets. First it went by pack horse
down the mountain to the road; it was then taken by cart to the
quays on the Traeth Bach where it was loaded into flat-bottomed
boats;[2] these unwieldy vessels, which could not beat against the
prevailing south-westerlies, had then to wait for a favourable wind
to take them across to Ynys Cyngar, Madocks' 'port' which was
still little more than a natural haven. Only here, under the lee of
the rocky headland, was the slate finally loaded.

This was a tedious and uncertain business but it answered the
immediate need and there was little inclination to look ahead:
there seemed to be no more that could be done to improve the
communications between these remote quarries and the outside
world. But it was at this stage that Port Madoc, or rather the idea
of a harbour at the Towyn end of the Embankment, was germi-
nating in Madocks' mind.

For the first time since the start of the ill-fated Embankment he had been blessed by unexpected luck. It had become apparent that the river, which had been diverted by the Bank to flow through the sluice-gates at the Towyn end, was scouring out a deep hole between Towyn island and the shore and an admirably sited natural harbour was being formed.[3] This was an improvement in every way on the site of Ynys Cyngar (which, anyway, was now beginning to silt up, probably also as a result of the new Embankment). Towyn was already connected by both canal and a good road to the town of Tremadoc which lay barely a mile inland; it was conveniently placed by the toll-house of the important north-south turnpike which was to pass over the Embankment itself; it was much more accessible to the slate boats from Traeth Bach which, having come down on the tide, could run up to Towyn before a south-west wind; it also offered, or could be made to offer, far surer shelter to vessels at anchor.

But its greatest advantage was then scarcely evident: if the railway track which was already laid on the Embankment, and which had so far only been used for its own construction and maintenance, could be connected with the quarries high up above Ffestiniog, slate could be loaded into waggons at the face and unloaded into ships lying alongside the quays of this as yet non-existent harbour. One swift operation could replace the three slow stages of the journey. Thus these two ideas of a new port and a railway, if both could be realised, would form a grand culmination to Madocks' plan for the whole region. Just how important they would prove to be lay beyond even his most optimistic imagination.

Before anything could be done on the ground, both the harbour and railway projects had to be sanctioned by Parliament. They were so clearly to the advantage of the whole district that it might be imagined that the Bills would go through easily enough but this was far from being the case.[4]

In addition to those who wanted no change as a matter of general principle, others had their grievances or were simply irked by Madocks' good fortune: 'Mr. Maddocks has accidentally caused deep water sufficient for Vessels to ride in by means of the flow through the Sluice in his Embankment,' some complained peevishly. But their main objection was to the payment of tolls on the Embankment should a railway ever be constructed from the Ffestiniog quarries. Since export costs were obviously going to be much reduced it is hard to see grounds for this objection. The proposed dues do not seem excessive:

'For slates coming along the rail road and loading
from the Quay of Ynys y Towyn   6d. per ton.
For do. loading from the Quay without coming
along the rail road   3d. per ton.'

This, with those to be paid on every conceivable object that might be imported or exported from the new harbour, Port Madoc, was printed in the schedule at the end of the Bill.[5] (Starting with A for *Ale*, it passed quickly through *Anchors, Anvils, Apples and Pears* through unexplained articles such as *Bares, made of old Junk, the Dozen 2d.* and had only reached pretty things like *Bast Bonnets and Birds, Singing*, at the top of the second page with ten more to go before it wound up more practically with *Wood, Wool and Yarn of all sorts*.) The Bill needed careful nursing through the Commons since although eventually the more important neighbouring landlords were described as 'warm friends to the whole concern' they did not give up without a fight. It was unfortunate that there should again be damage to the Bank just when the second reading was due. 'Make as *little* fuss as you can about the Injury done,' Madocks directed in an urgent postscript. At the beginning of May, Williams received an important call to come up to Westminster: 'I send this Express and hope you will have it on Friday, and if you were to set out that night, you should be in London on Sunday. *The Sooner the Better.*' So much for the easy pace of pre-Victorian England. After riding posthaste to catch the mail at Capel Curig, and being rattled in the fast coach on the not yet completed Holyhead–London mailroad, John Williams was to 'Enquire for me at Reed's Hotel, Lower Grosvenor St. No. 75. If I am not there . . . at Dunn's Hotel, Bridge St., *Close to Westminster*, and if I am not there come to Messrs. Jones & Dysons Office at the Election Committee Office in the House of Commons.'

In the Lords' Committee, Madocks' opponents succeeded in reinserting their pet clause which would exempt from toll slate brought along the Embankment railway to the port; but there was little option but to agree if the Bill was to be passed before the end of the session.[6] It was also laid down that no rates or duties should be payable until one third part of the £1,200 estimated to be necessary for the completion of the harbour had been laid out, and that the whole should be completed within five years.

The first part of the Bill had dealt with amendments to the original Traeth Mawr Act.[7] A new commissioner[8] was appointed to set out the boundaries of the newly reclaimed land. Owing to the death of the original commissioner, Benjamin Wyatt, these had never been settled so it was still in a sorry state being as yet neither drained nor irrigated.

Although the Bill was passed without more delay there seems to have been less sense of urgency on the site. Madocks writing over a year later urged 'As to the *Port*, It is high time it began.' But by Michaelmas (1824) the harbour was ready to receive vessels up to 60 tons' burden so application could be made to levy dues. More quays were needed and the activities of Griffith, the stone-mason who with his four sons had undertaken the job, were constantly questioned in Madocks' correspondence:

'Pray let me know if Griffith Griffith keeps the *new Southern Quay* out enough in the River as the Companies suggest not, as many rocks are left in the Channel which will prevent ships coming alongside the Quay. . . . Griffiths must not hug the Garth too much to save his pocket.'

John Williams, who was now officially styled Director of Works in the Harbour of Port Madoc, was soon to be employed in yet another capacity. The wave of mineral speculation which was to break over North Wales in 1825 was gradually gathering force and with it, and the opening of Port Madoc, interest in the projected Ffestiniog railway grew. Madocks, whose health had been even worse since a severe attack of jaundice, had to leave more and more of the work on the spot to Williams whom he continued to shower with ideas and instructions.

The problem was to choose the best line to connect the quarries with the new harbour; a distance of some twelve miles and a drop of 700–800 feet. At this time two roughly parallel schemes[9] were mooted by different speculators and Williams had now to turn railway surveyor and advise as to which line would be better. He had also to report all gossip and rumour which he might pick up as he rode over the country investigating the projected lines and, if possible, he was to meet the companies' surveyors in person. 'Pray fall in his way, be very civil to him and find what he is about,' wrote Madocks urgently of one of these gentlemen. Both companies went ahead and their railway Bills were petitioned in February 1825, Madocks himself sponsoring one of them. On the same day, he petitioned to introduce a Bill to amend the Harbour and Traeth Mawr Acts. Its chief purpose was to adjust the Embankment tolls but a clause was also inserted to prove that the Traeth Mawr enclosures had been ratified. The land would otherwise automatically revert to the Crown in two years' time (within twenty years of the passing of the original act). An appalling prospect.

While these matters were before Parliament another slate company appeared at Ffestiniog. Madocks, knowing the enormous untapped resources and the extreme poverty of the district, was delighted that more much-needed capital should be forthcoming to develop the area. 'Each of these agents should be personally attended to and made much of. There is a 3d. Company on the scent, the agent's name is Skinner,' he wrote. This rumour came to nothing but yet another concern, boasting the grand name of the Welsh Slate, Copper and Lead Company, showed lively interest. Its Chairman, Lord Palmerston, found its quarry to be a remarkably fine one. 'All we want is a railroad to the sea, as at present the slates are sent twelve miles along an infamously bad road,' he wrote enthusiastically. 'Bubble' Wilks, notorious in connection with other doubtful companies, was among the directors. Like other waves of speculation, slate was attracting its chancy characters.

In March, feeling a good deal better, Madocks wrote to ask Williams to come down to Tregunter bringing all his papers: 'I am most anxious to see you and have prepared much for our deliberation and decision, as to the future, which may be *nothing*

218

or everything, according to how it is managed.' There was certainly plenty to be managed: Griffith was to be urged on with the building of the quays; the quarry owners still had to be encouraged to use the new port rather than Ynys Cyngar; they somehow failed to see that it not only gave a shorter voyage but avoided 'the going down with the boats to Y, so far in the teeth of the Wind', while if they used the new harbour it would be 'all in their favour and blow them in to Port'.

The day-to-day business of the harbour now took up a good deal of time. Shipbuilding, which had long been traditional on the Traeth, was now concentrated at Port Madoc where the deeper water made for easy launching. A fishing smack, the *Ermine*, and a coaster, the *Two Brothers*, had already been built and now something bigger was in mind: 'Is the keel of the great vessel laid down?' Madocks asked Williams, who was also to deal with Embankment tolls and the letting of the toll-gates. If they were made too high the road would not be used, if too low, the gate would not be let. It was decided to raise the toll on draught and saddle horses but not on cattle or pigs, which could too easily slosh across the mud. Estimates were still being got for the Traeth Bach Bridge as Madocks was again pressing for an improved route down to Barmouth and both the Porthdinllaen turnpike acts (which had recently been revised by another Act of Parliament) needed attention. On top of all this he also had new ideas for the town. 'I want very much to establish a wool fair at Trè Madoc, soon after the shearing. The Loomery is a famous place for storing it for Exportation. . . . It requires only a good Sorter to bring the wool into its different qualities.'

Money remained an anxious preoccupation. Madocks was very concerned whether harbour dues should be subject to parish rates, and he spent a lot of time working on the legal aspect of this problem. There was still work to be done on the value of the reclaimed land and its rental which was made particularly complicated by the fact that the value of such land depended so much on what work went into it from year to year.

Remaining records of the estate business are scanty and are impossible to unravel, but Madocks was once again optimistic:

'The ladies are sure to be at Morva Lodge in July, by which time, and long before, I trust Trè Madoc will be on its Legs, and the Box filled with five Parchments. Then we shall all go on in high glee. Improvements, Leases, Buildings. But no Hollowing now.'

This injunction proved timely. Both the railway Bills which were before Parliament were dying in committee. To make matters worse a new company was causing loss of confidence among the other speculators. The Royal Cambrian Company, which included the great banker Meyer Rothschild among its directors, had obtained a lease to work mines and quarries on the Crown lands in Wales; it claimed that minerals under all estates in Wales were held by the Crown, unless already exempted by special grant. (It should be remembered that slate around Ffestiniog is mined, not quarried, although the term quarry is commonly used.) Such claims did not go unchallenged and Madocks, among others, was angry at the intrusion of this seemingly all-powerful company. 'I should soon be well enough to get into North Wales for Rail way & everything,' he wrote, 'if my spirits are not damped by a failure in the projected affairs, & seeing some Jew, or Stranger coming to interfere with every thing, & throwing all into confusion.'

However, no landowner was likely to allow the Royal Cambrian to sniff round his land and when Benjamin Smith, its agent, made some trials on the sheep-walk above one of the quarries, he was quickly served with a notice of trespass. He then went over to prospect on the Moelwyns—the block of mountains which separates the Vale of Ffestiniog from Traeth Mawr. He was thus adjacent to Madocks' own country. If good slate were found here, a quite separate railway system would be needed since the quarries would be on the wrong side of the watershed to make use of the Ffestiniog system.

After some reflection Madocks came to see the possibilities of the immense wealth such a company could pour into the Principality (the Royal Cambrian's capital already stood at half a million). It now seemed that all the companies might work simultaneously and so could be of inestimable value to the region.

'I long to get all the companies possible to bear down on our little *dear* counties of Carnarvon and Merioneth,' he wrote.

No sooner had Smith made his survey of possible quarries for the Royal Cambrian—and all this happened within a few weeks of the formation of the company— than it transpired that he was already planning to build a separate railway down the west side of the mountain, into Traeth Mawr and direct to Portmadoc. If this had been no threat to the Ffestiniog railway, Madocks would have been delighted, and none of his fellow supporters of the Ffestiniog scheme would have been much interested, but unfortunately the Royal Cambrian also had some mad scheme to carry branch lines over the mountain to the Ffestiniog quarries, thus destroying the reason for the projected Ffestiniog railway. Everyone was muddled, worried and uncertain whether this extraordinary scheme could be serious. The railway plan itself consisted of an unconvincing series of straight lines, nearly four miles of which were the steep branch inclines which brought the track from the projected Moelwyn quarries near the two thousand foot contour to the valley floor.[10]

The Harbour was now causing great anxiety. It had been rumoured that the Royal Cambrian was also manœuvring to get control of Portmadoc by terminating the railroad in such a way that it would have access to the quays at the expense of any other line; the company was said to regard Towyn as common ground (it had never been fenced) and to be aiming to gain from this. Madocks was furious. The situation was further complicated since the five years allowed for the port's completion in the Harbour Act would soon be over (as it turned out, Griffith seems to have finished in the nick of time) and this, coupled with the Royal Cambrian's scheme, was a gnawing uncertainty. 'I am alarmed in the greatest degree. Our enemies are all on the watch,' Madocks wrote wearily, but with something of his old zest he was also planning to get the Moel Wynn Bill 'properly altered. . . . Never was such *Robbery* contemplated.' Sheer exhaustion may have been partly responsible for his anxiety but he was not alone in his fears of the company's intentions. Faced with a common danger, the two rival Ffestiniog companies now amalgamated and appointed William Provis, who had recently been Telford's resident engineer on the Menai Bridge, to draw up a plan. He did this in time for a meeting which was arranged in Tremadoc a month later (12 December 1825). Here, to its supporters' amazement and subsequent bitterness, Provis' line (which was very similar to that which the railway now follows: its lower part was identical) was thrown over in favour of the unrealistic Royal Cambrian plan. It seems that some of the Ffestiniog quarry owners were persuaded that they might use the Harbour on better terms if the Moel Wynn Bill were adopted.[11] Only after the Ffestiniog line was dropped, was it realised, too late, that they were now entirely at the mercy of Rothschild and his improbable branch lines over the Moelwyns to connect their quarries to the port. A spirited battle followed; protagonists attacked each other with withering invective but the Ffestiniog scheme sank into oblivion leaving only the Moelwyn plan in the field.

But by this time suspicion of Rothschild's intentions had roused other landowners; it was folly to allow this all-powerful financier to prowl the sheep-walks unhindered. They petitioned against the Moel Wynn Bill in committee. In April Madocks' opponents also petitioned successfully against his Bill. As a result both were soon to sink without trace. Thus after seven years' struggle only half of his great plan for the region was approaching reality: Portmadoc might be growing in importance but the projected railway seemed as distant as ever.

As a background to this period of illness and frustration William had the comfort of Eliza's company and the domestic order of Tregunter. In London, too, when he was well enough there was time for entertainment and social life. It was very different from those dismal years immediately preceding his marriage, but his greatest joy had been the birth of their daughter, Eliza Anne Ermine.[12] As might be expected, he was a most devoted father. Even in business letters he could not imagine that his agent would not want the news that 'The Baby [has] a little cold but grows famously, and eats and sleeps like a True Welch Woman.' For-

tunately John Williams had himself recently married and his wife
was expecting a child so such information would have sympathetic reading.

William happened to be at Tremadoc on the occasion of his
daughter's first birthday and he wrote a long letter to
'My dearest *Eliza Anna Maria Ermine*,

I hope this will reach you by the 14th with my most affectionate
congratulations on your having completed one journey round the
Sun. . . .

. . . I conclude with an injunction to love tenderly your Mama,
your Aunt and your Sister. Remember always to your Mama
you owe the greatest of all gifts–Existence. It is that, without
which you could not enjoy any thing in this world, or be entitled
to anything of the good promised in the next–Life is the gift of
God, and if he has graciously vouchsafed to your mama to
bestow this invaluable gift on you, next to your God you are
bound to honour your Mama.

When you have been whisked round the Sun a few times more
in this agreeable public Conveyance called the Globe, your mind
will become more accessible to these ideas. . . .'
Meanwhile her mother, for whom the letter was naturally
intended, was delighted and, years later, it was carefully copied
and tied up with silk cord.

Tremadoc itself had also picked up. A recent *Tour* had described
it, perhaps optimistically, as a town of between eighty and a
hundred houses. 'Here is a handsome new Church, a Market-
Place, a comfortable Inn, and a great number of good shops. . . .
Here is an excellent Salmon Fishery–a good Shore for Bathing–
and a safe harbour for vessels under 120 Tons burthen.'[13]

With the revival of the neighbourhood Madocks was determined to make it as attractive to his family as he could. Eliza, who
loved the sea, preferred Morva Lodge, with its splendid view out
to Cardigan Bay and up the estuary to the Moelwyns, rather than
Tan-yr-allt which still looked over the dank half-drained marsh.
As John Williams was fully occupied, one John Etheridge was
appointed caretaker and became the recipient of the usual spate of
letters which heralded Madocks' arrival. 'Have dinner ready at all

events at 6 o'clock on Tuesday, namely, a joint of Mutton roasted. One boiled Chicken and one roast Duck, and a rice Pudding. If we do not come by *Four* o'clock on Tuesday keep the things till Friday' or 'Before you put the Hangings on the best Bed in the Bow Window Room, Sleep in it on the Feather Bed and Bolsters to air it well, and it should be put in the sun if the weather is hot and fine' or 'We bring a Cook but want a cleanly girl to wash the Dishes. Do *not* get Mrs. Roberts from Penmorva She will not do at all. Some clean young person. I hope the flag will be Flying at the Tower and the other at Towyn if large enough. If not get one from the Ships. I hope to get a cask of Porter from Daniel. Williams lends feather Beds & Blankets. I hope the Dove is arrived & that a Looking Glass will be put over the Chimney in the Dining Room. There must be 2 servants Beds over the Stable.' Comfortable family holidays had replaced those exuberant parties at Tany. The garden was a great interest and cuttings and plants were constantly exchanged between Morva Lodge and Tregunter. A conservatory was put up; grapes grown; a melon frame made: '. . . The fruit is so great an object to my Ladies, and I find they miss fruit in North Wales more than anything else. They are remarkably fond of it.'

Etheridge carried out sowing experiments which had been abandoned for so many years on the new land. He was responsible, too, for such things as the building of the look-out tower (whose pinnacles went mysteriously awry) from which the harbour could be admired; and he was also appointed gamekeeper. He gave satisfaction in these varied activities, and William was particularly happy in Eliza's delight in the house and new garden: 'I am *much pleased* to find you take so much *care* of Morva Lodge . . . as *Mrs.* Madocks is very fond of it, and, Please God, we shall be there a great deal the next Summer.'

In that boom year of speculation, 1825, Etheridge had to find accommodation for the various companies' surveyors and agents. Tremadoc, and particularly the Tap Room of the Madocks Arms, hummed with speculation and William, tied more than ever to his room at Tregunter, thirsted for news: 'Write by Thursday's post and let me hear, *all* you hear and know. How are the trials going

in Moel Wynn? Has Mr. Smith good prospects? Have many
fresh Ships *come into* Port, since I left? How is the Gray Horse?–
Who is at Twntyr Bwlch now?–Pray write on Thursday.–

Your friend

W.A.M.

Is Sir Joseph Huddart at Brynkir? Let me know all about the
Ships and how many there are now.
Plant Ivy *all round the Church* and Scotch Firs on each side the
Gate going to Morva Lodge from Towyn–
  I hope you got the £8 I sent the other day.'
Ready cash still presented a constant personal problem. This post-
script and notes such as 'I sent you two guineas by the last post,
I now enclose five more' give some gauge of William's pocket.
Presumably all his resources were expended on the port and, since
borrowing from private individuals or moneylenders was still a
usual way of raising money, he had naturally incurred debts. So
precarious was the position that in order to foil any attempted
seizure of the Morva Lodge furniture an agreement was discussed
whereby it might legally belong to John Williams; it would
indeed have been embarrassing to find bailiffs in possession when
the family arrived from Tregunter.
  The financial and legal affairs of both the Tremadoc and
Tregunter estates become even more difficult to disentangle. They
seem to have been primarily concerned with the mortgage on the
Tremadoc estate and the investment of a large part of the Hughes
inheritance in some big project (slate quarries or a railway in
North Wales?). Tens of thousands of pounds were concerned:
a nice contrast to the sums involved in William's private affairs.

  The 1820s which, if William had so chosen, could have been
comfortable years of consolidation, had been filled with the
anxious business of industrial expansion and improvement of
communications; the port and the railway, quarries, roads and the
Traeth Bach Bridge had all proved more controversial than he
could have believed possible. Nor did the doctors seem to be able
to decide on a cure for his own ailments. Even Dr. Bogeheda, the
celebrated Liver doctor in Cheltenham, was only temporarily

225

successful. Also the lawyers seemed as far as ever from settling his estate affairs. If it had not been for his beloved Eliza and for young Eliza Anne (now rising four), William might have been very low indeed. Even so, he was too often ill and dispirited. It was probably Eliza, sensible, kind and agog to see the world that lay beyond Wales, London, Cheltenham and Bath, who decided that for the first time in twenty-five years he should have a prolonged holiday.

13

The Italian Holiday
1826 – 1828
and the Realisation of the Dream

ON 31 MAY, 1826, the Madocks party landed at Le Havre on the first leg of their long journey across France and Switzerland to Italy. They travelled in style with their own carriages; William and Eliza, Eliza Anne aged four and her step-sister Eleanora now a young woman of twenty, Miss Anna Maria Hughes and Eliza's governess, Miss Caroline; two maids and a manservant accompanied them.

Although the destination was so distant, there was no great hurry to arrive. William was an eager sightseer. June was spent in Paris; by the end of July they had reached Geneva and had been able to gaze in amazement at the romantic grandeur of the Alps competing, it had to be admitted, with Snowdonia. They wintered in Florence where the English community was well established, and probably renewed acquaintance with Colonel Wardle who, finding his financial problems in England insoluble, had been there for some years. They left in early spring, and in May 1827, close on a year after leaving England, checked in with the British Consulate in Rome. Here were various acquaintances and one or two relatives to visit besides a mass of marvellous monuments, but the Italian roads would soon become chokingly dusty and hot so, after a few weeks, they pressed on with the last stage of their journey to Naples where they arrived thankfully nine days later.

They booked in at the Gran Brettagna Hotel where it was

agreed to pay the proprietors, the Brothers Magatti, 640 ducats for the whole of the second floor. This was to include 'Breakfast with fruit, Dinner, and Tea in the evening for four Masters, Board for the young Lady and her Governess, the board for 4 Servants, 60 wax candles, that is 2 a day, a lamp with oil and a Carriage'. Friends could be invited to dinner, not exceeding three, at a ducat a head.

This does not seem to be the style of an impoverished man, fleeing from his creditors, as has been generally assumed during the last hundred years, nor do William Madocks' letters suggest, even momentarily, that he had forgotten Tremadoc or the problems of the Embankment and port. It is clear from his continued correspondence with John Williams that he had every intention of returning.[1] Throughout the journey he was in touch with Williams about estate affairs; discussions about likely tenants, the possibilities of various slate quarries, and the endless business of lawsuits still filled his letters to his agent, leaving little room for anything else. From Florence, after dealing with the ungratefulness of the captains who were evidently complaining about the payment of harbour dues, he had sent one of those all-too-rare references to his everyday doings and impressions. 'I am examining the great works of the Romans and Buonoparte. Miraculous Engineers!' he wrote, but although he was enthralled by all he saw, Wales was never much out of mind. Perhaps this was not quite the respite Eliza had envisaged for her husband. Some important business matters were in hand which affected both the Hughes property and his own debts. Part of his sister-in-law's estate was involved and with loans from some other parties this was to make up an advance of £10,000. 'Miss Hughes will get us out of all scrapes that threaten us,' he wrote, but the transactions were very slow and the delay may have been the reason for the Madockses' prolonged stay abroad. William himself was rearing to return to the fray and did not intend to spend long in Naples. He wrote soon after his arrival to reassure his agent about two writs that had been sent in to secure the furniture at Morva Lodge: 'They do *not* wish to sell only to *secure* the property for their further safety against all other assailants until my return, which now will be very shortly. The Steam Boat will soon be here, by which we shall shorten our journey, and I shall see you in July, depend on it.' But this date gradually receded. William had hoped for one of the Irish seats in the November elections but when the time came they were still in Naples and so, for the first time in nearly twenty-five years, he was not a member of the House of Commons.

In addition to this ceaseless attention to affairs at home, sightseeing, entertaining and being entertained, William found time, with the help of Eleanora, to transfer a number of his impressions to his commonplace books.[2] The volume which he had started in 1825 began: 'Little Eliza Madocks's own particular Book, to be read through before she is 21 years old, being the History of the World and especially of Europe just before the French Revolution (1787) and the Grand Era of the Independence of South America ratified August 1825.' It did not live up to its title but turned out to be much more lively; the jottings give an idea of his current interests and sympathies which were as varied as ever. There were observations about Napoleon's road over the Simplon, with the note: 'We have but one masterly work of this nature' referring to Telford's new Holyhead Road; that Tiryns was the best specimen of military architecture of the heroic age; that 'Simplicity is the characteristick of profound knowledge'. There were appreciations of Byron's work which he greatly admired, notes from the *Electric Review*, and quotations ranging from Pope to the Book of Proverbs. There was a loose bit of paper on which it was noted that he considered Job to be the first drama of the world: 'I had an idea of writing a Job but found it too sublime'; and somewhere else was scrawled 'Wisdom & Love, before the world began, Assisted God, er' God created man.' The title-page of the last book, 'Man proposes; God disposes,' perhaps summed up a philosophy which many set-backs had instilled. Interspersed with these quotations were unfinished drafts of other verses which, whatever their poetic quality, show his homesickness and romantic longing for Wales, and sometimes a fear that he would never return. But this was only one side of the picture. He also copied, and doubtless delighted in reciting, quite different rhymes:

'That you should have so many women, I am
Shocked, says a Lady to a Prince of Siam
Madam, quoth he, we never should have two
Did every woman but resemble you.'

Young Eliza was herself making good progress with her lessons
and wrote, in beautiful copperplate three-quarters of an inch high,
to Master Williams, Ynys Towyn:
'Dear Little John,
    I hope you are well as I am. I write this at the foot of a great
smoking mountain almost as high as Snowdon, sometimes it
throws out fire from the top. I hope soon to be in Wales and shall
be glad to see Morva Lodge and Port Madoc again; and all the
ships. Remember me to Mr and Mrs Williams and believe me to
remain always
                        Yours sincerely
                    Eliza–Anna–Maria–Ermine Madocks.
I should like to see the new school.'
    During the winter Madocks and John Williams seem to have
had a serious row. Probably it was about the proposed schemes
for the estate or the industrial development of the area and
Williams, doubtless rightly, thought that Madocks' plans were
over ambitious. They usually were, and it was he, as agent, who
was caused so much trouble when means were not forthcoming
for their implementation. It seems that Williams had at last lost
patience and decided to quit. This provoked six closely written
pages from Madocks, telling him that he must stay: 'It is not
only the best and only thing for your interest, and mine . . .
I beg you if you value for your own sake our future.' He had
been planning ahead for the next twenty years relying on
Williams, and went on: 'force from your mind all little narrow
minded ideas of "being able to manage me" . . . "holding the
candle to the devil" and such like trumpery. Take a good dose
of Physic & get rid of them for such paltry mean motives of
action are only worthy of the lowest, & *worst constructed* minds.
They would never have carried Brindley & the Duke of Bridg-
water through their great job, nor would any of the stupendous

works of the Romans which I have witnessed & admired with awe in my travels, ever have been accomplished. Therefore away with all other notions but drawing together in an open, frank, manly manner. . . . I have no personal benefit but have had the fatigue & anxiety for 17 years of keeping all together. . . .

always most sinc. & affect. W.A.M.'

With typical optimism Madocks seems to have assumed that this settled the matter. He wrote again three days later to tell Williams about an antique statue which he had found: 'Let us proceed hand & heart to distinguish 1828 in such a manner as to make it worthy of being *recorded* by chisel, on the face of the perpendicular Rock, by the Embankment, for which I am preparing a piece of Old Roman Marble here, which starts next week, or very soon, for Liverpool in a Ship, by a Captain who will deliver it at Carnarvon. This old piece of marble is taken from a celebrated work against the Sea, made by Julius Caesar, & his General Agrippa, who made a large dam to shut in the Seas, to form a deep, safe, and landlocked Harbour for the Roman Fleet. I have had a suitable inscription engraved on it. . . .'

Like so many of their contemporaries the Madockses had been looking out for antique sculpture since their arrival in Italy, but William also believed in patronising living artists. He consulted Sir William Gell, a noted classical archaeologist and traveller, about commissioning a work and was told that John Gibson, a young sculptor of Welsh origin who was working in Rome, 'would be too happy to do anything You might like for Trè Madoc, but very difficult it will be to get a subject proper for the purpose. Neptune ought to be struggling with you for possession of the soil. . . .' Gell made various other less original suggestions and advised against temples as too costly, but promised some drawings. William entered into a lively correspondence with Gibson, sketches were exchanged (perhaps Eliza drew William's) and they settled for Neptune, on his own, with his trident uplifted in 'some energetic attitude with terrific majesty . . .' with the possibility of a 'light elegant' Venus rising from the sea as a second work. These they were later to discuss in frequent visits to Gibson's studio on their return to Rome.[3]

Meanwhile there were also more practical matters needing attention. The old worry about turning the river concerned them once more. It had been abandoned when the Embankment was repaired in the hope that the river would cut out a new course for itself towards the sluice; but this proved to be wishful thinking and Madocks had news that the river was still gnawing the back of the Bank. He wrote four pages to Williams on the immediate necessity of turning, trusting it could be effected before he came home. They were at last preparing for the long journey: the carriages were serviced and the baggage sorted and packed; it was to be another long drive overland as the idea of travelling by the Liverpool steam packet seems to have fallen through. By the end of March 1828 they were in Rome once more where Madocks, still a confirmed anglican but with sympathies ranging from his Methodist fellow-countrymen to the Pope, longed to see the pomp and splendour of St. Peter's at Easter.

Here he had great pleasure in a letter that he found from John Williams, who also seems to have forgotten their quarrel. It gave him 'new life and spirits' and he replied at once: 'I cannot lose a moment to express to you my joy & *gratification* at your dispatch received today. . . .' With Madocks in good heart it was inevitable that fresh plans would be forthcoming. The letter went on, true to form: '. . . a NEW IDEA has struck me lately . . . which is to have a good sized flat bottomed *Ferry Boat* of 15–18 Tons with a small steam engine to go between Ty Gwyn & Traeth Mawr. A Barmouth Stage Coach comes along the Commission Road to Ty Gwyn. The Passengers & Luggage are popped into the Ferry Boat. Another Coach is ready to receive them at Port Madoc & away they go to Carnarvon & Bangor or to Pwlhelly, or to Tan-y-Bwlch. What an immense saving . . .' (a sum then demonstrated that the journey would be thirty-three instead of fifty-four miles). He was also optimistic about the revival of the slate trade which had recovered from its temporary set-back and wrote again the next day, full of ideas for the future (which included an unexpected scheme for breeding oysters on the Traeth): '. . . and then we may sleep on a bed of roses without Any more thorns.'

Throughout their stay in Italy John Etheridge had received long letters about personal estate matters and now there were instructions about the decoration of the drawing-room at Morva Lodge which was to be ready for their return:

'. . . I mean the Paper with little Birds on a flower pattern. Put this in the Drawing Room (the room that looks to Towyn). Put it all round the room above the Dado only; & *below* the dado to be the present paper *light green*. . . . Put also the Bird Paper upon the Ceiling under the arch by the East window. You can cut the paper so as not to injure the prints upon the walls. . . . Messrs Morlands will send you *some more money*. . . . Stock the garden well for July & Aug. Plenty of Peas & Beans & Lettuces. . . . How are the Strawberries & Raspberries?'

A week later news came at last that the turning of the river,[4] about which anxious inquiries had been sent from Naples throughout the winter, was in hand and Madocks wrote his last surviving letter to John Williams: 'I am much gratified by your letter of 30th March' it began and went on to discuss details of the river bed and referred to a map of the Iron Rail Way and the construction of a new bridge. Unlike so many of the letters which were signed off at top speed ('Yr. fr. in gt. Haste WAM') this one ended with a strangely appropriate finality:

'God Bless you & God Prosper the Colony!!! Amen!
Ever yrs. mo. affecty, W. A. Madocks.'

But to William this was the opening of a new era. At last he was on his way home, eager once more for the fray. He had in his baggage the opening of a speech which had been composed in readiness: 'Accidentally looking over a map of Wales on my return from Italy . . .' it began. But he was never to see the bird wall-paper in the drawing-room nor to enjoy those peas, beans and strawberries fresh from his kitchen garden; the speech was to lie unspoken among his papers. The Madockses travelled up through Italy across Switzerland and France to Paris where they stayed at 109, Faubourg Saint-Honoré, thankful no doubt for a pause after so long on the road. There on September 15 1828 William Madocks died.

The circumstances of his death are obscure; no mention of them was made in the obituary notices which appeared in the *Gentleman's Magazine* or the *North Wales Chronicle*, and strangely enough no plaque was put up to his memory, even in Tremadoc Church.[5] This would not have been so surprising in an age when such memorials were less customary, or in a family which had no such tradition. But in his case some record certainly would be expected, if not at Tremadoc, in the family chapel in Gresford Church, or, as Eliza went home to Tregunter, perhaps at Talgarth or among her own family in St. Mary's, Brecon (now Brecon Cathedral).[6]

So inconclusive was the evidence of William Madocks' death and so unwilling were the people of Tremadoc to believe that they would never see him again that, as time went by, a rumour wove itself into a legend to the effect that he had in fact returned.

The stories varied as rumours do, and his own longing and determination to return may have been one of the threads on which they were spun. He had always intended to be buried in a vault in Tremadoc Church, but his body was not brought home: how then could the people believe that their warm-hearted founder was actually dead? Instead, some thought that in spite of his great longing to come home to Wales, he had been unable to do so openly because of his debts. So he had crossed over to England in disguise, and made his way to a remote farm in the hills above Tremadoc, where 'in some love-nest forgot by the world' he had happily lived for the rest of his life with some Welsh country woman. A slightly less romantic version tells how William, tired and sick, had made his way to this distant valley where a farmer and his wife had taken him in. She was said to be his illegitimate daughter, and the legend has it that she nursed him and cared for him for his remaining days. Another story tells how Eliza brought his body back to Wales and had it buried secretly at night in Talgarth Churchyard.

It is very difficult to account for the fact that Eliza had no memorial erected to her husband: but it is heartening to know from later letters that she remembered him and Tremadoc with affection and happiness and brought up their daughter (who was six when he died) to think of him in that same way. It is just possible that the gout which had plagued William from early manhood, could have 'attacked his brain' (as in the case of his eldest brother); but there is nothing, except lack of church memorials, to suggest that he took his own life in a delirium as the unfortunate John Edward had done.

These legends, even when completely refuted, have their own kind of reality in showing what people wanted to believe of the man: he would not desert them by quietly dying, among strangers, in a foreign land. Whatever their lack of foundation they give a sidelight on William's character: that he should become so soon a legendary figure is illuminating.

However, the French authorities, with typical Gallic thoroughness and clarity, have supplied the bare facts of his death, and have produced a certificate to the effect that the 'malheureux Madocks', as one of their twentieth-century officials so realistically and charmingly describes him, was buried on September 17 1828 in that most romantic and unexpected of cemeteries, Père Lachaise. The inscription on the stone can no longer be read; it is broken and has fallen and the grave 'est tout envahi par le lierre'. For one who wrote so anxiously from the brilliant Mediterranean sun of Naples to inquire how the ivy flourished in his distant Welsh churchyard, this state of affairs seems to be peculiarly fitting. Those young Chaotics in the carefree days of Doly could hardly have imagined a memorial or a setting more suited to his taste for picturesque melancholy.

If William Madocks' mortal remains were soon to be forgotten, he needs no memorial to describe his life's work. Back in 1814 when his fortunes were at their lowest ebb, he had written of his plans: 'If I can only give them *birth*, *shape* and *substance* before I die, they will work their own way to posterity.' This they surely did. Although, when he died, William's personal affairs were chaotic and his debts were not cleared for many years, his ideas for the whole region were soon to prosper beyond his wildest hopes.

The Embankment survived: today it carries both the main coast road and the original railway which now has a thriving tourist traffic. Three years after Madocks' death the duties on coastal coal against which he had struggled so long, and with them those on slate, were at last abolished by Parliament. This meant a great revival in the slate trade which had undergone a slump since the boom years. The Festiniog Railway was completed in 1836, and trade in Portmadoc increased enormously as a result of both these events. By 1845, twenty years after its opening, 43,000 tons of slate were exported in one year and 29,000 tons of shipping were required to clear the cargoes handled by the harbour.[7] This was a far cry from that day when John Williams had been instructed: '*Detain* a Captain or two and fill the Port' in order that Eliza might be impressed on her first visit. Portmadoc was now a forest of masts and its streets were impregnated with the smell of tar and new rope just as Boston had been after its young M.P. had piloted its Harbour Bill through Parliament.

The town of Portmadoc grew rapidly but, without its founder's guiding hand, it is relatively formless and architecturally of no great interest when compared with his own little town of Tremadoc. But the whole region prospered through the port's existence; at last this corner of the Principality had an outlet for its products and, before the century was out, Welsh slate was to roof buildings from the Baltic to Buenos Aires, Cape Town and even Western Australia. In return consumer goods were imported and the people no longer lived on the verge of famine.

Nor was Porthdinllaen forgotten, but its fortunes never revived. When the new railway was planned to connect London with a port for the Irish capital, schemes for this harbour were seriously put forward in preference to Holyhead. Had they succeeded, Robert Stephenson's mighty Britannia Bridge would never have been built to take the railway across the Menai Straits; and to Madocks, with an enthusiasm for the great engineering works of his time as keen as that for his regional plans or picturesque landscapes, that would have been a great loss.

Tremadoc itself, although it never grew beyond a village in size because of the prosperity of Portmadoc close by, was a thriving town in every other respect and markets, fairs and the Quarter Sessions were regularly held there. It has recently become a mecca for architectural and planning students who survey and appraise its buildings and layout. But the schemes for the reclaimed Traeth were never realised. This would have been a great disappointment to William with his keen eye for landscape and interest in agricultural improvement but there is now a haunting fascination in its lonely islands stranded in the sea of grass.

Other causes close to his heart were to flourish even more quickly than his planning projects. The Bill for Catholic Emancipation was finally passed by the Lords in the year following his death, while the first reformed parliament, something for which he had striven throughout his whole political career, was to meet only three years later (with his nephew John as one of its members).

John Williams was anxious to confirm young Eliza's connection with Tremadoc and one of the last glimpses of him is on the occasion of the splendid festivities there which marked her coming-of-age. The letters he then wrote might well have come from Madocks himself, reflecting as they do all his master's enthusiasm and zeal. Despite the activities of several 'vile wretches' who opposed his 'harmless frolic' and whom he declared he would fight 'as long as I have a single shot in the locker', the celebrations went with tremendous verve, beginning with processions and salutes of cannon and ending with a Ball in the Town Hall. There her father's portrait, wreathed in laurel, crowned the scene.

During the succeeding years, the usual mixture of judgements was passed on William Madocks. Most forgot the constant financial straits which so nearly wrecked him. They spoke of him as a rich man and remembered his achievements out of context. There was the full-blown rhetoric of the mid-Victorian admirer who wrote: 'If Russia may boast her Peter the Great, Wales may boast her Madocks' or the colleague who remembered him as 'a stanch friend of liberty both civil and religious'. To the Welsh it was unnecessary to record that he was a God-fearing man; that they took for granted, but his faith may have surprised some of his English contemporaries who knew only of his strong radical leanings.

There were also those who recorded his character more simply, not fussing over the apparently contradictory nature of the qualities they found in him: wide compassion; ready wit; boundless energy; patriotism; gentleness; unyielding stubbornness; love of ceremony. . . . It was probably these contrasts in temperament that rubbed against each other to produce a creative and effective personality out of a character which was in so many ways equipped for the pleasant life of a drifting dilettante. His resilient determination must have been as surprising to his colleagues as his impulsive spontaneity was attractive or, to those who had to implement those impulses, perhaps exasperating. His zest for life and amateurish inability to recognise both his and its limitations were part of the secret of the eventual success of his plans. But without the loyalty and friendship which he inspired in John Williams, little could have been achieved. Their mutual love for Wales and faith in what they were creating was the great bond between them and was their sheet anchor when things were at their darkest. Some years later Mrs. Williams was to write to young Eliza from Tremadoc: 'It has looked all this Summer, rain and fine, a Paradise. . . .' That was how William Madocks and John Williams had seen the Traeth and all they had planned between this lonely estuary and the empty hills, from the very beginning.

NOTES

Abbreviations

Davies: Davies, The Rev. Walter. *A General View of the Agriculture and Domestic Economy in North Wales.* 1813.

Dodd: Dodd, A. H. *The Industrial Revolution in North Wales.* 2nd ed. 1951.

Fenton: Fenton, Richard. *Tours in Wales 1804–13.* Ed. Rev. J. Fisher. Cambrian Arch. Ass. 1917.

Nicholson: Nicholson, George (ed.). *Cambrian Travellers' Guide.* 1808.

Nimrod: *Fraser's Magazine,* 1842. *My Life and Times,* Nimrod.

N.W.G.: North Wales Gazette.

Pennant: Pennant, Thomas. *Tours in Wales* (1773–1781). Ed. John Rhys 1883.

Richards: Richards, W. Morgan. 'Some Aspects of the Industrial Revolution in South East Caernarvonshire'. N.L.W. MS. thesis.

C.R.O.: Caernarvon Record Office.

GEO. III, GEO. IV: Acts of Parliament in the reigns of George III and George IV.

N.L.W.: National Library of Wales.

U.C.N.W.: University College of North Wales, Bangor.

This book is chiefly based on unpublished letters and papers of Madocks and his contemporaries. Those which are not annotated in the text are in the W.A. Madocks Collection, County Record Office, Caernarvon, or the Portmadoc Papers, National Library of Wales. A substantial part of the Porth-yr-aur and Glynllifon MSS., in the library of the University College of North Wales, Bangor, has also formed the background to this book.

Introduction

Note

1 Defoe, Daniel. *Tours through England and Wales*. Everyman edition, 1948.

2 Wyndham, Henry Penruddocke. *A Gentleman's Tour through Monmouthshire and Wales in the Months of June and July 1774. 1775.*

3 Davies.

4 In 1784 La Rochefoucauld had recorded how in England 'the humblest peasant has his tea twice a day just like a rich man'.

5 Dodd.

6 Davies.

7 Pennant.

8 Bingley, The Rev. W. *North Wales*, 2nd ed. 1814.

9 *The Cambrian Register*, 1795.

10 Ibid, 1796.

11 Hall, Edmund Hyde. *A Description of Caernarvonshire, 1809–11.* Caern. Historical Soc. Records. Series No. 2.

12 Nicholson.

13 Ibid.

14 Ibid.

15 Nimrod.

16 Davies.

Chapter 1

Note

1   By R. Pio.
2   Now demolished. The present house stands on the same site.
3   The Clwyd was surveyed by a professional engineer in 1778 with a view to embanking it against floods, but no Act of Parliament was applied for. Dodd.
4   *Kentish Travellers' Companion*. London, 1794.
5   The writer was proved correct: 'The whole district has, within the last 50 years, become studded, as it were, with villas, ornamented cottages, and fanciful habitations of every description.' Ireland, W. H. *History of Kent*. London, 1830.
6   Sale catalogue. Mount Mascall was demolished during the 1950s. It had a cupola-capped turret at each corner of its slightly austere four-storeyed façades; the windows were of late seventeenth-century proportions and the Madockses probably altered it further. A pentagonal bay had been added at some stage and this may have housed the private theatre.
7   John Edward Madocks married (firstly) in 1781 Frances, daughter of Sir Richard Perryn, Knight, Baron of the Exchequer. She died in 1790.
8   Ackermann, R. *History of the Colleges of Winchester, Eton and Westminster; with the Charter House.* 1816.
9   Davies, G. S. *Charter House in London.*
10 Mary-Anne Wainhouse, a ward of John Madocks, who lived at Mount Mascall. Portmadoc Papers, N.L.W.
11 Lloyd, J. W. *History of Powys Fadog, Vol. V.* Whiting & Co., 1885.
12 March 25 1782.
13 British Museum MS 19242.
14 The college was 'so completely cramm'd that shelving garrets and even unwholesome cellars, were inhabited by young gentlemen in whose fathers' families the servants could not be less liberally accommodated'. Colman, George. *Reminiscences of Oxford.*
15 Nimrod, *Life of Mr. Mytton.*

16 Mallet, C. E. *History of the University of Oxford*. 1924.
17 Several future statesmen were then members of Christ Church. Robert Jenkinson (later Lord Liverpool) had preceded William from Charterhouse; George Canning came up from Eton the following year; Henry Fox (the third and most famous Lord Holland) was a contemporary.
18 Nimrod.
19 John Edward Madocks *m.* secondly, 1793, Elizabeth, eldest daughter of William Baron Craven of Coombe Abbey by Elizabeth his 2nd wife. Elizabeth (the mother) married secondly Frederick, Margrave of Anspach; she was an exceptionally attractive and eccentric woman, and a renowned amateur dramatist. Shortly after this marriage her husband had sold Anspach and they had set up in great style at Brandenburg House, Hammersmith, where a private theatre, grandly named The Brandenburg, was built; here her plays were performed and the Madocks brothers often took part. See Craven, Elizabeth, *Memoirs of the Margravine of Anspach*, 1826.
20 Hasted, Edward. *History of Kent, Vol. 2*. 1797.
21 Llay Hall was left to the Puleston cousins to whom it had belonged in the seventeenth century. They had recently run into hard times and John Madocks seems to have been trying to set them on their feet; the Madocks brothers may have regretted this generosity, but they had the consolation that the property was to revert if Richard Puleston had no heir, which it apparently did.
22 Paris, Mathew. *Tour*. 1797.
23 Now the property of the National Trust. The path to the falls leaves the main road just to the north of the bridge.
24 Paris, Mathew. *Tour*. 1797.
25 Madocks' house has gone. Dolmelynllyn Hall, now a hotel, is almost certainly on the same site.
26 Fenton.
27 Ibid.
28 *Archaeologia Cambrensis*. Vol. XIX, Part 4, page 527. The translation is that given by the contributor, Egerton Philimore; it is not certain how much of the poem was inscribed; certainly the first two verses; he translates three in order to give the sense.
29 N.L.W. Portmadoc Papers 438 — Salt Box MSS of W. A. Madocks.
30–36 Ibid.

37 N.L.W. Portmadoc Papers 428.

38 The identity of Miss Hayman is uncertain. A. H. Palmer in *The History of the Town of Wrexham, its Houses, Streets and Old Families*, 1890, mentions only one sister of Watkin Hayman, Anne. She would certainly be known to William but seems unlikely to have been this Miss Hayman. Anne Hayman was twenty years older than himself. She was Privy Purse to Queen Caroline as Princess of Wales and did not marry.

39 N.L.W. Portmadoc Papers 428.

Chapter 2

Note

1 Quoted in Nicholson.

2 Ibid.

3 Warner, The Rev. Richard. *A Second Walk through Wales*, 1798.

4 Fenton.

5 They formed part of the estate of Richard Tavistock Price of Rhiwlas near Bala.

6 *Communications to the Board of Agriculture*, publ. 1808.

7 Jeffrey Holland.

8 For about half its length it ran parallel to, but outside, an earlier embankment (traditionally ascribed to William Wynn of Wern) which presumably had proved ineffectual. The failure of this embankment may have influenced those who opposed Madocks' scheme. It ran from Portreuddyn at the north of the estate, straight out into the Traeth for 300 yards; it then turned sharply through 90° to the south-west and ran in a nearly straight line across the Penmorfa inlet towards Clog-y-berth, where the town of Portmadoc now stands. Much of this embankment can still be traced on the ground: a stretch of the Croesor railway was later built along the line of the bank and this part is particularly easy to find. The top was about fifteen yards wide and it was reported to the Board of Agriculture that it 'is adapted only for a footwalk, as the materials being sea-sand confined by a coating of sward, laid with great care, it was deemed expedient to exclude beasts of

burden, and everything likely to tread it to its injury. Sheep are
pastured on it, much to its benefit.'

9 In a letter to *Byegones*, April 11 1900, William Payne, grandson
of Thomas Payne the Dolmelynllyn agent, gives an account of
embankment building on Traeth Mawr which seems to combine
the story of two different embankments. It states that wooden
rails were used to bring material from the high ground but there
is no mention of these elsewhere.

10 Creassy, James (Engineer). *Report on the Drainage and Improvement
of the Keyningham Level.* 1801.

11 These ballads alluded to any topical event, local or national, and
in the newspaperless country districts were particularly popular at
fairs and markets where they provided a way of passing on gossip
and news.

12 *Communications to the Board of Agriculture*, publ. 1808.

13 *European Magazine.* Vol. 153, February 1808.

14 Benjamin Wyatt was responsible for a number of buildings in and
around Bangor at this time. Doubtless he and Madocks, who were
colleagues on various local enterprises, exchanged ideas and notes.
But he was an older man with traditional ideas about architecture.
His fourth son, Lewis, who was only four years William's junior,
published, rather precociously at the age of twenty-one: *A Collection of Architectural Designs, Rural and Ornamental executed in a
Variety of Buildings upon the Estates of the Right Hon. Lord Penrhyn,
in Carnarvonshire and Cheshire, 1800.* This shows the inn at Port
Penrhyn with a shallow hipped roof and deep projecting eaves
supported on sprockets. Otherwise the design is conventional,
with symmetrically spaced windows and a pedimented porch,
but its bay windows suggest a touch of Brighton. Lewis was
at this time working in the office of one of his London uncles.
At twenty-one, he could hardly have gone home to Wales without
attempting to improve the design in his father's office.

15 Fenton.

16 The Hon. William Spencer, an Oxford friend of Madocks, wrote,
and later published, several poems while staying at Dolmelynllyn.
*From Sister Dolly in Cascadia to Sister Tanny in Snowdonia (Two
Country Seats in North Wales belonging to W. A. Madocks Esq.)*
reflects the prevailing interest and amusement in picturesque
landscape.
It began:

'Ods rocks and cascades! (God forgive me for swearing),
I vow, sister Tanny, your conduct's past bearing;
You know very well that this curs'd expedition
Would ne'er have been thought of without my permission:
You prest, and you plagued, till I gave you my leave,
Billy's friends, and himself, for two days to receive:
Now, time after time, new excuses you seek,
And keep the whole party away for a week!
In truth, sister Tan, you'll allow me to state
That you're grown rather proud and conceited of late;
Come, do yourself justice, indeed you must see
'Tis nonsense to vie in attraction with me;
. . . .
In vain you give out with an insolent swagger,
That you are an heiress, and I am a beggar.
What little I have is from Bankruptcy[1] free,
Your wealth, like a merchant's, depends on the sea;
My lands, as I've heard from surveyors of taste,
Are improv'd by the storm by which Yours are laid waste.
In vain, against me, winds and winter combine,
What ruins your prospects, embellishes mine!'

'[1]Alluding to the great embankment at Tanny-ralt-issa. Now called Tre-Madock.'

After more general observation on the delights of the beauties of the Dolmelynllyn woodlands and the muddiness of the newly reclaimed land, Spencer turned to the forestry and agricultural improvement which William was attempting:

'Whilst you to a nursery drag us, to see
Some poor baby Dryads as high as my knee!
In the place of Dianas, and Fairies, and Peris,
You shew us (oh fie!) that old workman, Ceres!
Whilst, proud to my rock-fretted realms to belong,
The torrent-king thunders my vallies along;
Your godling aquatic just makes a deposit
Sufficient to water a mill or a closet.
. . . .
So I hope you're not vex'd with my candour, dear Tan,

But send back my William as fast as you can;
And prithee give up this extravagant folly,
For Tanny can ne'er be the rival of Dolly!'
. . . .

17 All freemen who owned property worth £2 0s. 0d. per annum
were entitled to vote. The electoral list, as might be expected in
an up-and-coming seaport, contained its share of captains, merchants, cordwainers and others connected with shipping; the
town's building activity was reflected in the numbers of stone-
masons, bricklayers and carpenters. There was also an Organist, a
Captain Printer, a Surgeon and a surprising number of Hair-
dressers.

18 Marrat, *Lincolnshire*. 1814.

19 Ibid.

20 Ibid. The writer incidentally gives further insight into the way
many buildings of the day were designed: 'the model of this building was made from the Birmingham theatre.' It was to be a
handsome affair upon whose stage a Mr. Robertson always kept a
'respectable company', but this, together with the initial high cost
of the building, meant that for the first four years of its life the
theatre ran at a loss. After this it picked up. Modern management
might envy such support.

21 The theatre has gone, a new market and assembly rooms were
built in 1819, the chapels and congregational church have been
replaced. Even the Butter Cross, from whose upper chamber
candidates harangued and cajoled the electorate, has now been
demolished.

22 Lincolnshire County Archives. MS P.M.6/2.8. From Samuel
Leigh to Mr. and Mrs. George Leigh, Brigstock Northants.
31 October 1815.

23 Son of Sir Richard Perryn and brother of Frances, first wife of
John Edward Madocks.

24 Memorial in Twickenham Parish Church.

Chapter 3

Note

1 The A5 from Shrewsbury to Holyhead runs largely along the route engineered by Telford.

2 Pennant.

3 N.L.W. MS Peniarth 465.

4 By Bell Lloyd from near Bala.

5 See Davies. This project was published under the title: 'Proposals for making a Turnpike-Road from Llangynog, in Montgomeryshire, through Bala in Meirionyddshire, to Traeth Mawr; for Embanking and Draining the Sands of Traeth Mawr; and for continuing the said Road from thence to Porth-din-Lleyn in the Bay of Caernarvon'.

6 Golborne made two proposals. The first was for an embankment across the Traeth Mawr opposite Penmorfa; 2,000 acres would be reclaimed and the estimated cost was £20,000. His second proposal was to embank nearer the sea and thus enclose both Traeth Mawr and Traeth Bach (as the Dutch had suggested in 1719): in this case 3,000 acres would be enclosed at an estimated cost of £30,000. (There is something unconvincingly neat about Golborne's figures.) It was then proposed to form an incorporated company, each member having a share in proportion to his subscription. Dr. Worthington, vicar of Llanrhaidar, is said to have raised subscriptions amounting to £29,000, but in spite of this handsome figure the opposition of local landowners prevailed. An Act of Parliament was then proposed which would offer sufficient inducements and safeguards to overcome this opposition, but nothing came of it, despite Golborne's optimistic report on the value of the land which would be reclaimed. See N.L.W. MS thesis, 'Some Aspects of the Industrial Revolution in South East Caernarvonshire'. W. Morgan Richards.

7 See *Transactions of the Caernarvonshire Historical Society*, vols. 17 and 20, 'The Caernarvonshire Turnpike Trust' and 'The Porthdinllaen Turnpike Trust' by R. T. Pritchard.

8   See Carey's *Atlas*, 1794.
9   43 GEO. III CAP. 38.
10 Nicholson.
11 William Madocks, Thomas Parry Jones of Madryn (high sheriff) and Colonel G. Lloyd Wardle were among its leading supporters.
12 See Rogers, Thomas: *Documents addressed to W. A. Madocks Esq. M.P. relating to Porthdynllaen harbour, Caern, with a view to its improvement, for the better security of trade, and for a shorter and safer communication between Ireland and England*. Dublin, 1807.
    Rogers pointed out that the south-west wind which prevailed eight months of the year meant that Porthdinllaen vessels could run to Dublin without making a tack, nor was there any 'bar or rocks to intercept the passage', but 'a deep and extensive Bay to beat in and out . . .' while 'at Holyhead (a dry harbour) the tide must flow 3 hours at spring tides, and 4 hours at least, at neap tides, before packets have water enough to get in or out, by which . . . on going to Dublin, they lose the channel tide'. The Collector of Customs recorded that 656 vessels had put in at Porthdinllaen during the first six months of 1804 (but he did not specify their tonnage). The company went ahead to build a pier and, with more imagination than accuracy, Rogers described how 'a magnificent Hotel and accommodation for Travellers are preparing. . . .' He included for good measure in his report a curious design in which a town quite circular in plan was shown below the cliff.
13 46 GEO. III CAP. 34.
14 It cuts the embankment close to the present town of Portmadoc.
15 U.C.N.W. MS Glynllifon 5193.
16 47 GEO. III Sess. 2 CAP. 71.
17 Thomas Payne came up from Dolmelynllyn on his own account, living first at Tan-yr-allt Issa; he contracted to do some of the work on the 1800 embankment.
18 This word is still in use in parts of North Wales. Its use in this context may have Biblical origins.
19 At Llanfihangel Ysgeifog.
20 Anglesey seat of the Earl of Uxbridge, later 1st Marquess of Anglesey.
21 Peacock, T. L., *Headlong Hall*. 1816.

Chapter 4

Note

1 Loudon, J. C., *Designs for laying out Farms and Farm Buildings, in the Scotch Style; adapted to England*. 1809. In Loudon's plan the central street, which continues across the newly embanked land to what is now Portmadoc, remains the spine of the design and there is an open space on the site of the present Market Place. But the north wall of this square, on which the whole town is now focused, is shown as a nondescript broken line of buildings which is not even parallel to the square. The Town Hall and inn do not appear. One feature, probably intended in the eventual plan, was a short cross street or secondary 'square', to the south. The façades of the existing houses, now almost hidden by those in Church Street, suggest that this intention was abandoned rather late in the day (see note 10). As late as 1808, the *North Wales Gazette* refers to three intended squares, so yet another was presumably planned. The Ideal Plan is so different from that realised, it must either have been made very early in the life of the estate, or Loudon or his draughtsman can have paid little attention to the site. Tan-yr-allt is not marked, but a site for a house to be called Morva Lodge is, and also a marine hotel, and a fascinating pattern of standard smallholdings which cover the newly reclaimed land. This plan is weak compared with what was built. At twenty-four Loudon was even less experienced than Madocks.

2 When considering the site today, it should be visualised as it was when first built, alone on the edge of the Traeth. Portmadoc, which came as an unexpected by-product of the great Embankment, was unthought of.

3 Robert Owen, famed for the pioneer social work he did at New Lanark (largely built by his father-in-law), also planned 'villages of co-operation' in which the buildings, and the inhabitants' lives, were fitted round a central square. It is not known whether Madocks and Owen ever met; later they were both on the list of those to be sent Shelley's *A Proposal for putting Reform to the Vote*

throughout the Kingdom so they may have discussed parliamentary reform if not town-planning.

4 Presumably Madocks had not then realised that the Town Hall had somehow slipped slightly off the centre-line of London Street; a 'blunder' for which even he was unprepared with a solution.

5 An information office of the Snowdonia National Park now occupies the first floor.

6 The stone market-hall at Bala, on the other hand, may have been taken from Tremadoc: it was similar in intention but, unlike Tremadoc, it leaves the feeling that little affection has been felt by the designer for his building, and the result is very much less satisfying both in its general proportion and detail.

7 *A Dialogue between an Amateur Actor and a Hairdresser.*

8 N.L.W. Portmadoc Papers 444.

9 U.C.N.W. Porth yr aur. MS 18085.

10 The corner houses opposite the Town Hall are considerably larger. Mr. Williams, the Mayor and chief shopkeeper, had one of these. The main ground-floor room is 28' 0" × 25' 0" and there are two floors above. The houses which faced down London Street at the opposite end of the square were rather grander. They are now masked by the terrace houses in London Street. Their façades were decorated by blank arcading which went the full height of the house; the intention was evidently to make an entrance to the square which was in scale with the Town Hall at its far end; the domestic scale of the houses could not otherwise be expected to achieve this. The house on the west side has some charming Gothic detailing, as well as the coved and vaulted ceilings to which Madocks was so partial. The house walls are of roughly coursed rubble and average 2' 3" thick; roofs are of slate; the hall and lean-to floors are of slate slab.

11 Morva Lodge has a fine site, high up, commanding a splendid view of the estuary. It was built to be let to a Doctor Morris. Twnt'yr Bwlch was a farm conversion. It was owned by John Williams when the 1843 tithe map was made. Ty Nanney, opposite the Church, was scarcely mentioned in Madocks' correspondence. Although its site is dull compared with the others, it is in many ways the most accomplished architecturally, without having quite the charm of Tan-yr-allt. It has features in common with Vale Mascall and may be the house which John Madocks intended to build just before his death. Possibly David Ellis-Nanney (see ch. 9,

note 1) built it instead, but as he had inherited Gwynfryn in 1805, he cannot have intended to live there. He was well off and a lively character, so may have built it as a speculation and to help on the embryo town. Ynys Towyn house was originally built so that John Williams could have lodgings and an office near the Embankment.

12 From 1807 to 1809 John Randolph was Bishop of Bangor. He was succeeded by Henry William Majendie.

13 Pennant. Note added by David Pennant, 1813.

14 Fenton.

15 N.L.W. MS Puleston V 3565.

16 In Aberayron, for instance, the new town then building at the south of Cardigan Bay, services were held in warehouses until as late as 1830.

17 Belonging to Robert Pritchard the carpenter; it was superintended by Owen Williams, brother of John Williams. Probably Pritchard was responsible for the great timber roof which covered Peniel Chapel.

18 See *Peniel M.C.* by the Rev. R. G. Jones, a most informative publication written to mark the 150th anniversary of the Chapel. John Jones was ordained in 1814, became the first minister and remained in office until 1857.

19 Ibid.

Masons' wages	£150	9	6
Timber	£264	4	6½
Sawing the timber	£38	6	11
Carpenters' wages	£121	11	0
Lime and transport	£23	12	2
Nails	£14	8	1
Day work	£20	8	9
Glazing	£32	13	3
Slaters and plasterers	£66	0	8
Slates	£49	16	6
Transport	£21	5	3
Minor payments	£55	3	10½
	£858	10	6

20 One such described some trouble a vicar of the neighbouring parish of Llanfrothen was having with his parishioners, with

whom he was at loggerheads. For this interlude Twm o'r Nant was paid one guinea, but shortly after its début he was paid two more for withdrawing it from his repertoire.

21 See Davies. The scarcity of woollen mills at this time is emphasised by a footnote which was added just before going to press stating that 2 factories had been built (at Llangollen and Dolgelley) in 1809.

22 Dodd.

23 Davies describes webs: 'called by London drapers Welsh plains, or cottons. They are a coarse sort of white thick cloth, made in pieces from 90 to 120 yds. They are exclusively the production of *three* small districts: Dolgelly and the neighbourhood of 12 miles around, Machynlleth and the Vale of Dovey, (and) Glynn in Denbighshire around Oswestry.'

24 Walter Davies (ibid.) was very impressed by Bala market. When writing of markets generally he suggested that 'The hours of market should be limited by law: some commence at an hour when they should conclude, which serves as a cloak to ebriety, knavery, and a train of immoralities. In fine, many go to market with the moon and return with the sun. From this, however, Bala stocking-market is an exception in the extreme, which is generally over by morning candle-light in winter, and at all times cleared before breakfast.'

25 Fuller's earth (imported from Hampshire) was used to bleach and thicken the cloth. The word *pandy* (fulling mill), which commonly occurs in Welsh place names, shows how widespread these mills were.

26 Robert Owen moved out of New Lanark quite early in its history, perhaps because a large house was conveniently available. But as late as 1828 William Crawshay sited his house to overlook the great ironworks at Cyfarthfa.

27 Nimrod, who had been a brother officer of Wardle's, described him as 'a very good-natured person and a lively and agreeable companion' whose great mistake was to get mixed up in politics. It is easy to see that Madocks would find him good company.

28 *Dictionary of Welsh Biography.*

Chapter 5

Note

1 Nimrod.
2 Hall, Edmund Hyde. *A Description of Caernarvonshire, 1809–11.*
3 *British Public Characters 1802–3.* Elizabeth Billington was reputed to be paid the highest fee at Covent Garden (£2,500 for a season).
4 Kelly, Michael, (ed. T. E. Hook). *Reminiscences.* 1826.
5 N.L.W. MS Holland Papers IV. *A True Story.*
6 N.L.W. MS Portmadoc Papers 708.
7 Could be translated Boon Companions: a double superlative of friends.
8 In the Reign of the Royal Lady Caroline. If this is to be taken literally, the club would date from 1820–21. 1805–11 seems more likely.
9 The dinner provided by local inns on market day: a term still in use.

Chapter 6

Note

1 Hansard XIV. 1809.
2 These originated in a letter signed by Burdett in defence of a political writer imprisoned for contempt of the orders of the Commons; Perceval, then Prime Minister, regarded this letter as a breach of privilege and a warrant was issued for Burdett's arrest and conduct to the Tower. He waited peaceably at home in Piccadilly insisting on the warrant's illegality while outside the streets seethed both with sympathisers and the troops sent to quell them. When the unfortunate Serjeant-at-Arms called to deliver the warrant, he was politely told that Burdett was not at home; he and Madocks had in fact slipped out through the mob and military to take the air in the park. On other calls he was told with

equal civility that Burdett considered his arrest illegal. 'Sir Francis did not mean to evade caption by flight, but to show that resistance which would render it a forcible arrest, and then try its validity' (*Memoirs of the Life of Sir Francis Burdett*, 1810). Crowds in Piccadilly grew; the cavalry was sent to disperse them but they blocked the street by a ladder which the infantry was sent to break up. Eventually Burdett was formally arrested (with equal civility on both sides) and was conducted through immense crowds to the Tower by a splendid cavalcade of horse guards and dragoons which 'excited wonderful interest'; a spectacle much to Madocks' and Burdett's liking. The number of troops collected in and around London was numbered at 10,000. Burdett remained in the Tower for about 3 months until the end of the parliamentary session.

3 In 1807 Romilly reported that during a period of 3 years 19,178 prisoners had been tried on capital charges; of these, 9,150 had been convicted and 327 executed.

4 Charles Wynn, M.P., writing to his brother Henry said he had declined to dine with such red-hot radical reformers. N.L.W. MS 2791.

5 Hansard XIV. 1809.

6 Hansard XIV. 1809.

7 Romilly, Sir Samuel. *Memoirs.*

8 N.L.W. MS 2791.

9 Cobbett's *Political Register*, 20 May 1809.

10 Roberts, Michael. *The Whig Party 1807–12.*

11 Ibid.

12 Davies.

13 *N.W.G.* 16 January 1812.

Chapter 7

Note

1 Madocks' great Embankment has long been known as the Cob. *Cob* is the Welsh word for such a bank, but as he did not use it in his correspondence it has not been introduced here.

2   For the Porthdinllaen Harbour Act see 46 GEO. III CAP. 34.
3   *Gentleman's Magazine.* Vol. 76, 1806.
4   The source of this rumour can be seen in Thomas Payne's memorial in Dolgelley where it is stated that 'he designed and completed the Great Embankment across the estuary of Traeth Mawr with its floodgates (thought then to be one of the wonders in Wales)'. Engraved on brass and placed on the medieval walls of the parish church this statement has an air of authenticity which has led, naturally enough, to its being unquestioned. The plaque however is not contemporary but was put up many years after the events it records. Not surprisingly work on the two embankments of 1800 and 1808–11 had been confused. The memorial continues: 'This work begun in 1799, was not finished until 1810 owing to irruptions of the sea and of the floods of the river Glasllyn. His skill and perseverance as an enginner at last overcame all difficulties and the sites of the towns of Tremadoc and Portmadoc together with a large area of land were rescued from the sea. . . . This brass is placed here in loving memory by his grandsons

> William Payne J.P. ⎫
>   Thomas Payne ⎬ of Portsmouth'
>   Edward Payne ⎭

To add to the confusion William Payne, in a contribution to *Byegones*, 11 April 1900, confirmed this statement, but there is no other record of Payne, who was at that time a publican, taking part in the work.
5   47 GEO. III. Sess. 2, CAP. 36.
6   Ibid. In the preamble, the advantages were set out:
'Whereas a certain Tract of Sands in the Estuary called Traeth Mawr . . . extending from Pont Aberglaslyn to the Point of Gest, which in its present state is unproductive and incapable of being cultivated, and the passage over the same is frequently attended with great inconvenience, delay, difficulty and danger and expense — and whereas if the said sands were protected from the sea by Embankments and other necessary Works, the same might be cultivated and rendered productive, and the communication between the said two counties would be thereby greatly facilitated and improved . . . but the making and maintaining of the same will be attended with considerable difficulty and expense; and whereas William Alexander Madocks is desirous of making such Embankments, Sea Walls, Ramparts, Fences, sluices, bridges and

other works as may be necessary . . . at his own expense . . . His Majesty . . . being desirous of encouraging such Undertakings of Public Utility . . . has been most graciously pleased to . . . signify his royal pleasure that so much of the said Tract of Sands from the Point of Gest to Pont Aberglaslyn . . . shall be granted and confirmed to and vested in the said William Alexander Madocks, His Heirs and Assigns in fee simple. . . .'

7   By J. C. Loudon; J. P. Kennel; and Rennie Harrison in his report to the House of Lords. See notes 16 and 17.

8   *Proceedings at Committee on Private Bills*, Session 1821, 380 (House of Lords Record Office).

9   Lewis, M. J. T. *How Ffestiniog got its Railway.*

10 Pennant. Contemporary reports of the width of the Embankment varied from 6–12 yards at the top and 30–60 at the base.

11 Today travellers can see the toll list beside the gate which is now on the Merioneth side of the Embankment.

12 It was unusual enough to be described in some detail in a footnote added to the 1810 edition of Pennant's *Tours*. 'It was soon discovered that these materials sunk into the sand, or were removed by the action of the tides. To obviate this difficulty, a strong and thick species of matting was invented, made of the rushes which cover the adjacent marsh; this, secured by stakes driven into the sand, constitutes a solid foundation.'

13 50 GEO. III CAP. 216.

14 Fenton.

15 Marriot, J. A. R. *Castlereagh.*

16 J. C. Loudon's *Report on the Intended Embankments and Shorelands of Tremadoc* is quoted by W. Morgan Richards in his thesis (N.L.W. MS).

17 J. P. Kennels's MS 'Report and Valuation of the Estates in Caernarvonshire belonging to W. A. Madocks Esq.' C.R.O. The unfortunate Kennel, land-surveyor, was in the King's Bench Prison for debt by the time the Embankment was completed (*N.W.G.* 8 August 1811).

18 *The Embankment, Traeth Mawr . . . in the autumn of 1810*, drawn by H. W. Billington, engraved by M. Dubourg. Copies in N.L.W., British Museum, and Portmadoc Council Offices. The *N.W.G.* advertised coloured and plain prints.

19 Peacock, T. L. *Headlong Hall.* 1816.

20 *N.W.G.* July 1811.

Chapter 8

Note

1 The well-known Jubilee Tower on Moel Fama above the Vale of Clwyd was built by subscription from the local gentry; the list included Madocks' family. He may have had such enterprises in mind when the idea of the Trè Madoc Jubilee originated.

2 *N.W.G.* 26 September 1811.

3 N.L.W. MS Puleston V 3565. *Diary of a Lady, 1811.* It is anonymous but she was most probably a Puleston cousin.

4 Probably John Clementson Junior, deputy Serjeant-at-Arms.

5 Bathing off the North Wales coast was becoming popular. An advertisement in the *N.W.G.* (22 March 1810) ran:
   'WANTED TO PURCHASE
   On any part of the Sea Coast of Carnarvonshire or Merionethshire
   A BATHING LODGE with 30 or 40 acres of land adjoining it; also an Estate of two or three HUNDRED POUNDS per annum contiguous to the Lodge, or within a short distance from it.'

6 U.C.N.W. Porth yr aur MS 18244.

7 Ibid. The kitchen with its large Quantity of Earthen Ware was also provided with '1 Bellows, 1 Time Piece, (£3) 1 Oak Table, 11 Pairs of fire irons with 11 Copper Pans with lids, 7 Tin Covers, 1 Copper Pot, 1 Dutch Oven, 5 Pudding Pots, 2 Plated do., 3 Oak chairs, 1 Warming Pan, 1 Iron Stool, 1 Tea Kettle, 1 large Iron do., 1 smoke jack, 2 Coffee Mills, 1 large Fender.' The inventory of the housekeeper's room brings home the scale of the parties which were catered for, particularly when it is borne in mind that all the laundry was done at home so linen was quickly in use again. Besides a few items for the comfort of the housekeeper herself, there was a 'Quantity of Teathings & Earthen Ware, 50 Pairs of Sheets (valued at £42.10.0), 55 Pillow Cases, 60 Damask Dinner Cloths, 36 Do. Breakfast Do., 5 Napkins for Supper Tray, 60 Dinner Napkins, 8 Homemade Table Cloths for Servants, 12 do. Towels, 24 Bedroom Table Cloths, 47 Cotton Diaper Towels, 15 Linen do. and 12 White [?] Cloths'.

8 N.L.W. MS *Portmadoc Papers* 435.

9 This seems to have been very similar to J. C. Loudon's scheme referred to on p. 83.

10 See introduction to the Porth yr aur Collection in U.C.N.W. by Owen Parry, M.A.
John Evans took over the practice in 1808 and at the same time became Clerk to the Magistrates of Caernarvon district. In 1810 he became deputy Protho-Notary of the North Wales Circuit.

11 Nimrod: 'This little upstart town was, for its size perhaps the scene of more mirth and jollity than any other of three times its size in Great Britain. In as much as the fame of Scott is said to have directed all men's eyes to the border, so did that of William Madocks and his embankment induce numbers—tourists without numbers, on their road to Snowdon to visit Tremadoc in the summer. . . .'

Chapter 9

Note

1 David Ellis-Nanney (1759–1819) was Attorney-General for North Wales under the Great Sessions dispensation. In 1805 he inherited Gwynfryn from his father and, in 1812, the Nanney property of Bachwen and Elernion on condition that he assumed the surname Nanney. At this stage therefore he is still Mr. Ellis. He was a lawyer of great reputation and a very likeable man. Ten years Madocks' senior, he had a wide experience of affairs and a keen legal mind, coupled with a zest for life and easy manner that Madocks would find particularly congenial. He was the first to be at any trouble spot, but the last to get into an unnecessary fuss. (Twice in his few surviving letters he refused to keep the messenger waiting because he did not think the contents of a letter could be sufficiently important to answer by return of post, 'dinner being on the table'.) The sight of his flowing handwriting gives a sense of civilised ease. Without his support it was unlikely that the Embankment would survive.

2 High springs fell on 18 March in 1812 so the tides would be growing dangerously the previous week.

3 U.C.N.W. Porth yr aur MS 35786.

4 *Gentleman's Magazine*, Vol. 82, p. 380. 1812.

5 The Hon. Robert Leeson, son of the Earl of Milltown, an Irish presbyterian landowner, who had opened and managed a quarry (probably near Towyn) which provided stone for the Embankment. He became a tenant of Morva Lodge.

6 See notice in *N.W.G.* 9 April 1812. It has been assumed the wording of the two notices was the same.

7 Henry William Paget, who became 1st Marquess of Anglesey after the Battle of Waterloo where he was second-in-command of the British Army.

Chapter 10

Note

1 *N.W.G.* 1 October 1812. The meeting was held in May 1812.

2 *N.W.G.* 25 June 1812.

3 The story of the murder has been told in several printed books. A detailed account appears in *From Merioneth to Botany Bay* by Hugh J. Owen, 1952.

Thomas Edwards, a 6 ft. 2 ins. 'giant' known locally as the King of the Mountains or the great South Walian (Hwntwr Mawr), was convicted of the murder of Mary Jones in the Court of Great Sessions 1813. David Ellis-Nanney was the prosecuting counsel. Edwards might not have been suspected had he not been surprised digging up the loot which he had buried in a sheepfold near the farm. He broke cover and was caught trying to cross Traeth Bach at low tide below Portmerion. Six constables were appointed to take him to Dolgelley by night. He complained that the straps holding him were too tight, escaped his escort and was only recaptured after several days in the woods near Penrhyndeudraeth.

4 Peacock, T. L. *Memoirs of Shelley*.

5 *N.W.G.* 1 October 1812. The paper seems to have run into trouble over its long and enthusiastic report, perhaps through jealousy on the part of others who coveted some of the space given to the Beaumaris meeting. In the next issue (8 October 1812) it was

noted: 'We are desired to state, that the account of what passed at the Corporation meeting at Beaumaris on the 28th ult. in consequence of Mr. Sh. and Mr. Wms. having made a visit there from Tremadoc, has been made much more than the real truth would warrant. The Meeting of the Anglesey Agricultural Society on the 1st inst. was most numerously and respectably attended. . . .'

6 Hogg, T. J. *Life of Shelley.*
7 Ibid.
8 Ibid.
9 Ibid.
10 Boas, L. S. *Five Long Years.*
11 Hogg, T. J. *Life of Shelley.*
12 See Dowden, Edward. *Life of Shelley.*

Harriet Shelley's account was written to Hookham from Dublin.

'35 *Cuffe Street, Stephens' Green, Dublin,*
                                    March 11 [1813]

My Dear Sir,

We arrived here last Tuesday, after a most tedious passage of forty hours, during the whole of which time we were dreadfully ill. I'm afraid no diet will prevent us from the common lot of suffering when obliged to take a sea voyage.

Mr. S. promised you a recital of the horrible events that caused us to leave Wales. I have undertaken the task, as I wish to spare him in the present nervous state of his health, everything that can recall to his mind the horrors of that night, which I will relate:

On Friday night, the 26th February, we retired to bed between ten and eleven o'clock. We had been in bed about half-an-hour, when Mr. S. heard a noise proceeding from one of the parlours. He immediately went downstairs with two pistols, which he had loaded that night, expecting to have occasion for them. He went into the billard room, where he had heard footsteps retreating; he followed into another little room, which was called an office. He there saw a man in the act of quitting the room through a glass window which opens into the shrubbery. The man fired at Mr. S., which he avoided. Bysshe then fired, but it flashed in the pan. The man then knocked Bysshe down, and they struggled on the ground. Bysshe then fired his second pistol, which he thought wounded him in the shoulder, as he uttered a shriek and got up, when he said these words: "By God, I will be revenged! I will murder your wife; I will ravish your sister! By God. I will be revenged!" He then fled—as we hoped for the night. Our servants were not gone to bed, but were just going, when this horrible affair happened. This was about eleven o'clock. We all assembled in the parlour, where we remained for two hours. Mr. S. then advised us to retire, thinking it impossible he would make a second attack. We left Bysshe and the manservant, who had only arrived that day, and who knew nothing of the house, to sit up. I had been in bed three hours when I heard a pistol go off. I immediately ran downstairs, when I perceived that Bysshe's flannel gown had been shot through, and the window curtain. Bysshe had sent Daniel to see what hour it was, when he heard a noise at the window. He went there, and a man thrust his arm through the glass and fired at him. Thank Heaven! the ball went through his gown and he remained unhurt. Mr. S. happened to stand sideways; had he stood fronting, the ball must have killed him. Bysshe fired his pistol, but it would not go off; he then aimed a blow at him with an old sword, which we found in the house. The assassin attempted to get the sword from him, and just as he was pulling it away, Dan rushed into the room, when he made his escape.

This was at four in the morning. It had been a most dreadful night; the wind was as loud as thunder, and the rain descended in torrents. Nothing has been heard of him, and we have every reason to believe it was no stranger, as there is a man of the name of L[ee]son, who the next morning that it happened went and told the shopkeepers of Tremadoc that it was a tale of Mr. Shelley's to impose upon them, that he might leave the country without paying his bills. This they believed, and none of them attempted to do anything towards his discovery.

We left Tanyrallt on Saturday, and stayed till everything was ready for our leaving the place, at the Solicitor-General of the county's house, who lived seven miles from us. This Mr. Leeson has been heard to say that he was determined to drive us out of the country. He once happened to get hold of a little pamphlet which Mr. S. had printed in Dublin; this he sent up to Government. In fact, he was for ever saying something against us, and that because we were determined not to admit him to our house, because we had heard of his character; and from many acts of his we found that he was malignant and cruel to the greatest degree. . . .

Yours truly,

H. Shelley'

13 See *Notes and Queries*, 1954 and 1955. Dowling, H. M. *The Alleged Attempt to Assassinate Shelley*.

14 Spencer Perceval had been shot by a 'madman' (Bellingham) who after calmly giving himself up stated that it was a private grievance. Madocks, who hated violence of any kind, probably shared Romilly's anger when no time was allowed for Bellingham's relatives to come from Liverpool to testify to his insanity at his trial. He was convicted before they arrived and hanged shortly afterwards. Madocks' nephew, John, took up his place early to watch the execution with Lord Byron.

15 Fenton.

16 Inglis-Jones, Elisabeth. *Peacocks in Paradise*.

17 Davies, Edward. *Hanes Portmadog*.

18 Fenton.

19 Will of Joseph Madocks, 5 November 1816.

20 Hansard XXXII. 1816.

21 Hansard XXXV. 1817.

Chapter 11

Note

1 Tregunter was demolished during the 1920s; its splendid staircase was shipped to America.

The plaque in Talgarth church to Thomas Harris records that in him 'the Poor always Found a most Bountiful Benefactor, his Heart and his Mansion being ever open to the feelings of Humanity. . . .'

Thomas had numerous children but since he never married he left his fortune and his recently completed house to his niece, the same Mrs. Samuel Hughes, and she in her turn divided it between her two surviving daughters.

Had Thomas Harris married and had a legitimate heir, William Madocks would never have found himself living at Tregunter; on the other hand the life of at least one young woman might have been considerably happier. One of Thomas Harris' sons, a spendthrift youth named Thomas Robinson, married the girl who was to become the famed eighteenth-century actress, Perdita.

She imagined him to be 'the legal heir of a handsome fortune and estate in South Wales'. On arrival at Tregunter she was quickly disillusioned, finding her husband to be deep in debt and without prospects. She left a picture of dashing Thomas Harris, then High Sheriff and Justice of the Peace, wearing 'a brown fustian coat, a scarlet waistcoat edged with narrow gold, a pair of woolen spatter-dashes, and a gold laced hat'. After barely two sad years in Wales, where a daughter was born to them, she returned to London where the feckless Thomas had been arrested for debt. Sheridan befriended her and she acted at Drury Lane and the Haymarket. There, as Perdita, she caught the eye of the Prince of Wales. As a result he set her up with an annuity of £500 a year but luck was against her; not long after, she was crippled by rheumatic fever, and she died at Windsor some years later.

2 Malkin, Benjamin Heath. *The Scenery, Antiquities and Biography of South Wales.* 1804.

3 Lincolnshire County Archives. Pamphlet: *A History of the Boston Election, June 1818.* 1818.

4 Ibid.

5 Leighton, Rachel. *Correspondence of Lady Williams Wynn.*

6 See Marriot, J. A. R. *Castlereagh.* 1936.

7 *Gentleman's Magazine,* 1820.

Chapter 12

Note

1 For a detailed account of matters concerning the Festiniog Railway, see *How Ffestiniog got its Railway* by M. J. T. Lewis.

The first slate quarry had been bought in 1800 by three enterprising Englishmen, William Turner and two Casson brothers whose work as quarry managers in Ireland had come to an end during the rebellion. They had worked and speculated with well-earned success and, in conjunction with their mining activities, had opened up communications with the sea by building a road on their own account to connect with the Ffestiniog and

Maentwrog turnpike, for which the Cassons were also commissioners. Since this road benefited considerably from the slate trade it is hardly surprising that they were not much interested in railway projects.

The second Ffestiniog quarry was the property of young Lord Newborough, still a minor, so it was in the hands of his trustees. This working had everything to gain from better communications as had that which had been newly opened by a Liverpool slate dealer, Samuel Holland, who had leased it from Madocks' colleague, Oakeley of Tan-y-Bwlch. He had sent his eighteen-year-old son over as manager and things were just beginning to get under way.

2 'Their crews were a hardy race known locally as Philistines, who dressed like gamekeepers and wore tall felt hats.'
   Lewis, M. J. T. *How Ffestiniog got its Railway.*

3 The fact that the river had not been turned higher up and was still running along the back of the Embankment to the sluice would make little difference to this scouring.

4 None of the slate companies was at this stage enamoured of Madocks' proposals and Lord Newborough's trustees were particularly active in their objections to the payment of tolls. Madocks' solicitors reasonably pointed out: 'There is already a railroad over the embankment and therefore Mr. M. wishes Lord N. to have a right to use the one already made and if that should be out of repair to make a new one and he also wishes the dues to be in the schedule in the following way. . . .' He, himself, seems to have been on good terms with the Madockses and was often at Tregunter. N.L.W. Glynllifon MSS 481–488, 3451, 5192–5220.

5 Port Madoc Harbour Act 1 & 2, GEO. IV CAP. 115.

6 A discrepancy of the wording concerning these dues in the schedule and in the bill itself remained, presumably overlooked by those responsible for its redrafting.

7 Instead of receiving one-fifth of the rent of the reclaimed marshland, Madocks was to receive one fifth part of the land itself. It was also laid down that if a breach should occur in the Embankment the land should revert to its former owners. Thus adjoining owners' interests were considered.

8 John Matthews of Mold.

9 Both lines followed the Vale of Ffestiniog from the quarries to the Embankment. One ran along the valley bottom and finished at the

Penrhyn end of the Embankment; the other took a higher contour and crossed the Embankment to end at Portmadoc. Madocks eventually sponsored the low-level scheme (surveyed by Overton who had done a considerable amount of work in S. Wales, where they may have first met). The second was sponsored by Oakeley of Tan-y-bwlch who owned the land leased to Holland for his quarry.

It was exceedingly frustrating for Madocks, laid low by illness, not to be in the fray, but John Williams entered fully into the spirit of the battle between the two lines. Tied to bed and as impatient as ever, Madocks wrote concerning some property wanted by both railway parties 'about which you may conceive I am not a little anxious to hear. In several of your letters, and very properly, you say the Motions of the Enemy must be watched. But what is the use of watching their Motions, if it is only to follow them, when it is too late?'

10 N.L.W. Glynllifon MS 2489.

11 Madocks' amendment to the Port Madoc Harbour Act seeking adjustment of the dues was still before Parliament.

12 Eliza Anne (Maria) Ermine Madocks, only child of William Alexander and his wife Eliza Anne, is said to have married twice. Her first husband had the same name as her mother's first husband, Roderick Gwynne. He died in 1849 and they had no children. She married secondly John Webb Roche of County Cork (whose first cousin Edward was father of the 1st Baron Fermoy) and died shortly after the birth of their fourth child in 1859. She had intended to write a biography of her father, and material from a few letters which had been written to her by his friends and colleagues has been used in this book. Unfortunately her descendants have not been traced.

13 Williams, The Rev. P. B. *Tourists' Guide through the County of Caernarvon.* 1821.

Chapter 13

Note

1 Letters took 2 days from Tremadoc to London and 14 from London to Florence.
2 N.L.W. Portmadoc Papers 434.
3 See *Byegones*, February 1881.
4 The river seems never to have been turned; it may have temporarily run direct to the sluice gates but the Ordnance Survey map of 1838 shows it meeting the Embankment near the Merioneth side.
5 The brass in Tremadoc Church appears to be of much later date: probably mid-Victorian or later.
6 During extensive nineteenth-century rebuilding at St. Mary's, Brecon, a plaque could have been lost.
7 Richards.

BRIEF BIBLIOGRAPHY

Contemporary Manuscripts and Drawings

COUNTY RECORD OFFICE, CAERNARVON
Kennel, J. P. *Report and Valuation of Estates in Caernarvonshire belonging to W. A. Madocks, Esq.* 1809
W. A. Madocks Collection
Map: *Traeth Mawr and Traeth Bach at Low Water* (Breese, Jones and Casson additional deposit)
Traeth Mawr Enclosure Maps and Awards, 1823

NATIONAL LIBRARY OF WALES
Portmadoc MSS and Papers
Griffith, Moses. Water-colours of Tremadoc Church and Tremadoc Market Hall. 1812

COUNTY RECORD OFFICE, MERIONETH
Dolmelynllyn Deeds

UNIVERSITY COLLEGE OF NORTH WALES, LIBRARY
Glynllifon MSS
Porth-yr-Aur MSS

Contemporary Printed Sources

Ackermann, R. *University of Oxford.* 1793
Bill of Rights, Act of Settlement etc., in which the representations of Sir Francis Burdett, Mr. Maddox, and others are considered. Their ignorance and their falsehood exposed and their real view detected . . . by the Gresham Lecturer in Civil Law
Boston, Papers concerning the Election of. 1812
Burdett, Sir Francis. *Life.* 1812
Burdett, Sir Francis. *Parliamentary Reform.* 1809
Craven, Elizabeth. *Memories of the Margravine of Anspach.* 1826

Brief Bibliography

Davies, Walter. *A General View of the Agriculture and Domestic Economy of North Wales.* Board of Agriculture, 1813

Drakard, John. *Colonel Wardle.* 1810

Fenton, Richard. *Tours in Wales 1804–13.* 1813
   Now reprinted: Archaeologia Cambrensis, 6th series, Vol. XVII

Hall, Edmund Hyde. *A Description of Caernarvonshire, 1809–11*
   Printed by Caernarvonshire Historical Society Records, 1952

History of the Colleges of Eton, Winchester, etc. 1816

Jones, Theophilus. *History of Brecknockshire*

Kelly, Michael (ed. T. E. Hook). *Reminiscences.* 1825–1826

Loudon, J. C. *Designs for Laying Out Farms and Farm Buildings, in the Scottish style; adapted to England.* 1811

Moore, Thomas (ed.). *Letters and Journals of Lord Byron.* Murray. 1833

Nicholson, George (ed.). *Cambrian Travellers' Guide & Pocket Companion.* Stourport. 1808

Noble, J. *History of the 1818 Election.* Boston. 1818

Palmer, J. *Principles of Revolution.* 1809

Peacock, Thomas Love. *Headlong Hall.* 1816

Peacock, Thomas Love. *Memoirs of Shelley.* 1855

Rogers, T. *Documents addressed to W.A.M. relating to Portdynllean Harbour.* 1807

Spencer, W. R. *Poems.* Cadell. 1808

Contemporary Issues of:

Annual Register
Chester Chronicle
Communications to the Board of Agriculture. 1808
Fraser's Magazine. 1842. *My Life & Times.* Nimrod
Gentleman's Magazine
Hansard. *Parliamentary Debates*
North Wales Gazette
Political Register

Contemporary Printed Drawings and Maps

NATIONAL LIBRARY OF WALES
Billington, Horace. *The Embankment as it appeared in the Autumn of 1810.* 1811
Cary, J. Road map of Caernarvonshire and Merioneth. 1794
Loudon, J. C. *Ideal Plan of Part of the Trè Madoc Estate, Caernarvonshire.* 1811
Ordnance Survey Sheet 75, 1838
Sandby, Paul. *Traeth Mawr in the road to Caernarvon from Festiniog.* 1777
Tithe Map of *Ynys Cynhaiarn Parish.* 1843

Manuscripts and Drawings

Dalby, Michael. *The Caernarvonshire Estate of the late W. A. Madocks.* 1952. (Architectural thesis)
Richards, W. M. *A Dissertation on the History of Traeth Mawr and the Industrial Results of the Formation of the Embankment* (M.A.Thesis). 1927. N.L.W.
Rowntree Kenneth. *Tan-yr-allt* and *Tremadoc Chapel*; water-colours made for the Recording Britain Series. 1941
School of Architecture, Liverpool University. Measured drawings of Tremadoc. Made in survey of Tremadoc. 1955
Tremadoc Estate, Sale Map. 1921

Printed Books

Abbot. *Diary and Correspondence of Lord Colchester by his Son.* Murray. 1861
Boas, Louise S. *Harriet Shelley: Five long years.* Oxford University Press. 1962
Byegones Relating to Wales. 1881 and 1900
Cameron, K. N. *Young Shelley.* 1951

Davies, Edward. *Hanes Porthmadog*

Dodd, A. H. *Industrial Revolution in North Wales.* University of Wales Press

Dowden, E. *Life of Percy Bysshe Shelley.* London. 1886

Dowling, H. M. *The Alleged Attempt to Assassinate Shelley. Notes & Queries.* July, September, December 1954, December 1955

Eifion, Alltud. *Y Gestiana.* 1892

Ellis, Megan. Merioneth Historical Transactions 1954. *Some recorded impressions of Merioneth*

Ellis, S. M. *Life of Michael Kelly.* 1930

Griffiths J. E. *Pedigrees of Anglesey & Caernarvonshire families.* 1914

Ingpen, R. *Life of Shelley. Vol. I.* London. 1917

Jenkins, Dr. R. T. *Etifдddion Harrisiaid Trefeca*

Jones, R. J. *Hanes Cychwyn Yr Archos Yn Nhremadog.* Peniel M.C.

Leighton, Rachel (ed.). *Correspondence of Lady Williams Wynn.* 1920

Lewis, M. J. T. *How Ffestiniog got its Railway.* 1965

Mallet, C. E. *History of University of Oxford.* London. 1924

Marriot, J. A. R. *England since Waterloo.* Barnes & Noble. 1954

Marriot, J. A. R. *Castlereagh.* Methuen. 1936

Medwin, Thomas. *Life of Shelley.* 1847

Morris, Owen. *Portmadoc and its Resources.* 1856

Owen, H. J. *From Merioneth to Botany Bay.* Privately published. 1952

Richards, W. M. *Caernarvonshire Historical Society Transactions.* Vol. IV. 1943. Vol. V. 1944

Rigby, E. *Life of John Gibson.* 1870

Roberts, Michael. *The Whig Party 1807–1812.* 1939

Romilly, Sir Samuel, Memoirs of. Ed. by his sons. 1840. Murray. 1842

Russell, Lord John. *Memoirs of Thomas Moore.* 1853

Smythe, R. *History of the Charterhouse.* 1908

Index

Index